Hypercomputation

To my son Demetrios-Georgios
and my parents
Georgios and Vassiliki

Apostolos Syropoulos

Hypercomputation

Computing Beyond the Church–Turing Barrier

 Springer

Apostolos Syropoulos
366 28th October Street
GR-671 00 Xanthi
Greece
asyropoulos@gmail.com

ISBN 978-0-387-30886-9   ISBN 978-0-387-49970-3 (eBook)
DOI 10.1007/978-0-387-49970-3

Library of Congress Control Number: 2008923106

ACM Computing Classification System (1998): F.4.1, F.1.1, F.1.0
Mathematics Subject Classification (2000): 03D10, 03D60, 03D99, 68Q05, 68Q10, 68T99

Printed on acid-free paper

9 8 7 6 5 4 3 2 1

springer.com

Preface

Hypercomputation in a Nutshell

Computability theory deals with problems and their solutions. In general, problems can be classified into two broad categories: those problems that can be solved algorithmically and those that cannot be solved algorithmically. More specifically, the design of an algorithm that solves a particular problem means that the problem can be solved algorithmically. In addition, the design of an algorithm to solve a particular problems is a task that is equivalent to the construction of a Turing machine (i.e., the archetypal conceptual computing device) that can solve the same problem. Obviously, when a problem cannot be solved algorithmically, there is no Turing machine that can solve it. Consequently, one expects that a *noncomputable* problem (i.e., a problem that cannot be solved algorithmically) should become *computable* under a broader view of things. Generally speaking, this is not the case. The established view is that only problems that can be solved algorithmically are actually solvable. All other problems are simply noncomputable.

Hypercomputation deals with noncomputable problems and how they can be solved. At first, this sounds like an oxymoron, since noncomputable problems cannot really be solved. Indeed, if we assume that problems can be solved only algorithmically, then this is true. However, if we can find other ways to solve noncomputable problems nonalgorithmically, there is no oxymoron. Thus, hypercomputation is first about finding general nonalgorithmic methods that solve problems not solvable algorithmically and then about the application of these methods to solve particular noncomputable problems. But are there such methods? And if there are, can we use them to solve noncomputable problems?

In the early days of computing, for reasons that should not concern us for the moment, a Turing machine with an *oracle* was introduced. This oracle was available to compute a single arbitrary noncomputable function from the natural numbers to the natural numbers. Clearly, this new conceptual computing device can be classified as a *hypercomputer* since it can *compute* noncomputable functions. Later on, other variants of the Turing machine capable of *computing* noncomputable functions appeared in the scientific literature. However, these extensions to computability theory did not gain widespread acceptance, mainly because no one actually believed that one could *compute* the incomputable. Thus, thinkers and researchers were indirectly discouraged from studying and investigating the possibility of finding new methods to solve problems and compute things. But the 1990s was a renaissance for hypercomputation since a considerable number of thinkers and researchers took really seriously the idea of *computing beyond computing*, that is, hypercomputation. Indeed, a number of quite interesting proposals have been made ever since. And some of these proposals, although quite exotic, are *feasible*, thus showing that hypercomputation is not to the theory of computation what perpetual motion machines are to physics!

The success of the Turing machine in describing everything computable, and also its simplicity and elegance, prompted researchers and thinkers to assume that the Turing machine has a universal role to play. In particular, many philosophers, psychologists, and neurobiologists are building new theories of the mind based on the idea that the mind is actually a Turing machine. Also, many physicists assume that everything around us is a computer and consequently, the whole universe is a computer. Thus, if the universe is indeed a Turing machine, the *capabilities* of the mind and nature are limited by the capabilities of the Turing machine. In other words, according to these views, we are tiny Turing machines that live in a "Turing-verse"!

Hypercomputation poses a real threat to the cosmos described in the previous paragraph. Indeed, even today it is considered heretical or even unscientific to say that the mind in not a Turing machine! And of course, a universe where hypercomputation is possible renders certain beliefs and values meaningless. But then again, in the history of science there are many cases in which fresh ideas were faced with skepticism and in some instances with strong and prudent opposition. However, sooner or later, correct theories and ideas get widespread appreciation and acceptance. Thus, it is crucial to see whether there will be "experimental" verification of hypercomputation. But this is not an easy task, since hypercomputation is practically in its infancy. On the other hand, it should be clear that there is no "experimental" evidence for the validity of the Turing-centered ideas presented above.

Reading This Book

Who Should Read It?

This book is a presentation, in a rather condensed form, of the emerging theory of hypercomputation. Broadly, the book is a sort of compendium of hypercomputation. As such, the book assumes that readers are familiar with basic concepts and notions from mathematics, physics, philosophy, neurobiology, and of course computer science. However, since it makes no sense to expect readers to be well versed in all these fields, the book contains all the necessary definitions to make it accessible to a wide range of people. In particular, the book is well suited for graduate students and researchers in physics, mathematics, and computer science. Also, it should be of interest to philosophers, cognitive scientists, neurobiologists, sociologists, and economists with some mathematical background. In addition, the book should appeal to computer engineers and electrical engineers with a strong interest in the theory of computation.

About the Contents of the Book

The book is based on material that was readily available to the author. In many cases, the author directly requested copies of papers and/or book chapters from authors, and he is grateful to everyone who responded positively to his request. It is quite possible that some (important?) works are not discussed in this book. The reasons for any such omission are that the author did not really feel they were that important, that the author did not have at his disposal the original material describing the corresponding piece of work, or that the author simply was unaware of this particular piece of work.

For the results (theorems, propositions, etc.) that are presented in the book we have opted not to present their accompanying proofs. Since this book is an introduction to the emerging field of hypercomputation, it was felt that the proofs would only complicate the presentation. However, readers interested in proofs should consult the sources originally describing each piece of work.

The subject index of the book contains entries for various symbols, and the reader should be aware that there is only one entry for each symbol, and the unique entry corresponds to the page where the symbol is actually defined.

Mathematical Assumptions

At this point it is rather important to say that the discussion in the next nine chapters assumes that the Axiom of Choice holds. In other words, many of the ideas presented do not make sense without this axiom being valid. This axiom states that

Axiom of Choice There exists a choice function for every system of sets [88].

Assuming that S is a system of sets (i.e., a collection of sets only), a function $g : S \rightarrow S$ is called a *choice function* for S if $g(X) \in X$ for all nonempty $X \in S$. After this small but necessary parenthesis let us now describe the contents of each chapter.

The Book in Detail

The first chapter is both an introduction to hypercomputation and an over-view of facts and ideas that have led to the development of classical com-putability theory. In addition, there is a short discussion explaining why hypercomputation is so fascinating to many thinkers and researchers.

The second chapter can be viewed as a crash course in (classical) com-putability theory. In particular, we discuss Turing machines, general recur-sive functions, recursive predicates and relations, and the Church-Turing thesis, where we present not only the "classical" version, but even quite recent versions that encompass "modern" views.

In the third chapter we begin the formal presentation of various ap-proaches to hypercomputation. In particular, in this chapter we present early approaches to hypercomputation (i.e., proposals that were made be-fore the 1990s). Although some proposals presented in this chapter are quite recent, we opted to present them here, since they are derivatives of certain early forms of hypercomputation. More specifically, in this chap-ter we present trial-and-error machines and related ideas and theories, in-ductive Turing machines, coupled Turing machines, Zeus machines, and pseudorecursiveness.

Conceptual machines that may perform an infinite number of opera-tions to accomplish their computational task are presented in the fourth chapter. Since the theory of these machines makes heavy use of cardinal and ordinal numbers, the chapter begins with a brief introduction to the relevant theory. Then, there is a thorough presentation of infinite time Tur-ing machines and a short description of infinite time automata. In addition, there is a description of a "recipe" for constructing infinite machines, and the chapter concludes with a presentation of a metaphysical foundation for computation. Notice that infinite-time Turing machines are the ideal conceptual machines for describing computations that take place during a supertask. Thus, it should be more natural to present them alongside the supertasks; however, it was felt that certain subjects should be presented without any reference to related issues. On the other hand, other subjects are presented in many places in the book so as to give a thorough view of them.

Interactive computing is known to every computer practitioner; what is not known is that interactive systems are more powerful than Turing ma-chines. The fifth chapter begins by explaining why this is true and contin-ues with a presentation of various conceptual devices that capture the basic characteristics of interactive computing. In particular, we discuss interaction machines, persistent Turing machines, site and Internet machines, and the π-calculus.

Is the mind a machine? And if it is a machine, what kind of machine is it? What are the computational capabilities of the mind? These and other similar questions are addressed in the sixth chapter. However, it is rather important to explain why we have opted to discuss these questions in a book that deals with hypercomputation. The main reason is that if one can show that the mind is, among other things, a computational device that has capabilities that transcend the capabilities of the Turing machine, then, clearly, this will falsify the Church–Turing thesis. In other words, hypercomputation partially falsifies computationalism. In this chapter we discuss various approaches to show that the mind is not just a Turing machine, but a *device* with many capabilities both computational and noncomputational. In particular, we discuss arguments based on Gödel's incompleteness theorems, arguments from the philosophy of mind, the relation between semiotics and the mind, and the mind from the point of view of neurobiology and psychology.

The theory of computation deals primarily with natural numbers and functions from natural numbers to natural numbers. However, in physics and analysis we are dealing with real numbers and real functions. This implies that it is important to study the computational properties of real numbers and real functions. And real-number computation leads to hypercomputation in unexpected ways, which we discuss in the seventh chapter of the book. In particular, we discuss various approaches to real-number computation and how they may lead to hypercomputation. We begin with the Type-2 Theory of Effectivity, and continue with a discussion of a special form of Type-2 machines. Next, we present BSS-machines, real-number random access machines, and we conclude with a presentation of a recursion theory on the reals.

In the eighth chapter we discuss relativistic and quantum hypercomputation. More specifically, we show how the properties of space and time can be exploited to compute noncomputable functions. Also, we show how quantum computation can be employed to compute noncomputable problems. In addition, we present our objections to a computational theory of the universe. There is also a brief discussion of supertasks in the framework of classical and quantum mechanics.

The last chapter is devoted to natural computation and its relationship to hypercomputation. It is worth noticing that natural computation includes analog computing, and that is why we present various approaches to hypercomputation via analog computation. In addition, we demonstrate how one may end up with noncomputable functions in analysis and physics and, thus, showing in an indirect way, that noncomputability is part of this world. The chapter concludes with a presentation of an optical model of (hyper)computation, membrane systems as a basis for the construction of hypermachines, and analog X-machines and their properties.

The book includes four appendices. The $P = NP$ hypothesis is discussed in the first appendix. In the second appendix we briefly discuss how hypercomputation affects complexity theory. In the third appendix, we discuss how noncomputability affects socio-economic issues. The last appendix contains some useful mathematical definitions, necessary for the understanding of certain parts of the book. Clearly, this appendix is not a substitute for a complete treatment of the subject; nevertheless, it can be viewed as a refresher for those already exposed to the concepts or as a very brief introduction to the relevant theory for those with no prior knowledge of the relevant definitions.

Acknowledgments

First of all, I would like to express my gratitude to Ioannis Kanellos for his many comments and suggestions. Our long discussions over the phone were quite stimulating and thought-provoking. Also, I would like to thank Wayne Wheeler, Springer's computer-science editor, for believing in this project and for all his help and assistance, and Ann Kostant, my editor at Springer, for her help and assistance. In addition, I am really thankful to Francisco Antonio Doria, Martin Ziegler, Joel David Hamkins, Benjamin Wells, Bruno Scarpellini, Dina Goldin, Peter Wegner, Mark Burgin, Tien D. Kieu, John Plaice, Mike Stannett, Theophanes Grammenos, and Andromahi Spanou for reading drafts of the book and providing me with many valuable comments and suggestions on how to improve the presentation. Also, I would like to thank the Springer reviewers for critically reading drafts of the book and providing me with their valuable comments and suggestions. In addition, I thank David Kramer for his excellent work in copyediting the manuscript. Naturally, for any omissions and/or remaining errors and mistakes one should blame only the author and nobody else! Furthermore, I would like to thank Barbara Beeton, Jaako Hintikka, Mike Stannett, Petros Allilomes, and Peter Kugel for providing me with copies of important papers. Last, but certainly not least, I would like to thank Yannis Haralambous for his help and Maria Douma for the drawing on page 8.

Apostolos Syropoulos
Xanthi, Greece

March, 2008

Contents

I. Introduction

Why do we generally believe that "modern" digital computers cannot compute a number of important functions? Do we believe that there is some fundamental physical law that prohibits computers from doing a number of things or is it that there is something wrong with the very foundations of computer science? I cannot really tell whether the universe itself has imposed limits to what we can compute and where these limits lie, but a number of indications suggest that the established way of viewing things is not correct, and thus, we definitely need a paradigm shift in order to alter, or at least expand, the theory of computability. In this introductory chapter I present the historical background that eventually led to the formation of the classical landscape of computability and its implications. And since every criticism must be accompanied by proposals, this introduction concludes with a discussion about the prospects of a new theory of computation.

1.1 On Computing and Its Limits

Originally, the word computing was synonymous with counting and reckoning, and a computer was an expert at calculation. In the 1950s with the advent of the (electronic) computer, the meaning of the word computing was broadened to include the operation and use of these machines, the processes carried out within the computer hardware itself, and the theoretical concepts governing them. Generally speaking, these theoretical concepts are based on the idea that a computer is capable of enumerating "things" and calculating the value of a function. A direct consequence of this specific view of computing is the so-called Church–Turing thesis, named after Alonzo Church and Alan Mathison Turing, who introduced concepts and ideas that form the core of what is known as computability theory. The thesis arose out of efforts to give an answer to a problem that was proposed by David Hilbert in the context of the program that he enunciated at the beginning of the twentieth century.[1] The eventual finding that this particular problem cannot be solved in a particular framework led to the formulation of this thesis. Since this thesis lies at the heart of computability theory, it has directly affected the way we realize computing and its limits. In particular, the thesis states that no matter how powerful a given computing device is, there are problems that this machine cannot solve. In other words, according to the Church-Turing thesis there is a limit that dictates what can and what cannot be computed by any computing device imaginable.

In order to fully apprehend Hilbert's problem and how it helped in the formation of the Church-Turing thesis, we need to be aware of the context in which Hilbert's ideas were born. However, the context in cases like this is not alien to the most general and abstract categories and concepts with which we think. In other words, it is more than important to have an idea about the various philosophies of mathematics. The established philosophies of mathematics are:

(i) intuitionism, according to which only knowable statements are true (Luitzen Egbertus Jan Brouwer is the founding father of intuitionism);

(ii) Platonism (or realism), which asserts that mathematical expressions refer to entities whose existence is independent of the knowledge we have of them;

(iii) formalism, whose principal concern is with expressions in the formal language of mathematics (formalism is specifically associated with Hilbert);

(iv) logicism, which says that all of mathematics can be reduced to logic (logicism is specifically associated with Friedrich Ludwig Gottlob Frege, Bertrand Russell, and Alfred North Whitehead).

In the Platonic realm a sentence is either true or false. The truth of a sentence is "absolute" and independent of any reasoning, understanding, or action. Because of this, the expression *not false* just means *true*; similarly, *not true* just means *false*. As a direct consequence of this, the Aristotelian *principle of the excluded middle* (tertium non datur), which states that a sentence is either true or false, is always true. According to Arend Heyting (the founder of intuitionistic logic), a sentence is true if there is a proof of it. But what is exactly a proof? Jean-Yves Girard [67] gives the following explanation:

---

1. Hilbert's program called for finding a general (mechanical) method capable of settling every possible mathematical statement expressed using abstract "meaningless" symbols. Such a method should proceed by manipulating sequences of "meaningless" symbols using specific rules. Roughly speaking, the rules and the way to encode the mathematical statements form a *formal system*.

By proof we understand not the syntactic formal transcript, but the inherent object of which the written form gives only a shadowy reflection.

An interesting consequence of the intuitionistic approach to logic is that the principle of the excluded middle is not valid, or else we have to be able to find either a proof of a sentence or a proof of the negation of a sentence. More specifically, as Heyting [82] observes:

$p \vee \neg p$ demands a general method to solve every problem, or more explicitly, a general method which for any proposition p yields by specialization either a proof of p or a proof of $\neg p$. As we do not possess such a method of construction, we have no right to assert this principle.

The *Curry-Howard isomorphism* states that there is a remarkable analogy between formalisms for expressing effective functions and formalisms for expressing proofs (see [187] for more details). Practically, this means that proofs in logic correspond to expressions in programming languages. Thus, when one constructs a proof of the formula $\exists n \in \mathbb{N} : P(n)$, where $\mathbb{N}$ is the set of natural numbers including zero, he or she actually constructs an effective method that finds a natural number that satisfies P. In other words, proofs can be viewed as programs (see [9] for a description of a system that implements this idea).

The great ancient Greek philosopher Plato argued that mathematical propositions refer not to actual physical objects but to certain idealized objects. Plato envisaged that these ideal entities inhabited a different world, distinct from the physical world. Roger Penrose [152] calls this world the *Platonic world of mathematical forms* and assumes that the mathematical assertions that can belong to Plato's world are precisely those that are objectively true. According to Penrose, Plato's world is not outside the world we live, but, rather, part of it. In fact, Penrose is actually a *trialist*, since he argues that there are three worlds that constantly interact: the physical, the mental and the Platonic worlds.

Generally speaking, mathematical formalism is about manipulation of symbols, regardless of meaning. Hilbert's formalism was the attempt to put mathematics on a secure footing by producing a formal system that is capable of expressing all of mathematics and by proving that the formal system is *consistent* (i.e., it is not possible to derive from a set of axioms two formally contradictory theorems). Within the formal system, proofs consist of manipulations of symbols according to fixed rules, which do not take into account any notion of meaning. Clearly, this does not mean that the mathematical objects themselves lack meaning, or that this meaning is not important. In summary, as Girard [66, page 426] notes:

Hilbert treated mathematics as a formal activity, which is a nonsense, if we take it literally... But what should we think of those who take thought as a formal activity?

Since logicism has played no significant role in the development of the theory of computation, I will not give a more detailed account of it. One may challenge this assertion by noting that logic programming is evidence of logicism in the field of computation, but the point is that its role in the development of the relevant theory was not important at all. Now we can proceed with the presentation of events that led to the formulation of computability theory.

At the *Second International Congress of Mathematics*, which was held in Paris during the summer of 1900, Hilbert presented ten unsolved problems in mathematics [213, 31]. These problems, and thirteen more that completed the list, were designed to serve as examples of the kinds of problems whose solutions would lead to the furthering of disciplines in mathematics. In particular, Hilbert's tenth problem asked for the following:

> **Determination of the solvability of a Diophantine equation.** Given a Diophantine equation with any number of unknown quantities and with integral numerical coefficients: To devise a process according to which it can be determined by a finite number of operations whether the equation is solvable in integers.

A Diophantine equation is an equation of the form

$$D(x_1, x_2, \ldots, x_m) = 0,$$

where D is a polynomial with integer coefficients. These equations were named after the Greek mathematician Diophantus of Alexandria, who is often known as the "father of algebra." But what is the essence of Hilbert's tenth problem?

Since the time of Diophantus, who lived in the third century A.D., number theorists have found solutions to a large number of Diophantine equations and have also proved the insolubility of an even larger number of other equations. Unfortunately, there is no single method to solve these equations. In particular, even for different individual equations, the solution methods are quite different. Now, what Hilbert asked for was a *universal* formal method for recognizing the solvability of Diophantine equations. In other words, Hilbert asked for a general solution to a *decision problem* (*Entscheidungsproblem* in German), which is a finite-length question that can be answered with *yes* or *no*.

During the Third International Congress of Mathematics, which was held in Bologna, Italy, in 1928, Hilbert went a step further and asked whether mathematics as a formal system is *finitely describable* (i.e., the axioms and rules of inference are constructable in a finite number of steps, while, also, theorems should be provable in a finite number of steps), *complete* (i.e., every true statement that can be expressed in a given formal system is formally deducible from the axioms of the system), *consistent* (i.e., it is not possible to derive from the axioms of the system two contradictory formulas, for instance, the formulas 3 > 2 and 2 ≥ 3), and sufficiently powerful to represent any statement that can be made about natural numbers. But in 1931 the Austrian logician Kurt Gödel proved that any recursive (see Section 2.2) axiomatic system powerful enough to describe the arithmetic of the natural numbers must be either inconsistent or incomplete (see [138] for an accessible account of Gödel's famous theorem). Practically, Gödel put an end to Hilbert's dream for a fully formalized mathematical science. Now, what remained to fully refute Hilbert was to prove that formal mathematics is not *decidable* (i.e., there are no statements that are neither provable nor disprovable). This difficult task was undertaken by Church and Turing, who eventually *proved* that formal mathematics is not decidable.

In order to tackle the decidability problem, Church devised his famous λ-calculus. This calculus is a formal system in which every expression stands for a function with a single argument. Functions are anonymously defined by a λ-expression that expresses the function's action on its argument. For instance, the sugared λ-expression $\lambda x.2 \cdot x$ defines a function that doubles its argument. Church proved that there is no *algorithm* (i.e., a method or procedure that is *effectively computable* in the formalist program in mathematics, but see page 21 for a short discussion of algorithms and their properties) that can be used to decide whether two λ-calculus expressions are equivalent. On the other hand, Turing himself proceeded by proposing a conceptual computing device, which nowadays bears his name, and by showing that a particular problem cannot be decided by his conceptual computing device, which, with our knowledge and understanding, implies that Hilbert's tenth problem is unsolvable. Finally, in 1970, Yuri Vladimirovich Matiyasevich proved that Hilbert's tenth problem cannot be decided by a Turing machine. In particular, Matiyasevich proved that there is no single Turing machine that can be used to determine the existence of integer solutions for each and every Diophantine equation.

One may wonder what all these things have to do with computer science, in general, and computability theory, in particular. The answer is that all new "sciences" need mathematical foundations, and computer science is no exception. Eugene Eberbach [55] gives the following comprehensive account of what computer science is:

> Computer science emerged as a mature discipline in the 1960s, when universities started offering it as an undergraduate program of study. The new discipline of computer science defined computation as *problem solving*, viewing it as a transformation of input to output—where the input is completely defined before the start of computation, and the output provides a solution to the problem at hand.

So, it was quite logical to adopt Turing's conceptual device as a universal foundation for computational problem-solving and, hence, for computer science. Also, this is the reason why computer scientists are so reluctant to adopt another notion as a foundation of computer science. A direct consequence of this choice is the assumption that Turing's machine describes what is actually computable by any computing device. More specifically, since any programming language is actually a formal system, it has to have all the properties of a formal mathematical system. Thus, every sufficiently rich programming language, as a formal system, is either incomplete or inconsistent and it has to be undecidable. Clearly, a computer program written in some programming language L is actually a formal solution ("proof") of a particular problem ("theorem"). In addition, many computer programs are solutions to decision problems. But there is one decision problem that cannot be solved "algorithmically": To write a computer program that takes as input another program and any input that second program may take and decide in a finite number of steps whether the second program with its input will halt. The negative response to Hilbert's Entscheidungsproblem implies that it is not possible to write such a computer program, though it may be possible to give a certain response for a particular class of simple computer programs such as the following one:[2]

```
#include <iostream>
using namespace std;

int main()
{
  while (true)
    cout << "Hello World!\n";
}
```

Naturally, in many cases (experienced) computer programmers are able to tell intuitively whether a program that is actually being executed by a machine will terminate. But we will briefly discuss the capabilities of the human mind in the next section.

1.2 From Computation to Hypercomputation

The notion of a computable (real) number was introduced by Alan Turing in his trailblazing paper entitled *On Computable Numbers, with an application to the Entscheidungsproblem* [206]. In this paper, Turing identified computable numbers with those that a Turing machine can actually compute. In particular, a real number is computable if its decimal digits are calculable by finite means. Formally, we have the following definition.

---

2. The code is a simple C++ program that continuously prints on a computer monitor the greeting *Hello World!*. Thus, it is a nonterminating program.

Definition 1.2.1 A real number $x \in [0, 1]$ is *computable* if it has a computable decimal expansion. That is, there is a *computable* function $f : \mathbb{N} \to \{0, 1, \ldots, 9\}$ such that $x = \sum_{i \in \mathbb{N}} f(i) \cdot 10^{-i}$.

Of course, most real numbers do not belong to the unit interval; however, if $x \notin [0, 1]$, then x can be written as $y + n$, where $y \in [0, 1]$ and $n \in \mathbb{Z}$, where $\mathbb{Z}$ is the set of integers. Thus, x is computable if and only if both y and n are computable.

Clearly, the definition of the notion of a computable number depends on Turing's model of computation. This implies that a particular number might be noncomputable by a Turing machine, but it might be computable by some other conceptual computing device. Obviously, not all numbers are computable under the Turing machine model. In fact, it can be shown that any "simple" Turing machine (i.e., one that manipulates exactly two distinct symbols) can compute at most $(4n + 4)^{2n}$ distinct numbers. Here n denotes the number of different internal states the machine can enter. In addition, by employing a *diagonalization argument* (see page 161 for a brief overview), Turing managed to prove that there are uncountably many noncomputable numbers.

It is a fact that the set of Turing-computable numbers is quite small. And this is just one aspect of the limits that the Turing machine imposes on what we can compute. These facts have prompted a number of researchers and thinkers to propose alternative models of computation that somehow have the power to compute not only more numbers than the Turing machine does, but also to transcend the limits imposed by it. Collectively, all these models of computation are known as *hypercomputers*. The term *hypercomputation*, which was coined by Brian Jack Copeland and Diane Proudfoot [37], characterizes all conceptual computing devices that break the Church–Turing barrier.[3] With his famous theorem, Gödel managed to show that there is an endless number of true arithmetic statements that cannot be formally deduced from any given set of axioms by a closed set of rules of inference. The parallel between Turing's results and Gödel's results is obvious: on the one hand the number of noncomputable numbers is boundless, and on the other hand, the same applies to the number of true but unprovable arithmetic statements. However, it is important to note that Gödel's results apply only to formalized axiomatic procedures that are based on an initially determined and fixed set of axioms and transformation rules. In principle, this means that for any true but "unprovable" arithmetic statement one may come up with a nonformalistic proof. For example, one may employ a nonconstructive method to prove the validity of a given statement (see [72] for a discussion on this matter). Similarly, noncomputable numbers could become computable if an alternative method of computation were employed. Practically, this means that hypercomputation

---

3. The alternative term *super-Turing* computability was introduced by Mike Stannett, and it was popularized by Peter Wegner and Eberbach [217].

Figure 1.1: An artist's impression of the Chinese Room Argument.

is about a paradigm shift in order to find new models of computation that will allow us to compute classically noncomputable numbers. After all, the formal framework of the theory of computation has been developed mainly for problems that are logical and discrete in nature (see [231] for a brief discussion of the matter).

So far, we have explained what hypercomputation is, but one important question remains: are there any real hypercomputers? The established view of computation is that it is mechanical information processing (i.e., a transformation of some input to output, where the input is completely defined before the start of the computation and the output produces a solution to a specified problem). However, in the age of the Internet this view of computation is too restricted–modern computers continuously interact with each other and interchange vast amounts of information, thus making the established model of computation simply inadequate. In addition, Robin Milner points out [131] that the world of sequential computing is much smaller than the world of concurrent programming and interactive systems. Later studies have shown that algebraic models of the world of concurrent programming and interactive systems contain the classical model of the world of sequential computing [130].

Many thinkers believe that the human mind is a machine with capabilities that transcend the capabilities of the Turing machine. Indeed, John Rogers Searle's much acclaimed *Chinese room argument* [172] aimed at refuting "strong AI" (AI stands for Artificial Intelligence). "Strong AI" is the claim that computers are theoretically capable of literally thinking, understanding, and generally possessing intentional content in the same sense that humans do. On the other hand, "weak AI" is the claim that computers are merely able to *simulate* thinking rather than literally think. Searle's argument, which is the most common argument against *computationalism* (i.e., the philosophy behind "strong AI"), is based on the remark that proponents of computationalism usually leave out some essential features of the mind in their account. In brief, the Chinese room argument goes as follows: Imagine that Anna, who cannot speak or read Chinese, is locked in a room with boxes full of Chinese ideograms. In addition, she has at her disposal a rule book that enables her to answer questions put to her in Chinese. One may think of the rule book as a computer program. Anna receives ideograms that, unknown to her, are questions; she looks up in the rule book what she is supposed to do; she picks up ideograms from the boxes, manipulates them according to the rules in the rule book, and hands out the required ideograms, which are interpreted as answers. We may suppose that Anna is able to fool an external observer, giving the impression that she actually speaks and understands Chinese. But clearly, Anna does not understand a word of Chinese. And if Anna does not understand although she appears to do so, then no computer will actually understand Chinese just because it is equipped with a computer program much like Anna's rule book. Thus, Turing computers cannot be intelligent. Ergo, human minds are hypercomputers!

The capabilities of the human mind are not "divine"; they are the result of neurobiological processes in the brain. However, the Chinese room argument has made it clear that the following analogy is not correct:

$$\text{Mind} : \text{Brain} = \text{Program} : \text{Hardware}.$$

On the other hand, the brain is indeed a machine, an organic machine that clearly transcends the capabilities of the Turing machine. Searle himself calls his approach to the philosophy of mind *biological naturalism*.

Naturally, every argument has a counterargument. Indeed, there have been many attempts at refuting Searle's argument, but we will examine this issue and related ones later on. Also, based on the hypothesis that computationalism is correct, one may easily conclude that even emotions and feelings are actually computable just because they play a functional role in the corresponding cognitive architecture. Later on, we will examine this issue in more detail, and we will see why feelings and emotions cannot be replicated.

1.3 Why Bother with Hypercomputation?

Digital computers are capable of accomplishing an incredible number of tasks. However, one may argue that we have not yet managed to exploit their full power and potential. To a certain degree this is true. For example, the SETI@home project has shown that one can get enormous computational power by quite simple methods. However, sooner or later it will become impossible to further advance the technology associated with digital computers.[4] To avoid approaching this doomsday for computing, we need to take radical measures. Such measures include the development of new computing paradigms and/or the refinement of existing computing paradigms that are inspired by nature.[5] Currently, there is ongoing research work in a number of promising new computing paradigms that include DNA computing [148], quantum computing [84], membrane computing [147], evolution computing [127], and evolvable hardware [128]. In addition, researchers working in these new, promising areas have managed to show that these computing paradigms are steps toward hypercomputation (e.g., see [95, 196]). Evidently, the future of computing depends on developments in all these computing paradigms and more. But are these computing paradigms feasible?

I am convinced that future advances in technology will allow us sooner or later to build computers based on these paradigms. However, the most important issue is whether these machines will offer capabilities that transcend the capabilities of digital computers. A number of thinkers believe that it is impossible to create computing devices that will transcend the capabilities offered by physical implementations of the classical model of computation (e.g., see [39], but see [222] for a response to Paolo Cotogno's arguments). I believe that the discussion so far has made it clear that hypercomputation is not the fictitious "Superman" of computer science, but at the same time, it makes no sense to believe that in a few years we will replace our personal computers with some sort of personal hypercomputers (whatever that means). The truth is always in the middle, and I agree fully with Christof Teuscher and Moshe Sipper [200] when they say:

> *So, hype or computation? At this juncture, it seems the jury is still out–but the trial promises to be riveting.*

---

4. In 1965, Gordon Earle Moore predicted that the number of transistors per square inch on integrated circuits would double every 18 months. In 1975, he updated his prediction to once every two years. This prediction is commonly known as *Moore's law*. Most experts, including Moore himself, expect Moore's law to hold for at least another decade but not much more.
5. We must insist on this, since nature is the best source of inspiration. After all, natural phenomena and processes have taken place for more than 10 billion years!

II. On the Church–Turing Thesis

The classical theory of computability is built around the idea that all *effectively* computable functions are those that can be computed by a Turing machine. This idea has come to be known as the *Church-Turing* thesis. The thesis is actually a definition (or rather a set of definitions) that set the limits of computability. In order to fully understand the meaning of the Church-Turing thesis, one should be familiar with basic concepts from computability. Basically, this chapter is a brief introduction to the relevant material that is necessary for rigorously stating the much acclaimed Church-Turing thesis. The exposition is based on standard references [18, 48, 63, 111, 166].

2.1 Turing Machines

A *Turing machine* (named after the British mathematician Alan Turing, who invented it in the 1930s) is a conceptual computing device that consists of an infinite *tape*, a *controlling device*, and a *scanning head* (see Figure 2.1). The tape is divided into an infinite number of cells. The scanning head can read and write symbols in each cell. The symbols are elements of a set $A = \{S_0, S_1, \ldots, S_n\}$, $n \geq 1$, which is called the *alphabet*. Usually, the symbol S_0 is the blank symbol, which means that when the scanning head writes this symbol on a cell, it actually erases the symbol that was on this particular cell. At any moment, the machine is in a *state* q_i, which is a member of a finite set $Q = \{q_0, q_1, \ldots, q_r\}$, $r \geq 0$. The controlling device is actually a lookup table that is used to determine what the machine has to do next at any given moment. More specifically, the action a machine has to take depends on the state the machine is in and the symbol that is printed on the cell the scanning head has just finished scanning. If no action has been specified for a particular combination of state and symbol, the machine halts. Usually, the control device is specified by a finite set of *quadruples*, which are special cases of *expressions*.

Definition 2.1.1 An *expression* is a string of symbols chosen from the list

$q_0, q_1, \ldots; S_0, S_1, \ldots; R, L.$

A quadruple can have one of the following forms:

$$q_i S_j S_k q_l \qquad (2.1)$$

$$q_i S_j L q_l \qquad (2.2)$$

$$q_i S_j R q_l \qquad (2.3)$$

Note that $L, R \notin A$. The quadruple (2.1) specifies that if the machine is in state q_i and the cell that the scanning head scans contains the symbol S_j, then the scanning head replaces S_j by S_k and the machine enters state q_l. The quadruples (2.2) and (2.3) specify that if the machine is in state q_i and the cell that the scanning head scans contains the symbol S_j, then the scanning head moves to the cell to the left of the current cell, or to the cell to the right of the current cell, respectively, and the machine enters the state q_l. Sometimes the following quadruple is also considered:

$$q_i S_j q_k q_l. \qquad (2.4)$$

This quadruple is particularly useful if we want to construct a Turing machine that will compute *relatively computable functions*. These quadruples provide a Turing machine with a means of communicating with an external agency that can give correct answers to questions about a set $A \subset \mathbb{N}$. More specifically, when a machine is in state q_i and the cell that the scanning head scans contains the symbol S_j, then the machine can be thought of asking the question, "Is $n \in A$?" Here n is the number of S_1's that are printed on the tape. If the answer is "yes," then the machine enters state q_k; otherwise it enters state q_l. Turing machines equipped with such an external agency are called *oracle machines*, and the external agency is called an *oracle*.

Turing machines are used to compute the value of functions $f(x_1, \ldots, x_n)$ that take values in $\mathbb{N}^n$. Each argument $x_i \in \mathbb{N}$, is represented on the tape by preprinting the symbol S_1 on $x_i + 1$ consecutive cells. Argument representations are separated by a blank cell (i.e., a cell on which the symbol S_0 is printed), while all other cells are empty (i.e., the symbol S_0 has been preprinted on each cell). Note that it is customary to use the symbol 1 for S_1 and the symbol "⎵" for S_0. Thus, the sequence $3, 4, 2$ will be represented by the following three blocks of 1's:

$$1111⎵11111⎵111$$

The machine starts at state q_0 and the scanning head is placed atop the leftmost 1 of a sequence of n blocks of 1's. If the machine has reached a situation in which none or more than one quadruple is applicable, the machine halts. Once the machine has terminated, the result of the computation is equal to the number of cells on which the symbol 1 is printed.

The Turing machine's scanning head moves back and forth along the tape. The number that the scanning head displays is its current state, which changes as it proceeds.

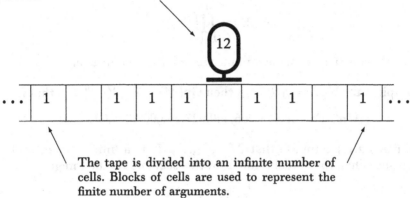

The tape is divided into an infinite number of cells. Blocks of cells are used to represent the finite number of arguments.

Figure 2.1: A typical Turing machine.

Let $\mathcal{M}$ be a Turing machine and let

$$\Psi_{\mathcal{M}}^{(n)}(x_1, x_2, \ldots, x_n)$$

be a partial function of n arguments. We say that $\mathcal{M}$ computes $\Psi_{\mathcal{M}}^{(n)}$ if for each tuple $(m_1, \ldots, m_n)$ of arguments, $\mathcal{M}$ halts after a finite number of steps. If $\mathcal{M}$ does not terminate on a tuple $(k_1, \ldots, k_n)$, then $\Psi_{\mathcal{M}}^{(n)}$ is undefined on this tuple. We say that $\mathcal{M}$ computes f if for all $(x_1, \ldots, x_n)$, $\Psi_{\mathcal{M}}^{(n)}(x_1, \ldots, x_n)$ is defined and equal to $f(x_1, \ldots, x_n)$. Now, it is possible to construct a Turing machine $\mathcal{M}'$ that will have as input the description of the controlling device of another Turing machine $\mathcal{M}$ and its arguments. Clearly, both the description of the controlling device and the arguments of the machine have to be encoded. Here are the relevant details. Suppose that we associate with each basic symbol of a Turing machine an odd number greater than or equal to 3 as follows:

$$
\begin{array}{ccccccccccc}
3 & 5 & 7 & 9 & 11 & 13 & 15 & 17 & 19 & 21 & \ldots \\
\uparrow & \uparrow & \uparrow & \uparrow & \uparrow & \uparrow & \uparrow & \uparrow & \uparrow & \uparrow & \\
R & L & S_0 & q_0 & S_1 & q_1 & S_2 & q_2 & S_3 & q_3 & \ldots
\end{array}
$$

For each i, S_i is associated with $4i + 7$ and q_i is associated with $4i + 9$. In order to define the encoding of a Turing machine, first we need to define the encoding of an expression and then the encoding of a sequence of expressions.

Definition 2.1.2 Assume that M is a string of symbols $\gamma_1, \gamma_2,\ldots,\gamma_n$ and that $a_1, a_2,\ldots, a_n$ are the corresponding integers associated with these symbols. The Gödel number of M is the integer

$$\text{Gn}(M) = \prod_{k=1}^{n}\Big(\text{Pr}(k)\Big)^{a_k},$$

where $\text{Pr}(k)$ is the kth prime number in order of magnitude.

Example 2.1.1 If $M = q_1 S_0 S_2 q_1$, then $\text{Gn}(M) = 2^{13}\cdot 3^7\cdot 5^{15}\cdot 7^{13}$, that is

$$\text{Gn}(M) = 52{,}974{,}066{,}440{,}027{,}250{,}000{,}000{,}000{,}000.$$

Definition 2.1.3 Suppose that $M_1, M_2,\ldots,M_n$ is a finite sequence of expressions. Then the Gödel number of this sequence is the integer:

$$\prod_{k=1}^{n}\Big(\text{Pr}(k)\Big)^{\text{Gn}(M_k)}.$$

Definition 2.1.4 Assume that $M_1, M_2,\ldots,M_n$ is any arrangement of the quadruples of a Turing machine $\mathscr{M}$ without repetitions. Then the Gödel number of the sequence $M_1, M_2,\ldots,M_n$ is a Gödel number of $\mathscr{M}$.

Clearly, a Turing machine consisting of n quadruples has $n!$ different Gödel numbers.

Definition 2.1.5 A universal Turing machine $\mathscr{U}$ is a Turing machine that can be employed to compute any function of one argument that an ordinary Turing machine $\mathscr{M}$ can compute.[1]

Practically, this means that given a Turing machine $\mathscr{M}$ with a Gödel number m that computes the function $f(x)$, then

$$\Psi_{\mathscr{U}}^{(2)}(m,x) = f(x) = \Psi_{\mathscr{M}}^{(1)}(x).$$

Thus, if the number m is written on the tape of $\mathscr{U}$, followed by the number x, $\mathscr{U}$ will compute the number $\Psi_{\mathscr{M}}^{(1)}(x)$. Also, the universal Turing machine can be used to compute functions with n arguments, but we are not going to describe how this can be done (see [48] for the relevant details).

The function $\Psi_{\mathscr{U}}^{(2)}$ is just an example of a function that has as arguments a "program" and its "input." Another interesting example of such a function is the so-called *halting function*:

$$h(m,x) = \begin{cases} 1, & \text{when } \mathscr{M} \text{ starts with input } x \text{ and eventually stops,} \\ 0, & \text{otherwise,} \end{cases}$$

1. The question regarding which functions can be computed by a Turing machine will be discussed in Section 2.4.

where m is the Gödel number of $\mathcal{M}$. Whether this function is computable is equivalent to the halting problem. This, in turn, can be summarized as follows: is there an *effective* procedure such that given any m and any x we can determine whether $\Psi^{(2)}_{\mathcal{U}}(m, x)$ is defined?

Although Turing machines are the standard model of the classical theory of computation, still their use is rather clumsy for practical purposes, for example, to specify how we can compute a particular function. Alternatively, we can use a *random-access machine* [111]. A random-access machine is an idealized computer with a random-access memory consisting of a finite number of idealized registers capable of holding arbitrarily long integers. The set of machine instructions is quite short; however, instead of presenting the standard random-access machine, we will present a sugared version of it that will appeal to those with a some knowledge of computer programming. Thus, a random-access machine will be an idealized computer capable of executing programs specified in a simple yet powerful enough programming language. The only data type that this language supports is the natural numbers including zero. However, numbers may be arbitrarily large. A program can employ an arbitrarily large number of variables, each capable of holding a single nonnegative integer. All variables will be initialized to 0. The language has only the following types of commands:

- **if** test **then** commands **else** commands **end**

- **while** test **do** commands **end**

- variable++ (increment)

- variable-- (decrement)

Note that decrementing a variable whose value is already zero has no effect. Also, the test will have the form variable = 0, and it will succeed only when the variable is equal to zero. In addition, commands is just a sequence of the commands presented above separated by at least one space character and/or one newline character. This language looks like a "real" programming language, though it appears to be a weak one. However, the language is equivalent in power to a Turing machine. In other words, this language is powerful enough to compute anything that can be computed by *any* algorithmic programming language.

2.2   General Recursive Functions

A basic exposition of the theory of general recursive functions is essential for a full appreciation of the Church–Turing thesis. The exposition of the theory presented in this section is based on a seminal paper by Kleene [100].

We start with a presentation of the notion of a primitive recursive function, since these functions are related to general recursive functions.

Primitive recursive functions are defined in terms of basic functions and function builders. There are three basic or initial functions:

(i) the *successor* function $S(x) = x + 1$,

(ii) the *zero* function $z(x) = 0$, and

(iii) the *projection* functions $U_i^n(x_1, \ldots, x_n) = x_i$, $1 \le i \le n$.

Primitive recursive functions can be defined by applying function builders, or schemas, to the basic functions. There are three function builders:

Composition Suppose that f is a function of m arguments and each of $g_1, \ldots, g_m$ is a function of n arguments. Then the function obtained by composition of f and $g_1, \ldots, g_m$ is the function h defined as follows:

$$h(x_1, \ldots, x_n) = f\Big(g_1(x_1, \ldots, x_n), \ldots, g_m(x_1, \ldots, x_n)\Big).$$

Primitive Recursion A function h of $k+1$ arguments is said to be definable by (primitive) recursion from the functions f and g, having k and $k+2$ arguments, respectively, if it is defined as follows:

$$h(x_1, \ldots, x_k, 0) = f(x_1, \ldots, x_k),$$
$$h(x_1, \ldots, x_k, S(m)) = g\Big(x_1, \ldots, x_k, m, h(x_1, \ldots, x_k, m)\Big).$$

Minimalization The operation of minimalization associates with each total function f of $k+1$ arguments a function h of k arguments. Given a tuple $(x_1, \ldots, x_k)$, the value of $h(x_1, \ldots, x_k)$ is the least value of x_{k+1}, if one exists, for which $f(x_1, \ldots, x_k, x_{k+1}) = 0$. If no such x_{k+1} exists, then its value is undefined.

Now we are ready to define primitive recursive and general recursive functions.

Definition 2.2.1 The functions that can be obtained from the basic functions by the function builders composition and primitive recursion are called primitive recursive functions.

Definition 2.2.2 The functions that can be obtained from the basic functions by all function builders are called general recursive functions.

Note that general recursive functions are also known as just recursive functions or μ-recursive functions.

We can easily extend the two previous definitions to define A-primitive recursive and A-recursive functions. However, in order to do this we need to know what the *characteristic* function of a set is.

Definition 2.2.3 Assume that X is a universe set and $A \subseteq X$. Then the characteristic function $\chi_A : X \rightarrow \{0, 1\}$ of A is defined as follows:

$$\chi_A(a) = \begin{cases} 1, & \text{if } a \in A, \\ 0, & \text{if } a \notin A. \end{cases}$$

Note that this particular way of defining a set is actually employed to define fuzzy subsets, multisets, etc., via different types of characteristic functions. We are now prepared to define A-primitive recursive and A-recursive functions. Assume that $A \subseteq \mathbb{N}$ is a fixed set.

Definition 2.2.4 A function f is a partial A-recursive function if $f = \Psi_{\mathcal{M}}^A$, where $\Psi_{\mathcal{M}}^A$ is a partial function that denotes the computation performed by an oracle Turing machine $\mathcal{M}$ with oracle A.

Definition 2.2.5 A function f is an A-recursive function if there is an oracle machine $\mathcal{M}$ with oracle A such that $f = \Psi_{\mathcal{M}}^A$ and $\Psi_{\mathcal{M}}^A$ is a total function.

Definition 2.2.6 A set B is recursive in A if χ_B is A-recursive.

2.3 Recursive Relations and Predicates

It is quite natural to extend the notion of recursiveness to characterize not only functions, but also sets, relations, and predicates. Informally, a set is called recursive if we have an effective method to determine whether a given element belongs to the set. However, if this effective method cannot be used to determine whether a given element does *not* belong to the set, then the set is called semirecursive. Formally, a recursive set is defined as follows.

Definition 2.3.1 Let $A \subseteq \mathbb{N}$ be a set. Then we say that A is primitive recursive or recursive if its characteristic function χ_A is primitive recursive or recursive, respectively.

Example 2.3.1 Suppose that Π is the set of all odd natural numbers. Then Π is primitive recursive, since its characteristic function

$$\chi_\Pi(a) = R(a, 2)$$

is primitive recursive. Here, $R(x, y)$ returns the remainder of the integer division $x \div y$.

Definition 2.3.2 A set A is called recursively enumerable or semirecursive either if $A = \emptyset$ or if A is the range of a recursive function.

Similarly, we can define A-recursively enumerable sets.

Definition 2.3.3 A set B is called A-recursively enumerable either if $B = \emptyset$ or if B is the range of an A-recursive function.

Definitions 2.3.1 and 2.3.2 can be easily extended to characterize *relations*. Note that an n-ary relation on a set A is any subset R of the n-fold Cartesian product $A \times \cdots \times A$ of n factors.

Definition 2.3.4 A relation $R \subseteq \mathbb{N}^m$ is called primitive recursive or recursive if its characteristic function χ_R given by

$$\chi_R(x_1, \ldots, x_m) = \begin{cases} 1, & \text{if } (x_1, \ldots, x_m) \in R, \\ 0, & \text{if } (x_1, \ldots, x_m) \notin R, \end{cases}$$

is primitive recursive or recursive, respectively.

Definition 2.3.5 A relation $R \subseteq \mathbb{N}^m$ is called recursively enumerable (or semirecursive) if R is the range of a partial recursive function $f : \mathbb{N} \to \mathbb{N}^m$.

Let us now see how the notion of recursiveness has been extended to characterize predicates. But first let us recall what a predicate is. Roughly, it is a statement that asserts a proposition that must be either true (denoted by tt) or false (denoted by ff). An $\mathbb{N}^n$ function whose range of values consists exclusively of elements of the set $\{tt, ff\}$ is a predicate.

Definition 2.3.6 A predicate $P(x_1, \ldots, x_n)$ is called recursive if the set

$$\{(x_1, \ldots, x_n) | P(x_1, \ldots, x_n)\},$$

which is called its *extension*, is recursive.

Definition 2.3.7 The predicate $P(x_1, \ldots, x_n)$ is called recursively enumerable (or semirecursive) if there exists a partially recursive function whose domain is the set

$$\{(x_1, \ldots, x_n) | P(x_1, \ldots, x_n)\}.$$

The Arithmetic Hierarchy Let us denote by Σ_0^0 the class of all recursive subsets of $\mathbb{N}$. For every $n \in \mathbb{N}$, Σ_{n+1}^0 is the class of sets that are A-recursively enumerable for some set $A \in \Sigma_n^0$. It follows that Σ_1^0 is the class of recursively enumerable sets. Let us denote by Π_0^0 the class of all subsets of $\mathbb{N}$ whose complements are in Σ_0^0. In other words, $D \in \Pi_0^0$ if and only if $\mathbb{N} \backslash D \in \Sigma_0^0$. The class Π_1^0 is knwon in the literature as the class of *corecursively enumerable* sets. In addition, let us denote by Δ_n^0 the intersection of the classes Σ_n^0 and Π_n^0 (i.e., $\Delta_n^0 = \Sigma_n^0 \cap \Pi_n^0$). The classes Σ_n^0, Π_n^0, and Δ_n^0 form a hierarchy that is called the *arithmetic hierarchy*. The classes that make up this hierarchy have the following properties:

$$\Delta_n^0 \subset \Sigma_n^0, \qquad\qquad \Delta_n^0 \subset \Pi_n^0,$$
$$\Sigma_n^0 \subset \Sigma_{n+1}^0, \qquad\qquad \Pi_n^0 \subset \Pi_{n+1}^0,$$
$$\Sigma_n^0 \cup \Pi_n^0 \subset \Delta_{n+1}^0, \forall n \geq 1.$$

Figure 2.2 depicts the relationships between the various classes of the arithmetic hierarchy.

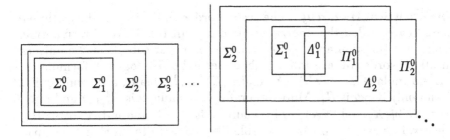

Figure 2.2: The relationships between the various classes of the arithmetic hierarchy.

The set-theoretic presentation of the arithmetic hierarchy is not the only possible presentation. Indeed, other presentations based on predicates or relations are also possible. Assume that φ is a formula[2] in the language of first-order arithmetic (i.e., there are no other nonlogical symbols apart from constants denoting natural numbers, primitive recursive functions, and predicates that can be decided primitive recursively). Then we say that φ is a Δ_0^0-formula if φ contains at most bounded quantifiers. We say that φ is Σ_1^0 if there is a Δ_0^0-formula $\psi(x)$ such that $\varphi \equiv (\exists x)\psi(x)$. Dually, φ is Π_1^0 if $\neg\varphi$ is Σ_1^0. More generally, a formula φ is in Σ_{n+1}^0 if there is a formula $\psi(x)$ in Π_n^0 such that $\varphi \equiv (\exists x)\psi(x)$. Dually, φ is Π_{n+1}^0 if $\neg\varphi$ is Σ_{n+1}^0. Note that Σ_0^0 is the class of all recursive predicates. Suppose that $Q_1 = P_1(x_1)$, $Q_2 = P_2(x_1, x_2)$, $Q_3 = P_3(x_1, x_2, x_3),\ldots$ are Δ_0^0-formulas. Then Table 2.1 gives a schematic representation of the classes Σ_n^0 and Π_n^0.

	$n = 1$	$n = 2$	$n = 3$	
Σ_n^0	$(\exists x_1)Q_1$	$(\exists x_1)(\forall x_2)Q_2$	$(\exists x_1)(\forall x_2)(\exists x_3)Q_3$	$\cdots$
Π_n^0	$(\forall x_1)Q_1$	$(\forall x_1)(\exists x_2)Q_2$	$(\forall x_1)(\exists x_2)(\forall x_3)Q_3$	$\cdots$

Table 2.1: A schematic representation of the classes Σ_n^0 and Π_n^0.

2. Very roughly: a term yields a value; variables and constants are terms; functions are terms; atoms yield truth values; and each predicate is an atom. An atom is a formula. Given formulas p and q the following are also formulas: $\neg p, p \vee q, p \wedge q, p \Rightarrow q, p \equiv q, \forall x p,$ and $\exists x p$. In the last two cases x is said to be a bound variable, while in all other possible cases it is said to be a free variable.

Assume that $R \subseteq \mathbb{N}^m$ is a relation. Then $R \in \Sigma_1^0$ (i.e., R is Σ_1^0-relation) if R is recursively enumerable. Similarly, $R \in \Pi_1^0$ if $\overline{R} \in \Sigma_1^0$ (i.e., if the complement of R with respect to $\mathbb{N}^m$ is a Σ_1^0-relation). In general, $R \in \Sigma_n^0$ ($n \geq 2$) if there are a $k \in \mathbb{N}$ and a Π_{n-1}^0-relation $S \subset \mathbb{N}^{m+k}$ such that

$$R = \{(x_1, \ldots, x_m) \mid \exists (x_{m+1}, \ldots, x_{m+k}) \in \mathbb{N}^k, (x_1, \ldots, x_{m+k}) \in S\}.$$

Also, $R \in \Pi_n^0$ if $\overline{R} \in \Sigma_n^0$.

The Analytical Hierarchy   The second-order equivalent of the arithmetic hierarchy is called the *analytical hierarchy*. In this hierarchy, quantifiers range over function and relation symbols and over subsets of the universe. In other words, we are talking about second-order logic. A formula φ is a Π_1^1-formula if $\varphi \equiv (\forall X)\psi(X)$ and $\psi(X)$ is Σ_1^0. Dually, a formula φ is Σ_1^1 if and only if $\neg\varphi$ is Π_1^1. More generally, a formula φ is Π_{k+1}^1 if and only if $\varphi \equiv (\forall X)\psi(X)$ and $\psi(X)$ is Σ_k^1. Dually, φ is Σ_{k+1}^1 if and only if $\neg\varphi$ is Π_{k+1}^1. Clearly, it is easy to construct a table like Table 2.1 to provide a schematic representation of the analytical hierarchy. Note that the Δ_1^1-sets are the so-called *hyperarithmetic* sets. In addition, a function $f : \mathbb{N} \to \mathbb{N}$ is hyperarithmetic if its graph[3] G_f is a hyperarithmetic relation.

The arithmetic and analytic hierarchies are used to classify functions, sets, predicates and relations. In particular, the higher the class an object belongs to, the more classically noncomputable it is. Alternatively, one can view these hierarchies as a means to classify hypercomputers.

2.4   The Church–Turing Thesis

The Church–Turing thesis is the cornerstone of classical computability theory, since it describes what can and what cannot be computed. The thesis can be phrased as follows.

Thesis 2.4.1 *Every effectively computable function is Turing computable, that is, there is a Turing machine that realizes it. Alternatively, the effectively computable functions can be identified with the recursive functions.*

Formally, a function $f : \mathbb{N}^n \to \mathbb{N}^m$ is Turing computable if there is a Turing machine $\mathscr{M}$ that computes it. But it is not clear at all what is meant by an *effective* procedure or method. For example, Copeland [36] gives four criteria that any sequence of instructions that make up a procedure or method should satisfy in order for it to be characterized as effective:

---

3. The graph of a function $f : X \to Y$ is the subset of $X \times Y$ given by $\{(x, f(x)) : x \in X\}$. A total function whose graph is recursively enumerable is a recursive function.

(i) Each instruction is expressed by means of finite number of symbols.

(ii) The instructions produce the desired result in a finite number of steps.

(iii) They can be carried out by a human being unaided by any machinery save paper and pencil.

(iv) They demand no insight or ingenuity on the part of the human carrying it out.

In his classical textbook [134], Marvin Minsky defines an effective procedure as "a set of rules which tell us, from moment to moment, precisely how to behave," provided we have at our disposal a universally accepted way to interpret these rules. Minsky concludes that this definition is meaningful if the steps are actually steps performed by some Turing machine. However, even this definition is not precise according to Carol Cleland. More specifically, she argues in [33, p. 167] that "Turing-machine instructions cannot be said to prescribe actions, let alone *precisely* describe them." Cleland has come to this conclusion by noticing that although it is perfectly legitimate to use the word "mechanical" to mean something that is done without *thought* or *volition*, still this usage does not capture the idea of a finite, constructive process.

Since an algorithm is roughly synonymous with an effective method, it is necessary to discuss the notion of an algorithm. The definition that follows, which was borrowed from [87], is roughly the one that is accepted by most computer scientists and engineers.

Definition 2.4.1 An algorithm is a finite set of instructions that if followed, accomplish a particular task. In addition, every algorithm must satisfy the following criteria:

(i) *input*: there are zero or more quantities that are externally supplied;

(ii) *output*: at least one quantity is produced;

(iii) *definiteness*: each instruction must be clear and unambiguous;

(iv) *finiteness*: if we trace out the instructions of an algorithm, then for all cases the algorithm will terminate after a finite number of steps;

(v) *effectiveness*: every instruction must be sufficiently basic that it can in principle be carried out by a person using only pencil and paper. It is not enough that each operation be defined as in (iii), but it must also be feasible.

Naturally, it is no surprise to hear that this definition is not a precise one. However, it is considered to be sufficient for most practical purposes. Also, Hartley Rogers [166] gives the following (imprecise) definition:

> [A]n algorithm is a clerical (i.e., deterministic, book-keeping) procedure which can be applied to any of a certain class of symbolic inputs and which will eventually yield, for each such input, a corresponding symbolic output.

The lack of a precise definition of what an algorithm is has prompted Noson Yanofsky [230] to define an algorithm as the set of computer programs that implement or express that algorithm. Unfortunately, even this apparently mathematical approach has its drawbacks. For instance, is it possible to be aware of all programs that implement an algorithm? And when Anna writes a computer program that implements an algorithm, what is, actually, the algorithm that she is programming? Clearly, one must be very careful to avoid entering a vicious circle.

A rather different idea regarding effectiveness has been put forth by Cleland who argues that even everyday procedures can be rendered as effective [33]. For example, she argues that if a recipe for Hollandaise sauce is to be carried out by an expert chef, then the whole procedure can be classified as effective. The core of her argument is that "...quotidian [everyday] procedures are bona fide procedures; their instructions prescribe genuine actions." However, we agree with Selmer Bringsjord and Michael Zenzen [26] when they say that

> By our lights, recipes are laughably vague, and don't deserve to be taken seriously from the standpoint of formal philosophy, logic, or computer science.

Gábor Etesi and István Németi [58] describe as effectively computable any function $f : \mathbb{N}^k \to \mathbb{N}^m$ for which there is a *physical computer* realizing it. Here, by "realization by a physical computer" they mean the following:

> Let P by a physical computer, and $f : \mathbb{N}^k \to \mathbb{N}^m$ a (mathematical) function. Then we say that P *realizes* f if an imaginary observer O can do the following with P. Assume that O can "start" the computer P with $(x_1, \ldots, x_k)$ as an input, and then sometime later (according to O's internal clock) O "receives" data $(y_1, \ldots, y_m) \in \mathbb{N}^m$ from P as an output such that $(y_1, \ldots, y_m)$ coincides with the value $f(x_1, \ldots, x_k)$ of the function f at input $(x_1, \ldots, x_k)$.

The same authors, after introducing the notion of *artificial computing systems,* that is, thought experiments relative to a fixed physical theory that involve computing devices, managed to rephrase the Church–Turing thesis as follows.[4]

Thesis 2.4.2 *Every function realizable by an artificial computing system is Turing computable.*

---

4. Actually, they call this "updated" version of the Church–Turing thesis the *Church–Kalmár–Turing* thesis, named after Church, László Kalmár, and Turing.

Since artificial computing systems are thought experiments relative to a fixed physical theory, the thesis can be rephrased as follows.

Thesis 2.4.3 *Every function realizable by a thought experiment is Turing computable.*

Note that according to Etesi and Németi, a thought experiment relative to a fixed physical theory is a theoretically possible experiment, that is, an experiment that can be carefully designed, specified, etc., according to the rules of the physical theory, but for which we might not currently have the necessary resources.

Others, like David Deutsch [51], have reformulated the Church-Turing thesis as follows.

Thesis 2.4.4 *Every finitely realizable physical system can be perfectly simulated by a universal model computing machine operating by finite means.*

In the special case of the human mind, this thesis can be rephrased as follows.

Thesis 2.4.5 *The human brain realizes only Turing-computable functions.*

This thesis is the core of computationalism. This philosophy claims that a person's mind is actually a Turing machine. Consequently, one may go a step ahead and argue that since a person's mind is a Turing machine, then it will be possible one day to construct an artificial person with feelings and emotions. The mind is indeed a machine, but one that transcends the capabilities of the Turing machine and operates in a profoundly different way. But we will say more about this in Chapter 6.

We have presented various formulations of the Turing-Church thesis. This thesis forms the core of the classical theory of computability. Hyper-computation is an effort to refute the various forms of this thesis. And the ambitious goal of this book is to show that this can actually be done!

III. Early Hypercomputers

Hypercomputation is not really a recent development in the theory of computation. On the contrary, there were quite successful early efforts to define primarily conceptual computing devices with computational power that transcends the capabilities of the established model of computation.[1] In this chapter, I will present some of these early conceptual devices as well as some related ideas and theories. In particular, I will present trial-and-error machines, TAE-computability, inductive machines, accelerated Turing machines, oracle machines, and pseudorecursiveness. However, I need to stress that I have deliberately excluded a number of early efforts, which will be covered later in more specialized chapters.

3.1 Trial-and-Error Machines

In this section I present the theory of trial-and-error machines, a model of the human mind based on these machines, and TAE-computability, a model of computation that is similar to trial-and-error machines.

3.1.1 Extending Recursion Theory

In 1965, the prestigious *Journal of Symbolic Logic* published in a single issue two papers [68, 160] by Mark Gold and Hilary Putnam that dealt surprisingly with the same subject—*limiting recursion*. This type of recursion can be realized in the form of *trial-and-error* machines. Typically, a trial-and-error machine is a kind of a Turing machine that can be used to determine whether an element x belongs to a set $X \subset \mathbb{N}$ or, more generally, whether a tuple $(x_1, \ldots, x_n)$ belongs to a relation $R \subset \mathbb{N}^n$. In the course of its operation, the machine continuously prints out a sequence of responses (e.g., a sequence of 1's and 0's) and the last of them is always the correct

---

1. Strictly speaking, Kalmár [93], Rózsa Péter [154], and Jean Porte [156] were probably the first researchers to challenge the validity of the Church–Turing thesis. Nevertheless, their arguments were not without flaws, as was shown by Elliott Mendelson [126].

answer. Thus, if the machine has most recently printed 1, then we know that the integer (or the tuple) that has been supplied as input must be in the set (or relation) *unless the machine is going to change its mind*; but we have no procedure for telling whether the machine will change its mind again. Suppose now that our trial-and-error machine prints out an infinite number of responses. Then after a certain point, the machine may converge to a particular response, and thus it will continuously print out the same response (1 or 0). Of course, this description is somehow vague, and so we need to define precisely limiting recursion. Let us begin with limiting recursive predicates.[2]

Definition 3.1.1 A function P is a limiting recursive predicate if there is a general recursive function f such that (for every $x_1, x_2, \ldots, x_n$),

$$P(x_1, x_2, \ldots, x_n) \iff \lim_{y \to \infty} f(x_1, x_2, \ldots, x_n, y) = 1,$$

$$\neg P(x_1, x_2, \ldots, x_n) \iff \lim_{y \to \infty} f(x_1, x_2, \ldots, x_n, y) = 0,$$

where

$$\lim_{y \to \infty} f(x_1, x_2, \ldots, x_n, y) = k \overset{\text{def}}{=} (\exists y)(\forall z)(z \geq y \to f(x_1, \ldots, x_n, z) = k).$$

The following theorem is proved in [160].

Theorem 3.1.1 *P is a limiting recursive predicate if $P \in \Delta_2^0$.*

Obviously, this means that one cannot use a Turing machine to check whether a limiting recursive predicate P is true or false. Thus, trial-and-error machines transcend the Church–Turing limit.

Assume now that we restrict a trial-and-error machine so it can change its mind only k times, irrespective of the particular input the machine has. As a direct application of this restriction, k-limiting recursion was introduced.

Definition 3.1.2 P is a k-limiting recursive predicate if there is a general recursive function f such that (for every $x_1, x_2, \ldots, x_n$):

(i) $P(x_1, x_2, \ldots, x_n) \iff \lim_{y \to \infty} f(x_1, x_2, \ldots, x_n, y) = 1$;

(ii) there are *at most k* integers y such that

$$f(x_1, \ldots, x_n, y) \neq f(x_1, \ldots, x_n, y + 1).$$

The following theorem is proved in [160].

---

2. Putnam calls these predicates *trial-and-error* predicates, but we have opted to use Gold's terminology.

Theorem 3.1.2 *There exists a k such that P is a k-limiting recursive predicate if and only if P belongs to $^*\Sigma_1^0$, the smallest class containing the recursively enumerable predicates and closed under truth functions.*

Limiting recursive functions can be defined similarly to limiting recursive predicates.

Definition 3.1.3 A partial function $f(x)$ will be called limiting recursive if there is a total recursive function $g(x, n)$ such that

$$f(x) = \lim_{n \to \infty} g(x, n).$$

Similarly, one can define limiting recursive sets and relations (see [68] for details).

It has already been noted that trial-and-error machines transcend the capabilities of ordinary Turing machines; thus they should be able to solve the halting problem. Indeed, Peter Kugel [103] describes an *effective method* (or *hyperalgorithm*) that can solve this problem. Here is his effective method to solve this problem:

> Given a program, Prog, and an input, Inp, output NO (to indicate that Prog(Inp) will not halt). Then run a simulation of Prog(Inp). (Turing [206] showed that such a simulation is always possible.) If the simulation halts, output YES to indicate that Prog(Inp) really does halt.
>
> Clearly the last output that this procedure produces solves the halting problem, if you are willing to accept results arrived at "in the limit." Which proves that limiting computation can do things no ordinary, or recursive, computation can.

3.1.2   A Model of the Human Mind

Another aspect of Kugel's work is a proposed model of intelligence, and consequently a model of the human mind, that is based on limiting recursion. In particular, Kugel is a strong advocate of the idea that the human mind is actually a trial-and-error machine. He has suggested a division of the human mind into four parts or modules [102]. Figure 3.1 depicts Kugel's division.

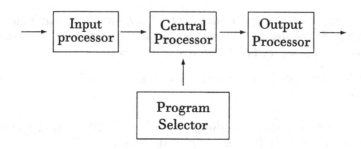

Figure 3.1: Kugel's division of the human mind.

The functionality of each module is briefly outlined below:

Input Processor This module gathers information from the environment and transforms it into a form suitable for further processing by the central processor. For example, suppose that Lila is a zoologist who studies a herd of zebras in an African savanna. Suddenly, she realizes that a tiger is approaching the place where she is standing. At once, her input processor takes this visual signal and turns it into the message, "This is a tiger."

Central Processor The transformed data that the input processor produces are further transformed into a form that is meaningful for the output processor. For example Lila's central processor might transform the message, "This is a tiger" into the message, "run."

Output Processor This module takes the information produced by the central processor and transforms it into something that can be used to affect the world. For example, Lila's output processor might take the message, "run" and turn it into messages to control specific muscles so as to remove Lila from the immediate area.

Program Selector In general, different situations demand different actions. In Kugel's model, the human mind has a set of (predefined?) actions, which he calls *programs*, that can be invoked to handle a particular situation. The program selector is the module that is responsible for the invocation of the appropriate program. For example, Lila's program selector will most probably decide that it is time to invoke the *animal-recognizing program* and halt the *zebra-studying program*.

Kugel argues that the input processor is a Π_1^0 process (i.e., it can be simulated by a machine capable of computing such functions), the output processor is a Σ_2^0 process, the central processor is a k-limiting recursive process, and the program selector is a Π_2^0 process.

Kugel has derived his results by tacitly assuming that all mental processes are mechanistic in nature and part of the arithmetic hierarchy. This observation explains the nature of his results, but not how he arrived at his conclusions. Therefore, to explain how he did so, I will briefly present the ideas that led him to this particular model of the mind.

Among other things, the input processor classifies what we see or observe. Based on earlier suggestions made by other researchers, Kugel has suggested that our ability to classify what we observe might involve the recognition of membership in productive sets. A set $A \subseteq \mathbb{N}$ is called productive when there is no computing procedure to determine whether some element x belongs to A. In addition, there is a computable function, the production function, that effectively finds a counterexample to the claim that some procedure will effectively recognize membership in A. Formally, productive sets are defined as follows.

Definition 3.1.4 Let W_i, $i \in \mathbb{N}$, be a numbering (i.e., a surjective assignment of natural numbers to the elements of a set of objects) of the recursively enumerable subsets of $\mathbb{N}$ such that $W_i = \text{dom}\,\varphi_i$ (i.e., the domain of φ_i), where φ_i is a recursive function whose Gödel number is i. A set $A \subseteq \mathbb{N}$ is called productive if there exists a computable function ψ such that for all $i \in \mathbb{N}$, $W_i \subseteq A$ implies that $\psi(i)$ is *convergent* (i.e., it is defined) and $\psi(i) \in A \setminus W_i$.

There are productive sets in Π_1^0. For instance, the set N of all pairs $(\mathcal{M}, x)$ such that $\Psi_{\mathcal{M}}^{(1)}(x)$ fails to halt is a productive set that is in Π_1^0. In addition, there is a nonhalting procedure to determine whether a pair $(\mathcal{M}, x)$ belongs to N. And according to Kugel, the input processor employs such a nonhalting procedure to recognize objects.

The human mind is able to derive general theories from specific evidence and to deduce specific facts from its ever changing knowledge of the world. In general, theories are assumed to be correct until some evidence forces us to alter the theory or even to abandon it in favor of a new theory. For instance, as Kugel [104] has pointed out if all swans that we have observed are white, then we will come up with the theory that all swans are white. Naturally, this theory will change the very day someone observes a *cygnus atratus* (a black swan). This scenario of scientific research suggests that our ability to develop theories from specific evidence is not really computable (i.e., one cannot "re-create" this procedure by using a conventional computing device). Indeed, Kugel has suggested that this ability might be actually a trial-and-error procedure. As such, it can evaluate predicates in Σ_2^0. Thus, Kugel has actually suggested that the output processor is a Σ_2^0 process.

A simple model of how the mind actually solves problems is based on the solution of the *problem of inverting computable functions*, that is, given a machine p and an output o, find an input i such that $\Psi_{\mathcal{U}}^2(p, i)$ equals o. This problem can be solved by employing a k-limiting recursive process, and so one may say that the central processor is actually a k-limiting recursive process, though it is not clear what the value of k shoulf be.

Usually, most computer programs decrease the amount of information involved during their execution. For example, a simple program that adds its (command line) arguments generates one number out of two. On the other hand, Kugel asserts that the selection of a program to perform a particular task increases the amount of information in an information-theoretic sense. This is an indication that this procedure cannot be computable. In general, a k-limiting recursive process can be used in association with a program-generating program to find a program that matches the evidence provided. This is clearly the task performed by the program selector. However, since many of the generated programs are not suitable for some particular task (e.g., they cannot handle all pieces of evidence), we need a mechanism to filter these programs. It is not possible to computably filter out all and only the totally computable programs from the list of all possible programs. But it is possible to perform this task noncomputably using a Π_2^0 filter, which explains why Kugel has suggested that the program selector is a Π_2^0 process.

The adoption of Kugel's model automatically implies the invalidation of the Church–Turing thesis. However, what is really puzzling about Kugel's model is that he asserts that most (if not all) vital mental processes are purely computational in nature. Obviously, a number of mental processes are indeed computational in nature, for instance, our ability to perform basic arithmetic operations.[3] However, it is one thing to be able to calculate the sum or the product of two numbers and another to fall in love and express it by saying "Sigga, I love you!" In other words, as has been already pointed out, no one has provided enough evidence to support the idea that feelings and affection are computational in their nature. Another aspect of Kugel's model is that it seems to be naive in the eyes of contemporary thinkers and researchers, for it lacks the "sophistication" of modern approaches to the philosophy of mind. Apart from this, it is really difficult to see why some machine that can solve the halting problem, can ipso facto feel angry, fall in love, or even worship God!

3.2   TAE-Computability

Jaakko Hintikka and Arto Mutanen [83, Chapter 9] present an alternative conceptual computing device that is similar to trial-and-error machines. The Hintikka–Mutanen abstract computing device is essentially a Turing machine with an extra tape, which is called the *bookkeeping* or *result-recording* tape. Both the working and bookkeeping tapes can be viewed as

---

3. Although it is not clear at all that our ability to perform basic arithmetic operations is computational, still, for the sake of argument, I will assume this is the case.

read–write storage devices, since the machine can print and erase information from either tape. Without loss of generality, one can assume that what appears on the bookkeeping tape are equations of the form $f(a) = b$, where $a, b \in \mathbb{N}$. These equations are used by the machine to define the function to be computed. In particular, this function is computed by the machine if and only if all (and only) such true equations appear on the bookkeeping tape when the machine has completed its operation. Practically, this means that each true equation $f(a) = b$ will be printed on the bookkeeping tape sometime during the operation of the machine and it will stay on it until the machine terminates. At that point, for each a, there has to be one and only one true equation on the bookkeeping tape. If no such equation has appeared on the bookkeeping tape for some a, or the equation for some a was changing continuously, then the value $f(a)$ is not defined.

A Hintikka–Mutanen machine cannot be simulated by a Turing machine, since these machines introduce a wider notion of computability compared to standard Turing machines. On the other hand, by imposing some restrictions on the operation of the machine, we obtain an abstract machine that is computationally equivalent to the Turing machine. More specifically, if we require that the machine never erase anything from the bookkeeping tape, the machine will behave like an ordinary Turing machine. In classical computability it is not enough to have each true equation $f(a) = b$ on the result-recording tape from some finite stage on, but it is necessary to know when the machine has reached this stage. If we allow the machine to erase data from the bookkeeping tape, then we could specify as a condition that $f(x)$ have the value b if and only if the equation $f(a) = b$ is the last equation of the form $f(a) = x$ produced by the machine. Clearly, this implies that we have at our disposal an effective procedure to determine when the last equation has been printed on the bookkeeping tape.

Hintikka and Mutanen call the resulting computability theory *TAE-computability*, short for trial-and-error computability. The following passage [83] gives an explanation of why this particular name was chosen:

> The name is motivated by the fact that erasure from the result tape is permitted by our definition. Such erasure can be thought of as an acknowledgement on the part of the machine that its trial choice of a line of computation has been in error and that it is using the recognition of an error to try a different line of computation.

TAE-computability is "arguably more fundamental theoretically than recursivity." In order to show this, the authors prove a theorem. But in order to fully comprehend it, one must be familiar with a number of definitions from logic. So, I will briefly present the notions of satisfiable formulas and Skolem functions as they are presented in [53]. Readers familiar with these concepts can safely skip the next paragraph.

Assume that L is a language (i.e., a countable set of nonlogical symbols). Then an *interpretation I of L* is characterized by the following:

(i) There is a *domain* of interpretation, which is a nonempty set D of *values*.

(ii) A function $f_I : D^n \to D$ is assigned to each n-ary function symbol $f \in L$. Constants are assigned values from D.

(iii) A proposition letter in L is assigned either the value $t\!t$ or $f\!f$.

(iv) A relation $P_I \subseteq D^n$ is assigned to each n-ary predicate symbol $P \in L$.

Suppose that L is a language, I an interpretation of L, D the domain of I, and α a formula of L. Now, if α has the value $t\!t$ in I for every assignment of the values of D to the free variables of α, then α is said to be valid in I or that I *satisfies* α. For any formula that is valid in an interpretation I, the interpretation I is called a model of α. Also, any formula α that has at least one model is called satisfiable, or else it is called unsatisfiable. A sentence is a logic formula in which every variable is quantified. A sentence is in prenex normal form if it has the following form:

$$Q_1 x_1 Q_2 x_2 \ldots Q_n x_n \alpha,$$

where Q_i is either a universal quantifier or an existential quantifier, x_i are distinct variables and each of them occurs at least once in α, and α contains no quantifiers. If σ is a sentence in prenex normal form, the Skolemization of σ is the procedure by which we eliminate each existential quantifier and its attached variable from the prefix of σ and then replace each occurrence of the attached variable in the quantifier-free part of the sentence with certain terms called Skolem functions. If the existential quantifier is in the scope of a sequence of universal quantifiers, then each free occurrence of the attached variable will be replaced by the term $f(x_1, x_2, \ldots, x_n)$, where f is a fresh function symbol and the x_i's are the variables attached to the universal quantifiers; otherwise, each free occurrence of the attached variable will be replaced by a new constant symbol.

In the 9th chapter of [83], Hintikka and Mutanen state and prove the following theorem.

Theorem 3.2.1 *Each satisfiable formula S of first-order logic has at least one model where its Skolem functions are TAE-computable.*

The essence of this theorem is that since there are satisfiable formulas for which there are no models with recursively enumerable relations (i.e., there are no sets of recursive Skolem functions) and we, on the other hand, can compute these sets using TAE-machines, these machines are clearly more powerful than Turing machines. Thus TAE-machines are hypermachines.

It is rather interesting to note that Hintikka and Mutanen conclude that the logic associated with TAE-computability is just classical logic. Going one (probably arbitrary) step ahead, one may say that classical logic is the logic of (one form of) hypercomputation.

Although TAE-computability is not as mature a theory as its classical counterpart, still there are certain aspects of the theory that have been addressed by its developers. For instance, a set is *TAE-enumerable* if and only if its *semicharacteristic* function[4] is TAE-computable. Also, a set is TAE-decidable if and only if both it and its complement are TAE-enumerable. The halting problem in the case of TAE-computability is formulated as follows: does the Turing machine with number n, which defines a partial function $f_n(x)$, TAE-compute a value for the argument m? It important to say that in the case of the TAE-"halting" problem we are not really concerned whether the machine will actually stop; instead, we are concerned about the constancy of the value the machine has reached.

For reasons of completeness, we present some results from [83, pp. 183–184].

Theorem 3.2.2 *If the sets A and B are TAE-enumerable, then so are $A \cap B$ and $A \cup B$.*

Theorem 3.2.3 *If the functions f and g are TAE-computable, then so is $f \circ g$.*

Theorem 3.2.4 *Being TAE-computable is an arithmetic predicate. In fact, it is a Σ_2^0 predicate.*

There are a number of interesting philosophical issues that are addressed by Hintikka and Mutanen. However, I will not discuss them here. The interested reader should consult [83] for more details.

3.3 Inductive Turing Machines

Inductive Turing machines were introduced by Mark Burgin and are described in detail in his recent monograph [28]. Generally speaking, a simple inductive machine is a Turing machine equipped with two additional tapes, each having its own scanning head. Burgin argues that the structure of a simple inductive Turing machine closely resembles the generalized architecture of modern computers. For instance, the input tape corresponds to the input devices of the computer (e.g., the keyboard, the mouse, the optical scanner), the output tape corresponds to the output devices of the

---

4. Given a set $A \subseteq X$, where X is some universe set, then for any $x \in A$, we have $c_A(x) = \chi_A(x)$, where c_A is the semicharacteristic function of A. When $x \notin A$, then $c_A(x) = \bot$, where $\bot$ denotes the undefined value. In other words, $c_A(x)$ is undefined when $x \notin A$.

computer (e.g., the video monitor, the printer), and the working tape corresponds to the central processing unit of the computer.

A simple inductive machine operates in a fashion similar to that of an ordinary Turing machine (e.g., the scanning heads read the symbol that is printed on a particular cell on the corresponding tape, then the machine consults the controlling device, and proceeds accordingly). However, their difference lies in the way they determine their outputs (i.e., the result of the computation). In the course of its operation, an inductive machine prints symbols on consecutive cells, which form sequences of symbols that form the result of the computation (Burgin calls these sequences *words*, but I prefer the term strings). Sometimes, the machine stops, provided it has entered its halting state, and thus operates like a normal Turing machine. Nevertheless, there are cases in which the machine does not actually stop. But this does not prevent the machine from giving results. When the machine has printed a string on the output tape that remains unchanged while the machine continues its operation, we can safely assume that this particular string is the result of the computation. Even in cases in which the result changes occasionally, it is quite possible that the output is adequate for our purposes. For example, when we compute a real number we are interested in computing it to a specific accuracy. Thus, when our machine has achieved computing the real number to the desired accuracy, we can fetch our result while the machine continues computing the number to even greater accuracy.

One can easily prove the following statement concerning the computational power of simple inductive machines.

Theorem 3.3.1 *For any Turing machine $\mathcal{T}$, there is an inductive Turing machine $\mathcal{M}$ such that $\mathcal{M}$ computes the same function as $\mathcal{T}$; that is, $\mathcal{M}$ and $\mathcal{T}$ are functionally equivalent.*

In order to classify simple inductive machines as hypermachines, they should be able to compute functions that ordinary Turing machines fail to compute. Clearly, in most cases we are interested in seeing how a potential hypermachine can solve the halting problem. Here is how this can be done: Assume that $\mathcal{M}$ is an inductive machine that contains a universal Turing machine $\mathcal{U}$ as a subroutine. Given a string u and a description $D(\mathcal{T})$ of a Turing machine $\mathcal{T}$, machine $\mathcal{M}$ uses machine $\mathcal{U}$ to simulate $\mathcal{T}$ with input u. In the course of its operation $\mathcal{M}$ prints a zero on the output tape. If $\mathcal{U}$ stops, which means that $\mathcal{T}$ halts with input u, machine $\mathcal{M}$ prints a 1 on the output tape. Now, according to the definition, the computational result of $\mathcal{M}$ is equal to 1 if $\mathcal{T}$ halts, or else it is equal to 0.

As has been demonstrated, simple inductive machines are hypermachines. However, the crucial question is, how much more powerful than ordinary Turing machines are these machines? It has been shown that these machines can compute functions that are in $\Sigma_3^0 \cap \Pi_3^0$, which is not really high in the arithmetic hierarchy. For this reason, Burgin has developed an advanced form of inductive machine called *inductive Turing machines with a structured memory*. We note that these machines were developed independently from the theory of limiting recursion. For reasons of brevity, in what follows, the term "inductive machine" will refer to inductive machines with a structured memory.

A typical inductive machine consists of three components: *hardware*, *software*, and *infware*. The term infware refers to the data processed by the machine. An inductive machine $\mathcal{M}$ operates on strings of a formal language. In other words, the formal languages with which $\mathcal{M}$ works constitute its infware. Usually, these languages are divided into three categories: input, output, and working language(s). Normally, a formal language L is defined by an alphabet (i.e., a set of symbols on which this language is built) and formation rules (i.e., rules that specify which strings count as well-formed). The language L of an inductive machine is a triple (L_i, L_w, L_o), where L_i is the input language, L_w is the working language, and L_o is the output language. Notice that in the most general case it holds that $L_i \neq L_w \neq L_o \neq L_i$.

The hardware of an inductive machine is simply its control device, which controls the operation of the machine; its operating devices, which correspond to one or several scanning heads of an ordinary Turing machine; and its memory, which corresponds to one or several tapes of an ordinary Turing machine. The control device has a configuration $S = (q_0, Q, F)$, where Q is the set of states, $q_0 \in Q$ is called the initial state, and $F \subseteq Q$ is the set of final (or accepting) states. The memory is divided into different, but usually uniform, cells. In addition, it is structured by a system of mathematical relations that establish ties between cells. On each cell the operating device may print any of the symbols of the alphabet or it may erase the symbol that is printed on the cell. Formally, the memory is a triad $E = (P, W, K)$, where P is the set of all cells, W is the set of connection types, and $K \subseteq P \times P$ is the binary relation that specifies the ties between cells. Moreover, the set P, and consequently the relation K, may be a set with structure. A type is assigned to each tie from K by the mapping $\tau : K \to W$.

In general, the cells of the memory may have different types. This classification is represented by the mapping $\iota : P \to V$, where V is the set of cell types. Clearly, different types of cells may be used to store different kinds of information, but we will not elaborate on this issue.

The set of cells P is actually the union of three disjoint sets P_i, P_w, and P_o, where P_i is the set of input registers, P_w is the working memory, and P_o is the set of output registers. In addition, K is the union of three disjoint sets K_i, K_w, and K_o that define ties between the cells from P_i, P_w, and P_o, respectively. For simplicity, one may consider P_i and P_o to be two different singleton sets (i.e., to correspond to two different one-dimensional tapes).

The software of an inductive machine is a sequence of simple rewriting rules of the following form:

$$q_h a_i \quad \longrightarrow \quad a_j q_k,$$
$$q_h a_i \quad \longrightarrow \quad C(l)q_k.$$

It is also possible to use only rules of one form,

$$q_h a_i \longrightarrow a_j q_k c.$$

Here q_h and q_k are states of the control device, a_i and a_j are symbols of the alphabet of the machine, and c is a type of connection from K. Each rule instructs the inductive machine to execute one step of computation. For example, the meaning of the first rule is that if the control device is in state q_h and the operating device has scanned the symbol a_i, then the control device enters state q_k and the operating device prints the symbol a_j on the current cell and moves to the next cell. The third rule is the same except that the operating device uses a connection of type c, and in the case of the second rule, the operating device moves to the cell with number l. Having described in a nutshell the structure of inductive machines as well as the way they operate, we can now proceed with the presentation of results concerning the computational power of inductive machines.

First of all, let us see whether it is ever necessary for an inductive machine to stop and give a result. The following statement gives a negative response to this requirement.

Lemma 3.3.1 *For any inductive machine $\mathcal{M}$, there is an inductive machine $\mathcal{G}$ such that $\mathcal{G}$ never stops and computes the same functions as $\mathcal{M}$; that is, $\mathcal{M}$ and $\mathcal{G}$ are functionally the same.*

Also, the following result is quite important.

Theorem 3.3.2 *For any Turing machine $\mathcal{T}$ with an advice function (see Section 5.4), there exists an inductive Turing machine $\mathcal{M}$ with a structured memory that computes the same function as $\mathcal{T}$.*

In order to present the next result we need a few auxiliary definitions.

Definition 3.3.1 The memory E of an inductive machine is called recursive if the relation $K \subseteq P \times P$ and all mappings $\tau : K \to W$ and $\iota : P \to V$ are recursive.

The following result is not the one promised above. Nevertheless, it is a useful one.

Theorem 3.3.3 *An inductive machine with recursive memory is equivalent to a simple inductive machine.*

Definition 3.3.2 The memory E of an inductive machine $\mathcal{M}$ is called 0-inductive if it is recursive. For every $n \geq 1$, an inductive machine $\mathcal{M}$ with structured memory E is said to be $(n-1)$-inductive when the relation $K \subseteq P \times P$ and all mappings $\tau : K \to W$ and $\iota : P \to V$ are defined by some inductive machines of order n.

And here is the main result.

Theorem 3.3.4 *For any arithmetic relation Y, there exists an inductive machine $\mathcal{M}$ such that it computes the characteristic function of Y. If $Y \in \Sigma_n^0 \cup \Pi_n^0$, there is an inductive machine $\mathcal{M}$ of order n that decides Y.*

It is important to note that inductive machines are not only more powerful than Turing machines, but also more efficient. In addition, it can be shown that for a model of computation based on recursive functions, it is possible to find a class of inductive machines that can compute the same result more efficiently (personal communication with Burgin, 2005). Roughly speaking, the term efficiency means that computations performed by inductive machines take less time than their Turing counterparts. Also, when an inductive machine has delivered its result, it does not necessarily stop but can continue to operate, or as Burgin has put it in a personal communication:

> They always finish computation in a finite number of steps when they give the result, but they can continue to function. For example, when you wrote your e-mail to me, you gave a result, but I hope that you did not terminate your functioning.

3.4 Extensions to the Standard Model of Computation

When Turing proposed the abstract computing device that bears his name, he also proposed two other conceptual devices that somehow extend the capabilities of the standard Turing machine. These conceptual devices were dubbed choice and oracle Turing machines. Here is how Turing defined choice machines [206]:

> For some purposes we might use machines (choice machines or c-machines) whose motion is only partially determined by the configuration (hence the use of the word "possible" in §1). When such a machine reaches one of these ambiguous configurations, it cannot go on until some arbitrary choice has been made by an external operator.

The external operator is supposed to be a human being that assists the machine in the course of its operation. Clearly, if the actions of the mind transcend the capabilities of the standard model of computation, then c-machines are hypermachines by definition. It is rather interesting to note that a c-machine cannot be mimicked by a nondeterministic Turing machine (see Appendix A), since nondeterminism does not confer additional computational power on a Turing machine.

As we have described on page 12, an oracle machine is equipped with an external agency that can give correct answers to questions about a set $A \subset \mathbb{N}$. Clearly, it is possible to posit the existence of an oracle (i.e., a physical oracle) that gives correct answers to questions about a noncomputable set B. In fact, this is how Copeland has interpreted Turing's writing. On the other hand, no one has ever formulated oracles this way. Obviously, a machine assisted by such an oracle can compute sets and functions that are classically noncomputable. For example, a physical oracle machine might solve the halting problem for ordinary Turing machines. Naturally, for Copeland the next step was to propose oracle machines as a model of the human mind [34]:

> As I argued in my [previous] paper, O-machines point up the fact that the concept of a programmed machine whose activity consists of the manipulation of formal symbols is *more general* than the restricted notion of formal symbol-manipulation targeted in the Chinese room argument. The Chinese room argument depends upon the occupant of the room–a human clerk working by rote and unaided by machinery; call him or her Clerk–being able to carry out by hand each operation that the program in question calls for (or in one version of the argument, to carry them out in his or her head). Yet an O-machine's program may call for fundamental symbol-manipulation processes that rote-worker Clerk is incapable of carrying out. In such a case, there is no possibility of Searle's Chinese room argument being deployed successfully against the functionalist hypothesis that the brain instantiates an O-machine–a hypothesis which Searle will presumably find as "antibiological" as other functionalisms.

However, Bringsjord, Paul Bello, and David Ferrucci totally disagree with this idea. In particular, these authors point out that oracle Turing machines process symbols just like ordinary Turing machines [24]. In other words, Copeland's argument *falls prey* to Searle's argument. After all, one can supply a Turing machine with an auxiliary infinite tape (instead of a physical oracle) on which are listed, in increasing order (as sequences of 1's) the members of some set X. These machines can correctly answer any question regarding X and thus have the computational power of oracle machines. Obviously, these machines can be used to refute Copeland's argument, since they are clearly symbol-manipulation devices. An interesting question is what happens when there is no auxiliary infinite tape, but a physical oracle, which leads naturally to the next question: do there exist physical oracles?

On page 15 we presented an alternative formulation of classical computability in the form of a random-access machine. An oracle Turing machine can be "simulated" by introducing a **read** command:

read variable

This command is an ordinary input command—nothing magical is assumed! However, the command is used only to assist the computation via an external operator (a physical oracle?), much as interactive systems take user feedback to proceed.

If we go one step further and introduce an *output* command (e.g., a **write** command) that can feed the "external world" with data, then we have a model of interactive computation. However, this model of computation is not general enough, since it suffers from the same drawbacks the classical model does. Nevertheless, it seems to be a step forward.

Coupled Turing machines, which were proposed by Copeland [38], are an extension of the notion of a Turing machine that exhibits interactive behavior. A coupled Turing machine is the result of coupling a Turing machine to its environment via one or more input channels. Each channel supplies a stream of symbols to the tape as the machine operates. In addition, the machine may also have one or more output channels that output symbols to the environment. The universal Turing machine is not always able to simulate a coupled Turing machine that never halts (think of a computer operating system, which is a system that never halts; nevertheless, sometimes some "operating systems" crash quite unexpectedly...).

It is not difficult to see that coupled Turing machines are actually hypermachines. Assume that C is a coupled Turing machine with a single input channel. The number of output channels will not concern us here. Also, suppose that $u \in [0, 1]$ is some "noncomputable" real number (i.e., a number that cannot be computed by a Turing machine) whose decimal representation can be written as follows: $0.u_1u_2u_3\ldots$. The digits of the binary representation of u will form the input of C. The input channel of C writes to a single square of the machine's tape, and each successive symbol u_i in the input stream overwrites its predecessor on this square. As each input symbol arrives, C performs some elementary computation (e.g., it multiplies the symbol by 3) and writes the result on some designated squares of the tape. In order to achieve constant operation time, the next result always overwrites its predecessor. No Turing machine can produce the sequence $3 \cdot u_1, 3 \cdot u_2$, etc. (for if it could, it could also be in the process of producing the binary representation of u).

Clearly, the important question is what numbers a coupled Turing machine can compute. To say that it can compute more than the Turing machine is not really useful. In addition, the vague description above is surely not a replacement for a rigorous mathematical definition of the machine and its semantics.

3.5   Exotic Machines

The term "exotic machines" refers to conceptual computing devices that assume that our universe has certain properties. For example, take the case of Thomson's lamp, which was "invented" by James Thomson and was first described in [202]. This is a device that consists of a lamp and an electrical switch that can be used to turn the lamp on and off. Assume that at $t = 0$, the lamp is off. At time $t = \frac{1}{2}$, we turn the lamp on. At time $t = \frac{1}{2} + \frac{1}{4}$, we turn the lamp off. At time $t = \frac{1}{2} + \frac{1}{4} + \frac{1}{8}$, we turn the lamp on. At time $t = \frac{1}{2} + \frac{1}{4} + \frac{1}{8} + \frac{1}{16}$, we turn the lamp off and so on. The problem is to determine whether the lamp will be on or off at time $t = 1$. Thomson provided the following solution to this problem: assume that $0 < t < 1$. (i) If the lamp is off at t, then there is a t' such that $t < t' < 1$ and the lamp is on at t', and (ii) if the lamp is on at t, then there is a t' such that $t < t' < 1$ and the lamp is off at t'. Thomson thought that it followed from (i) that the lamp cannot be off at $t = 1$ and from (ii) that the lamp cannot be on at $t = 1$. This is clearly a contradiction, and thus Thomson concluded that this device is logically or conceptually impossible. Paul Benacerraf [12] has pointed out the fallaciousness of this argument. He claimed that one should distinguish between the series of instants of time in which the actions of the *supertask*[5] are performed (which will be called the t-series) and the instant $t^* = 1$, the first instant after the supertask.

Thesis 3.5.1 *From a description of the t-series, nothing follows about any point outside the t-series.*

From a practical point of view, one may say that tasks like this are really meaningless if time is granular. However, if time and space are continuous, then this task has at least some physical basis (for more details, see the short discussion at the end of Section 8.3).

The so-called Zeus machine is an example of an exotic machine that has been popularized by Boolos and Jeffrey in their classical textbook [18]. A Zeus machine is operated by the superhuman being Zeus (i.e., the principal god of the ancient Greek pantheon), who can perform an infinite task in a finite amount of time. Actually, Zeus can enumerate the elements of an

---

5. In philosophy, a supertask is a task involving an infinite number of steps, completed in a finite amount of time. The term supertask was coined by James Thomson.

enumerable set[6] in one second by writing out an infinite list faster and faster. In particular, Zeus enumerates the elements of the set in a way that is identical to the operation of Thomson's lamp. Copeland has proposed a more formal version of a Zeus machine, which is called an *accelerating Turing machine* [34]. These are Turing machines that perform the second primitive operation in half the time taken to perform the first, the third in half the time taken to perform the second, and so on. If we assume that the first primitive operation is executed in one minute, then since

$$\frac{1}{2} + \frac{1}{4} + \frac{1}{8} + \cdots + \frac{1}{2^n} + \frac{1}{2^{n+1}} + \cdots < 1,$$

an accelerating Turing machine can execute infinitely many primitive operations before one minute of operating time has elapsed. It is interesting to see how accelerating Turing machines can compute the halting function. We assume that a universal accelerating Turing machine is equipped with a signaling device (e.g., a horn) that is used to send a signal when a computation is finished within one minute. In particular, given a Turing machine $\mathcal{M}$ with a Gödel number m that is supposed to compute the function $f(x)$, a universal accelerating Turing machine will take as input the numbers m and n (a possible argument to function f). If within one minute, the signaling device does not send a signal, the computation does not halt; otherwise, it does halt. Strictly speaking, this universal accelerating Turing machine is not a Turing machine at all, since it communicates with the external world. However, it is not really important to get into these details (the interested reader should consult Copeland's paper). Copeland claims that accelerating oracle Turing machines can be used to refute Searle's Chinese room argument. Again, this is not correct. Bringsjord, Bello, and Ferrucci [24] point out that

> After all, Zeus could be a pigeon. And a pigeon trained to move symbols around, even if blessed with the ability to carry out this movement at Zeus-level speeds, would still have the mental life of a bird, which of course falls far short of truly understanding Chinese.

Copeland responded to this argument by claiming that there is an *ascending hierarchy of symbol-manipulations* [35]. Thus, it is not possible to apply the Chinese room argument to all different levels of this hierarchy. However, symbol-manipulation is always the same kind of operation no matter how fast we perform it. Also, there are no recipes to construct a proof. Of course a brute-force search is not such a recipe, although it is employed by automated theorem-proving systems to prove truly interesting statements.

---

6. Although in the original description, Zeus is supposed to enumerate the elements of an enumerable set, it was pointed out to the author that a machine cannot so "easily" produce an enumeration of a countably infinite set. On the other hand, Zeus's job would make sense for any infinite recursively enumerable set.

But this approach is not always applicable. In addition, the general proof methodologies cannot be used to construct the proof or disproof of a particular mathematical statement. Also, mechanical symbol manipulation is a process that clearly lacks intentionality, and as Dale Jacquette remarks [90, p. 10]: "[T]he machine can only imperfectly simulate the mind's intentionality and understanding of a sentence's meaning." Now, whether machines have or do not have mental capabilities is an issue that I will address in Chapter 6.

The *Rapidly Accelerating Computer* (RAC), which was proposed by Ian Stewart [195], is actually equivalent to an accelerating Turing machine. In particular, the clock of an RAC accelerates exponentially fast with pulses at times $1 - 2^{-n}$ as $n \to \infty$. And just like accelerating Turing machines, an RAC can perform an infinite number of computations in a single minute. It can therefore solve the halting problem for Turing machines by running a computation in accelerating time and throwing a particular switch if and only if the Turing machine halts. Like all computations carried out by an RAC, the entire procedure is completed within one minute; and it siffices to inspect the switch to see whether it has been thrown. In Stewart's own words, "RAC can calculate the *incalculable*" (emphasis added). Interestingly enough, the RAC and accelerating Turing machines can be modeled by a classical (i.e., nonquantum) dynamical system, because classical mechanics poses no upper bound on velocities. Thus, it is possible to "accelerate" time so that infinite "subjective" time passes within a finite period of "objective" time. However, it is quite possible to achieve the same effect in special spacetimes, and we will say more on this matter on Chapter 8.

3.6   On Pseudorecursiveness

While working on his doctoral dissertation, Benjamin Wells constructed a particular nonrecursive set of algebraic equations, that his thesis advisor, Alfred Tarski declared to be decidable.[7] Thus Wells constructed a nonrecursive but decidable set. Clearly, the very existence of such a set jeopardizes the foundations of classical computability theory, which is of interest because it was constructed by someone without a negative attitude toward the Church-Turing thesis and its implications. Let us now see how one can construct such a set (the discussion that follows is based on Wells's two recent papers [224, 225]).

We want to construct a set of formal equations. Each formal equation

---

7. Any decision problem P is associated with a predicate F_P. In normal parlance, a problem P is decidable if F_P is computable; P is semidecidable if F_P is semicomputable; and P is cosemidecidable if $\neg F_P$ is semicomputable.

is a string that can be generated using the following formal grammar:

formal equation ::= term "=" term

      term ::= "(" term + term ")" | constant | variable

   constant ::= "a" | "b"

   variable ::= "v_1" | "v_2" | $\cdots$ | "v_i" | $\cdots$ $i \in \mathbb{N}$.

We usually drop the outermost parentheses for clarity.

An *equational theory* of such formal equations is a set T consisting of strings, generated by the grammar above, that necessarily includes the equation $v_1 = v_1$. In addition, T must be closed under the following two operations:[8]

Subterm replacement The replacement of a subterm t_1 that appears in an equation in T by a term t_2 when $t_1 = t_2$ or $t_2 = t_1$ belongs to T.

Variable substitution The substitution of a chosen but arbitrary term for every occurrence of a variable in an equation in T belongs to T.

A subset B of an equational theory T is an *equational base* for T if T is the smallest equational theory that includes B. We write $T = \mathrm{Th}(B)$. Thus, T is *recursively based* precisely when T is the closure under subterm replacement and variable substitution of a finite set, or an infinite recursive set, of equations. The class of algebraic models for an equational theory is called its *variety*. The equational theories that Wells considered in his work are equational theories for varieties of *semigroups*, that is, they contain equations that guarantee the associativity of the + operator. In other words, they contain

$$(v_1 + v_2) + v_3 = v_1 + (v_2 + v_3).$$

In addition, one can introduce an *additive identity* element by including the following equations:

$$0 + v_1 = v_1 = v_1 + 0.$$

Here 0 is a new distinguished constant or a particular term.

Assume that T_n is the subset of the equational theory T consisting of the equations in T with no more than n distinct variables. We say that T is *quasirecursive* if for every number n, T_n is recursive. The theory T is *pseudorecursive* if T is quasirecursive but not recursive.

Wells has constructed various pseudorecursive equational theories. In particular, he provides the following recipe for constructing such theories: start with a fixed but arbitrary nonrecursive, recursively enumerable set $X \subset \mathbb{N}$ and define a finite equational base $\Psi 1_X$ from a highly engineered Turing machine that accepts X [223]. The resulting theory $\mathrm{Th}(\Psi 1_X)$ is an

---

8. A set X is said to be closed under some operation or map L if L maps elements of X to elements of X.

equational theory of semigroups with identity and finitely many individual constants (the number of constants can be reduced to two or even to one or zero). This recipe can be formally summarized as follows.

Theorem 3.6.1 *For every nonrecursive recursively enumerable set X that is a subset of $\mathbb{N}$, $\text{Th}(\Psi 1_X)$ is a finitely based pseudorecursive equational theory that is Turing-equivalent to X.*

According to Wells [224], Tarski has suggested that a basis for a decision procedure of T (i.e., a method for telling whether an arbitrary equation is in T) can be constructed as follows: For each value of n, there is a procedure for deciding T_n; n can be used to index a catalog of these procedures. Given an arbitrary equation, count the number of variables in it, and then use the catalog to locate the correct procedure and apply it. Using this basis, we can construct a decision procedure for a finitely based or even just recursively enumerable pseudorecursive theory. We employ an oracle Turing machine, whose query tape lists the values of the characteristic function for X. The keying is performed by counting variables to n. Indexing depends on oracular information: the Turing index for the template used to build the machine M_n, which is used to decide T_n, and the first n items from the oracle are sent to an internal foundry to be recast as a functional equivalent of M_n, and its Gödel number, now computable, is returned. The last step sends this number with n to a universal Turing machine that simulates M_n computing with input n and "allows nature to take its course." This oracle Turing machine can decide T_n by looking only at the first n cells on the tape, which lists the characteristic function f_n of $X_n = \{0, 1, \ldots, n\} \cap X$. In addition, since this finite function is recursive, we can incorporate it into the control mechanism of the oracle machine to form M_n^*, an ordinary Turing machine that decides T_n. Clearly, for every n, $f(n) = f_n(n)$, where f is the characteristic function of X (therefore, there is no way to recursively recapture X from the X_n or synthesize an ordinary Turing machine to decide T).

The work on pseudorecursiveness has revealed the following (see the abstract of [225]):

> The dilemma of a decidable but not recursive set presents an impasse to standard computability theory. One way to break the impasse is to predicate that the theory is computable—in other words, hypercomputation by definition.

This statement should not be taken as an indication that hypercomputation is actually an empty word. On the contrary, the theory can be made computable once the very notion of computability is extended. Wells believes that one should expand a theory only when "real" problems need solutions. For example, our inability to find a number that is the square root of minus one led mathematicians to *invent* the imaginary numbers. Thus, Wells expects a new expanded theory based on nonrecursive yet decidable sets.

IV. Infinite-Time Turing Machines

Infinite-time Turing machines are Turing machines that can perform an infinite number of steps to accomplish their tasks. Since their theory relies heavily on the theory of infinite ordinal numbers, I will provide a brief introduction to the theory of infinite cardinal and ordinal numbers. Then, I will present the basic results concerning these machines and discuss the feasibility of a sort of infinite-time Turing machine. Also, I will briefly present infinite-time automata and "building instructions" for infinite-time machines. The chapter concludes with Eric Steinhart's metaphysical foundations for computation, since it seems to fit best in this chapter.

4.1   On Cardinal and Ordinal Numbers

The number of elements of a set A is called the *cardinality* of the set A, and it is expressed in *cardinal numbers*. The cardinality of a set A is denoted by card(A). For a finite set, its cardinality is simply a natural number equal to the number of elements in the set. For infinite sets, one has to use *infinite cardinal numbers* to express their size. The first infinite number is denoted by $\aleph_0$ (pronounced *aleph null*) and by definition it is the cardinal number of the set $\mathbb{N}$ of natural numbers. An infinite set that can be put into one-to-one correspondence with the set $\mathbb{N}$ is called a *countable* set. Clearly, the cardinality of a countable set is equal to $\aleph_0$. Examples of countable sets include the set of integers ($\mathbb{Z}$) and the set of rational numbers ($\mathbb{Q}$). Assume that A and B are two finite or infinite sets and that $a = \text{card}(A)$ and $b = \text{card}(B)$. Then one can define the arithmetic of cardinals as follows:

(i) $a + b := \text{card}(A \cup B), A \cap B = \emptyset,$

(ii) $a \cdot b := \text{card}(A \times B),$

(iii) $a^b := \text{card}(A^B)$ (recall that A^B is the set of all mappings from B to A).

Notice that the operations of subtraction and division are not defined in this arithmetic. Also, for every set X it can be proved that

$$\text{card}(2^X) = 2^{\text{card}(X)},$$

where 2^X is identified with the *power set* of X, or $\mathcal{P}(X)$, that is, the set of all subsets of X. Suppose that n is a finite cardinal number. Then it is easy to see that $\aleph_0$ has the following properties:

$$\aleph_0 + \aleph_0 = \aleph_0,$$
$$\aleph_0 \cdot \aleph_0 = \aleph_0,$$
$$\aleph_0 + n = n + \aleph_0 = \aleph_0,$$
$$\aleph_0 \cdot n = n \cdot \aleph_0 = \aleph_0, n > 0,$$
$$\aleph_0^n = \aleph_0, n > 0.$$

An infinite set A is called *uncountable* if $\operatorname{card}(A) > \aleph_0$. A classical example of an uncountable set is the set of real numbers ($\mathbb{R}$). The cardinality of this set is called c. Another uncountable set is the powerset of $\mathbb{N}$. The cardinality of this set is equal to $2^{\aleph_0}$. An important question is the following: is there an uncountable cardinal number λ such that $\lambda < 2^{\aleph_0}$? The hypothesis that there is no such cardinal number is known as the *continuum hypothesis*. Let us denote by $\aleph_1$ the least uncountable cardinal number. Then $\aleph_1 = c = 2^{\aleph_0}$, provided the continuum hypothesis holds. More generally, one can formulate a broader hypothesis and introduce a sequence $\aleph_0, \dots, \aleph_a, \dots$ of transfinite cardinals, but we will come to this at the end of this section. Now assume that n is a finite cardinal. Then the arithmetic of $\aleph_1$ obeys the following conditions:

$$\aleph_1 + n = n + \aleph_1 = \aleph_1,$$
$$\aleph_1 + \aleph_0 = \aleph_0 + \aleph_1 = \aleph_1,$$
$$\aleph_1 + \aleph_1 = \aleph_1,$$
$$\aleph_1 \cdot n = n \cdot \aleph_1 = \aleph_1, n > 0,$$
$$\aleph_0 \cdot \aleph_1 = \aleph_1 \cdot \aleph_0 = \aleph_1,$$
$$\aleph_1 \cdot \aleph_1 = \aleph_1,$$
$$\aleph_1^n = \aleph_1, n > 0,$$
$$n^{\aleph_0} = \aleph_1, n > 1,$$
$$\aleph_0^{\aleph_0} = \aleph_1,$$
$$\aleph_1^{\aleph_0} = \aleph_1.$$

The last three properties make sense only if the continuum hypothesis holds.

In von Neumann–Bernays–Gödel set theory, one deals with classes and sets. The notion of a *class* is more general than that of a set. Assume that P is some property. Then one can define the class of all objects that have this property. The elements of a class are called *sets*. Although a set is a class, not every class is a set (e.g., consider the class V of all sets). Two classes with the same elements are equal. A well-ordering is a linear order $(W, \leq)$

(i.e., the elements of the set W are comparable) that is irreflexive with the additional property that every nonempty $S \subseteq W$ has a least element. If $(\alpha, \in_\alpha)$ is a well-ordering, where α is a transitive set (i.e., if every set B that is an element of α has the property that all of its elements also belong to α) and $\in_\alpha$ is the relation *is an element of*, we call α an *ordinal number*. Thus we can define the first ordinal numbers as follows:

$$0 := \emptyset,$$
$$1 := \{0\} = \{\emptyset\},$$
$$2 := \{0, 1\} = \{\emptyset, \{\emptyset\}\},$$
$$3 := \{0, 1, 2\} = \{\emptyset, \{\emptyset\}, \{\emptyset, \{\emptyset\}\}\},$$
$$\vdots$$
$$\omega := \{0, 1, 2, 3, \ldots\}.$$

An ordinal number $x > 0$ is called a *limit ordinal* if it has no immediate predecessor (i.e., an ordinal number y such that $y + 1 = x$). One can prove that if $\alpha \neq 0$ and for all $\beta \in \alpha$, $\beta + 1 \in \alpha$ as well, then α is a limit ordinal. Indeed, all limit ordinals have this property, as can easily be seen. The first limit ordinal is ω. There are two rules for generating infinite ordinal numbers:

(i) if x is an ordinal number, then $x \cup \{x\}$ is the next ordinal; in fact, $x + 1$ is a suggestive notation for $S(x)$, where $S(x) = x \cup \{x\}$ is called the successor operation on ordinal numbers;

(ii) given the sequence $0, 1, 2, \ldots, x, x + 1, x + 2, \ldots$, where x is an ordinal number, the number following all $x + n$, $n \in \mathbb{N}$, is a limit ordinal number that can be understood as the set of all smaller numbers:

$$x \cdot 2 = x + x = \{0, 1, 2, \ldots, x, x + 1, \ldots\}.$$

For example, by applying the first rule to ω, we obtain the ordinal $\omega + 1$; then by applying the same rule to $\omega + 1$, we obtain $\omega + 2$, and so on. This way, we obtain the sequence

$$0, 1, 2, 3, \ldots, \omega, \omega + 1, \omega + 2, \omega + 3, \ldots .$$

Notice that while the ordinal numbers $\omega + 1, \omega + 2, \ldots$ are bigger than ω in the sense of order, they are not bigger in the sense of cardinality, since $\operatorname{card}(\omega) = \operatorname{card}(\omega + 1) = \operatorname{card}(\omega + 2) = \cdots = \aleph_0$. By applying the second rule to the previous sequence of ordinals we are led to the new limit ordinal $\omega + \omega$, equal to $\omega \cdot 2$:

$$0, 1, 2, 3, \ldots, \omega, \omega + 1, \omega + 2, \omega + 3, \ldots, \omega \cdot 2.$$

Notice that card(ω) = card($\omega \cdot 2$) = $\cdots$ = $\aleph_0$. Now, by combining both rules we obtain the following sequence:

$$0, 1, 2, \ldots, \omega, \omega + 1, \omega + 2, \ldots, \omega \cdot 2, \omega \cdot 2 + 1, \omega \cdot 2 + 2, \ldots, \omega \cdot 3, \omega \cdot 3 + 1, \ldots.$$

The rules of the arithmetic of ordinal numbers are rather tricky. For example, $1 + \omega$ is not equal to $\omega + 1$, since the latter is the next ordinal number after ω, but $1 + \omega = \omega$.

We define $\beth_0$ (pronounced *beth null*) to be the first infinite cardinal (that is, $\aleph_0$). For each ordinal α, we define $\beth_{\alpha+1} = 2^{\beth_\alpha}$. For each limit ordinal δ, we define $\beth_\delta = \cup_{\alpha \in \delta} \beth_\alpha$. The *generalized continuum hypothesis* is equivalent to the assertion that $\aleph_\alpha = \beth_\alpha$, for every ordinal α. An equivalent condition is that $\aleph_{\alpha+1} = 2^{\aleph_\alpha}$. Thus, if the generalized continuum hypothesis is indeed true, one can construct any possible infinite cardinal using this rule.

Let us conclude this section with the following important definition from [166, p. 211].

Definition 4.1.1 An ordinal α is a *recursive* ordinal if there exists a relation R such that:

(i) R is a well-ordering (of some set of integers);

(ii) R is recursive; and

(iii) the well-ordering given by R is order-isomorphic (see Appendix D.1) to α.

The least nonrecursive ordinal is denoted by ω_1^{CK}, the Church–Kleene ordinal.

4.2   Infinite-Time Turing Machines

Jeffrey Kidder initially defined infinite-time Turing machines in 1989, and later, together with Joel David Hamkins they worked out the early theory while they were graduate students at the University of California, Berkeley. Later, Hamkins and Andrew Lewis reworked the theory [74]. To put it very simply, an infinite-time Turing machine is a Turing machine that may perform an infinite number of steps to achieve its computational task. More precisely, the total number of steps that an infinite-time Turing machine may perform is characterized by some ordinal number α. When a machine enters stage α, then there is a unique next stage $\alpha + 1$, and all of these culminate in the stage that is characterized by the limit ordinal β (e.g., ω, $\omega \cdot 2$, etc.). The informal description of the operation of an infinite-time Turing machine that is presented in the next subsection is based on [73]. In addition, unless it is explicitly stated, the rest of the presentation is based on [74].

4.2.1   How the Machines Operate

An infinite-time Turing machine consists of three parallel right infinite tapes (i.e, all tapes are infinite to the right only). A scanning head simultaneously moves across all three tapes. The scanning head, as in the case of ordinary Turing machines, can read or write symbols or move left or right by following the commands of a finite program, thereby entering a new state. When the scanning head is atop a triplet of cells, it can read symbols from any cell or write symbols to any cell. The three tapes are called the *input* tape, the *scratch* tape, and the *output* tape. Initially, the head is on the leftmost cell, and the machine is in a special state called the *start* state. In addition, the (possibly infinite) input is written on the input tape, while the scratch and output tapes are filled with zeros. Figure 4.1 depicts an infinite-time Turing machine at its starting configuration.

start

input:	1	1	0	1	1	0	...
scratch:	0	0	0	0	0	0	...
output:	0	0	0	0	0	0	...

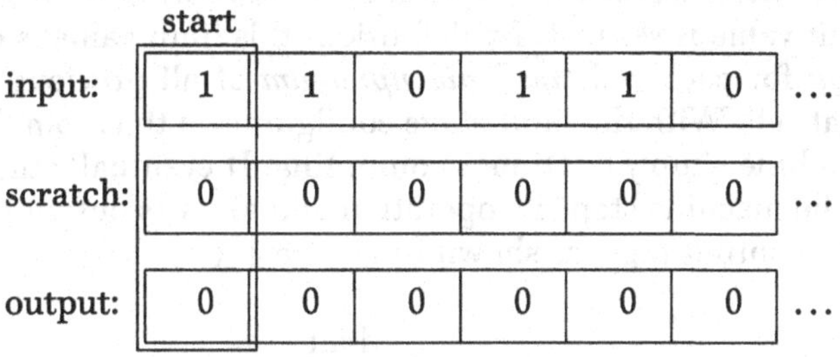

Figure 4.1: An infinite-time Turing machine at its starting configuration.

An infinite-time Turing machine operates in a purely deterministic fashion, since if we know the state of the machine, the position of the scanning head, and the contents of the tapes at any stage α, we can uniquely determine the configuration of the machine at stage $\alpha + 1$.

Assume that a Turing machine has entered an infinite loop. Clearly, this machine is performing a nonhalting computation and thus fails to compute the requested computation. However, it is quite possible that the symbols written on the tape constitute a noncomputable number. This means that useful information may be lost, since we usually discard the output of a nonhalting Turing machine. On the other hand, infinite-time Turing machines provide a mechanism by which we can avoid losing this "precious" information. The way they succeed is by taking some kind of limit of the earlier configuration and continuing the computation transfinitely. In particular, at any limit-ordinal stage, the scanning head resets to the leftmost cell; the machine enters the special *limit* state, which is just another of the finitely many states; and the values in the cells of the tapes are updated by computing a kind of limit of the previous values the cell has displayed. Figure 4.2 depicts an infinite-time Turing machine in the limit stage.

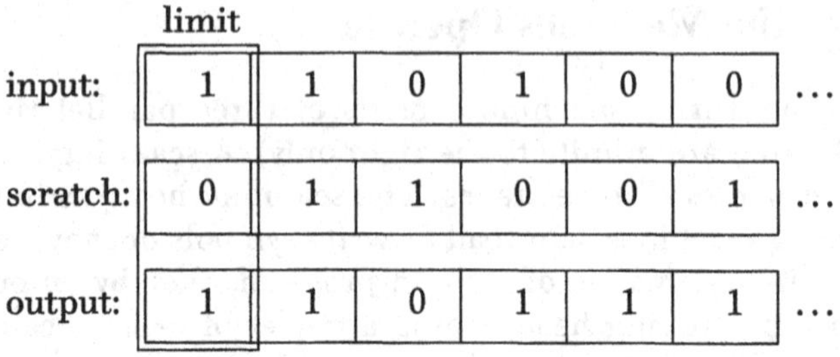

limit						
input:	1	1	0	1	0	0 ...
scratch:	0	1	1	0	0	1 ...
output:	1	1	0	1	1	1 ...

Figure 4.2: An infinite-time Turing machine in the limit stage.

Suppose now that the values in a cell have stabilized before a limit stage. Then the limit value displayed by the cell at the limit stage will be this stabilized value; otherwise, if the cell's value is alternating between 0 and 1, then the limit value is set to 1. By definition, this limit value is equivalent, to computing for each cell the *limit-supremum* of all previous values displayed in that cell. With the limit-stage configuration thus completely specified, the machine simply continues computing. If eventually the *halt* state is reached, the machine stops its operation and gives as output whatever is written on the output tape; as shown in Figure 4.3.

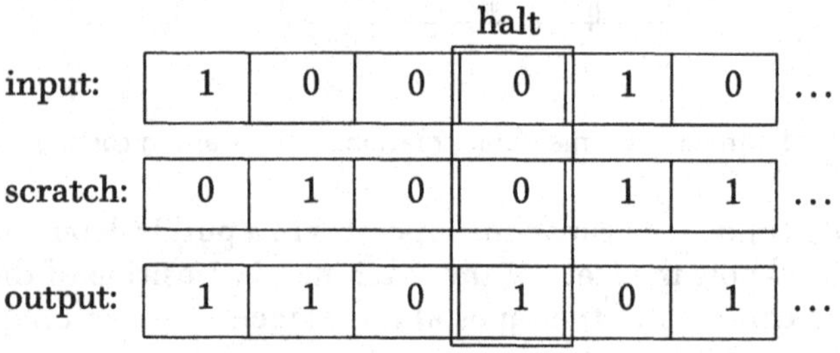

			halt			
input:	1	0	0	0	1	0 ...
scratch:	0	1	0	0	1	1 ...
output:	1	1	0	1	0	1 ...

Figure 4.3: An infinite-time Turing machine in the halt stage.

Obviously, in all other cases the machine will operate forever.

Assume that p (for program) is an infinite-time Turing machine; then clearly p determines a function. When the machine (or program) p is run on input x, the result of a halting computation will be denoted by $\varphi_p(x)$. Apparently, the domain of φ_p is the collection of all x that lead to a halting computation. Notice that the natural input for these machines is an *infinite* bit string $x \in 2^\omega$ (recall that $2 = \{0,1\}$). Thus, the functions computable by infinite-time Turing machines are partial functions on a Cantor space (see Appendix D.3). Since it is not too wrong to let $\mathbb{R}$ stand for 2^ω, in what follows the symbol $\mathbb{R}$ will stand for 2^ω.

From the discussion so far, it is not clear how one can use an infinite-time Turing machine to compute functions that take more than one argument. An obvious solution to this problem is to augment the machine with additional input tapes—one for each argument. On the other hand, it is possible to print the arguments on one tape using the following technique: Assume that $\langle a_1, a_2, \ldots \rangle$ and $\langle b_1, b_2, \ldots \rangle$ are the digits of two arguments. Then we print on the single tape the "number" $\langle a_1, b_1, a_2, b_2, \ldots \rangle$. In other words, the digits of the two inputs appear interleaved on the single tape (see also Section 4.2.5). By convention, the numbers 0 and 1 are represented by $\langle 0, 0, 0, \ldots \rangle$ and $\langle 1, 1, 1, \ldots \rangle$, respectively. Let us now proceed with a number of basic definitions.

Definition 4.2.1 Assume that $f : \mathbb{R}^k \to \mathbb{R}$ is a partial function. Then we say that f is *infinite-time computable* if there is a program p such that $f = \varphi_p$.

It is not a novelty to assume that the program of an infinite-time Turing machine is represented by some natural number n. Clearly, n can be generated by employing a coding mechanism. For example, one can use a coding mechanism like the one employed in the theory of universal Turing machines to represent the program of an ordinary Turing machine.

Definition 4.2.2 Let A be a set of reals. Then A is infinite-time *decidable* if its characteristic function, χ_A, is infinite-time computable. Moreover, A is infinite-time *semidecidable* if the partial function

$$g(x) = \begin{cases} 1, & \text{if } x \in A, \\ \text{undefined}, & \text{otherwise}, \end{cases}$$

is infinite-time computable.

Thus, a set is infinite-time semidecidable when it is the domain of an infinite-time computable function.

Definition 4.2.3 Suppose that A is a set of reals. Then A is α-decidable if its characteristic function χ_A can be computed by a machine that must perform no more that α steps on any input.

As a direct consequence of these definitions, we have the following result. If g is a function from $2^{<\omega}$ (the set of finite bit strings) to $2^{<\omega}$, then g is Turing-computable if and only if g is ω-computable with every computation of a value of g having a finite time bound. Note that there is an ω-computation of the Turing machine halting problem, but it requires ω time, as stated in the next section.

Imagine that an infinite-time Turing machine has performed an uncountable number of steps without halting. Then one may speculate that this machine will never terminate. Consequently, if an infinite-time Turing machine halts, then one may deduce that it has performed a countable number of steps. This conjecture has been proved by Hamkins and Lewis [74].

Theorem 4.2.1 *Every halting infinite-time computation is countable.*

An instantaneous description of a computation is a complete description of the configuration at some particular moment. An instantaneous description specifies the program being used, the state and position of the head, and the complete contents of each of the tapes. Before proceeding with the following definition, let us say that it is quite possible for a machine that has entered an infinite loop to break the loop and continue its computation or even halt. For example, this could happen if the limit of the instantaneous descriptions of the repeated commands is different from these instantaneous descriptions.

Definition 4.2.4 If an instantaneous description of some computation occurs at two limit-ordinal stages and between these two stages the cells that are 0 in the limit never turn to 1, we say that the computation repeats itself.

Notice that it is allowed for the ones to turn to zero. Based on this, one can prove the following statement.

Corollary 4.2.1 *Every infinite-time computation either halts or repeats itself in countably many steps.*

4.2.2   On the Power of Infinite-Time Machines

The first question that pops into one's mind regards the computational power of infinite-time Turing machines: are they more powerful than Turing machines or not? Clearly, one should notice that the halting problem for Turing machines is infinite-time decidable, since one can easily simulate an ordinary Turing machine computation with an infinite-time Turing machine. Either the simulation halts in a finite number of steps, or after ω steps the machine reaches the limit state. So by giving the output "Yes" or "No," respectively, in these two situations, the halting problem is solved. Thus, infinite-time Turing machines are more powerful than ordinary Turing machines, since they can decide sets that are undecidable by Turing machines. The next theorem gives a first hint as to the real computational power of these machines.

Theorem 4.2.2 *Any arithmetic set is infinite-time decidable.*

Assume that $\lhd$ is a relation in $X \times X$, where $X \subset \omega$; then $\lhd$ can be coded by the real number x such that $x(\langle n, k \rangle) = 1$ if and only if $n \lhd k$. Here $\langle .,. \rangle$ is some standard *pairing* function (i.e., a function that reversibly maps $\mathbb{N} \times \mathbb{N}$ onto $\mathbb{N}$). In this way every real x codes some relation $\lhd$. Suppose that WO is the set of reals coding well-orderings. The set WO is a complete Π_1^1 set, in the sense that if A is another Π_1^1 set, there is a recursive function f on the real numbers such that $x \in A$ if and only if $f(x) \in$ WO. The following statement gives a property of the set WO.

Theorem 4.2.3 *The set WO is infinite-time decidable.*

More generally, one can prove the following statement.

Corollary 4.2.2 *Every Π_1^1 set is infinite-time decidable, and hence every Σ_1^1 set is infinite-time decidable.*

But the properties of the collection of decidable sets extend further up the analytical hierarchy. Before elaborating on this matter, we need a definition from [52].

Definition 4.2.5 Assume that β is a recursive ordinal. Then $A \subseteq \omega^\omega$ is β-Π_1^1 if and only if $A_\alpha \subseteq \omega^\omega$ exists for each $\alpha \leq \beta$ with $A_\beta = \emptyset$ and there exists a recursive well-ordering of a subset E of ω with order type β such that if $|n|$ is the order type of $n \in \omega$ in this well-ordering, then

$$\left\{ (k,x) \in E \times \omega^\omega \;\middle|\; x \in A_{|k|} \right\} \in \Pi_1^1$$

and

$$A = \left\{ x \in \omega^\omega \;\middle|\; \exists \alpha \leq \beta \Big((\alpha \text{ odd}) \wedge \big(x \in \bigcap_{\gamma < \alpha} A_\gamma \setminus A_\alpha \big) \Big) \right\}.$$

An ordinal is even if and only if it has the form $\alpha + 2n$, and it is odd if and only if it has the form $\alpha + 2n + 1$, where $n \in \omega$ and α is a limit ordinal (see [167]).

Definition 4.2.6 Suppose that an infinite-time Turing machine starts with input the number 0 and when it halts, the real number x appears on its output tape. Then x is called *writable*. Also, an ordinal is writable if there is a writable real number that codes it.

Assume that A is β-Π_1^1, where β is a writable ordinal. Let us consider an algorithm that first writes the relation R coding β on a section of the scratch tape that is fed to the Π_1^1 algorithm in order to make a list of those numbers n with the property that the input x is in $A_{|n|}$. Finally, by counting through the relation coding β, the algorithm searches for an odd ordinal $\alpha < \beta$ such that $x \in \cap_{\delta < \alpha} A_\delta \setminus A_\alpha$. So the algorithm will decide whether x is in A, thus proving the following corollary.

Corollary 4.2.3 *If β is a writable ordinal, then every β-Π_1^1 set is decidable.*

The following statement gives a characterization of decidable and semidecidable sets.

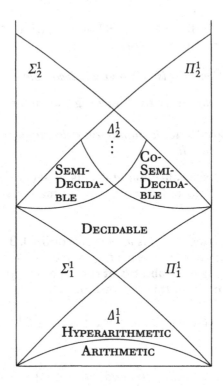

Figure 4.4: The semidecidable and cosemidecidable sets in the analytic hierarchy.

Theorem 4.2.4 *Assume that G is the graph of an infinite-time computable function. Then $G \in \Delta_2^1$. More generally, every decidable set and every semidecidable set is Δ_2^1.*

Every cosemidecidable set is also Δ_2^1, also the semidecidable sets form a proper subclass of the Δ_2^1 sets (see Figure 4.4). The following statement identifies the classes of sets that are decidable by algorithms that need to take relatively few limits.

Theorem 4.2.5 *The arithmetic sets are exactly the sets that can be decided by an algorithm using a bounded finite number of limits.*

In addition, the following result concerns the length of computation of hyperarithmetical sets:

Theorem 4.2.6 *If $A \in \Delta_1^1$, then A can be decided in some bounded recursive ordinal length of time.*

4.2.3 Clockable Ordinals

In order to measure the time it takes for a halting computation to finish, it was necessary to introduce the notion of clockable ordinals.

Definition 4.2.7 Let $\mathscr{I}$ be an infinite-time Turing machine with input the number 0. Then if $\mathscr{I}$ completes its computational task in exactly α steps we say that the ordinal α is *clockable*.

By the previous definition, any natural number is clockable. In addition, there are many other ordinals that are clockable. Indeed, the following theorem characterizes some clockable ordinals.

Theorem 4.2.7 *Every recursive ordinal is clockable.*

A direct consequence of this result is that the clockable ordinals extend at least up to ω_1^{CK}. However, the clockable ordinals extend even further.

Theorem 4.2.8 *The ordinal $\omega_1^{CK} + \omega$ is clockable.*

Another interesting fact is captured by the following statement.

Lemma 4.2.1 *If $\alpha + n$ is clockable for some natural number n, then α is clockable.*

It is quite surprising that there are openings in the sequence of clockable ordinals. In other words, there are intervals of ordinals that no infinite-time Turing machine can count. The following theorem makes this explicit.

Theorem 4.2.9 *There are openings in the sequence of clockable ordinals. In fact, the first opening above any clockable ordinal has size $\mathrm{card}(\omega)$.*

The following theorems reveal something of the structure of these openings.

Theorem 4.2.10 *The openings in the clockable ordinals become large. Indeed, for every clockable ordinal α, there are openings of size at least $\mathrm{card}(\alpha)$ in the sequence of clockable ordinals.*

Theorem 4.2.11 *There are many openings in the clockable ordinals. In particular, if α is a writable ordinal, there are at least $\mathrm{card}(\alpha)$ openings of size at least $\mathrm{card}(\alpha)$ in the sequence of clockable ordinals. In addition, if α is either clockable or writable, the "number" of openings of size at least $\mathrm{card}(\alpha)$ is neither clockable nor writable.*

Theorem 4.2.12 *There are no openings in the sequence of writable ordinals.*

The following two results are quite interesting.

Theorem 4.2.13 *If α and β are clockable, then $\alpha + \beta$ and $\alpha \cdot \beta$ are also clockable.*

Theorem 4.2.14 *If α is either clockable or writable, the set of reals coding well-orderings of length less than $\mathrm{card}(\alpha)$ is decidable.*

4.2.4   On Infinite-Time Halting Problems

Just like ordinary Turing machines, infinite-time Turing machines have their own halting problems. We say "problems" and not "problem" because the two sets $H = \{(p, x) \mid p \text{ halts on input } x\}$ and $h = \{p \mid p \text{ halts on input } 0\}$ are not equivalent as in the classical case. Let us start by stating a theorem that characterizes these problems.

Theorem 4.2.15 *The halting problems h and H are semidecidable.*

The following classes of sets are called approximations to the halting problems:

$$H_\alpha = \{(p, x) \mid p \text{ halts on input } x \text{ in fewer that } \alpha \text{ steps}\},$$
$$h_\alpha = \{p \mid p \text{ halts on input } 0 \text{ in fewer that } \alpha \text{ steps}\}.$$

It is clear that if $\alpha < \beta$, then $H_\alpha \subseteq H_\beta$. In addition, it can be proved that if $\alpha < \beta$, then $H_\alpha \subset H_\beta$. The following statements provide more insight into the halting problems of infinite-time machines.

Theorem 4.2.16 *For any limit nonclockable ordinal α, neither H_α nor h_α is α-decidable. In case α is clockable, then both H_α and h_α are α-semidecidable and $(\alpha + 1)$-decidable.*

Theorem 4.2.17 *If α is writable or clockable, then H_α and h_α are decidable.*

Theorem 4.2.18 *The set h_α is decidable for every α below the supremum of the clockable ordinals.*

Theorem 4.2.19 *Assume that γ is the supremum of the clockable ordinals. Then H_γ is semidecidable.*

4.2.5 Machines with Only One Tape

Assume that we have an ordinary Turing machine that operates in transfinite ordinal time. A natural question that comes up is whether this machine is as powerful as the infinite-time Turing machine with three tapes. This question has been addressed by Hamkins and Daniel Evan Seabold [76]. Here are their main results.

(i) A set is decidable if and only if it is one-tape decidable.

(ii) A function $f : \mathbb{R} \to \mathbb{R}$ whose range is not dense in $\mathbb{R}$ is computable if and only if it is one-tape computable.

(iii) There is a computable function $f : \mathbb{R} \to \mathbb{R}$ that is not one-tape computable.

(iv) The class of one-tape computable functions is not closed under composition; closing it under composition yields the class of all computable functions.

(v) Every clockable ordinal is one-tape clockable, except certain isolated ordinals that end gaps in the clockable ordinals.

4.2.6 Infinite-Time Machines with Oracles

An infinite-time oracle Turing machine is an infinite-time machine equipped with an auxiliary tape. The oracle of an infinite-time Turing machine can be either a single real number or, more generally, a set of reals. However, for reasons I will explain later, in general it is not possible to print the elements of a set of real numbers on the cells of this auxiliary tape. Assume that p is a machine using an oracle tape. Then φ_p^x will denote the resulting function that uses a real number x as an oracle. Such functions will be referred to as infinite-time x-computable functions.

Assume that A is a closed interval of real numbers in $\mathbb{R}$. Then A is uncountable, and so it is not possible to print out the elements of A on an oracle tape. Therefore, for this (not particularly rare) case, we need a different method for using such a set of real numbers as an oracle. Hamkins, in a personal communication has suggested that one may think of the oracle tape as a *buffer* on which a number x is printed out during a computation in order to allow the machine to query whether x belongs to A. Depending on what gets printed on the cell that lies beneath the scanning head at this given moment, it is assumed that the oracle gives the response either *Yes* or *No*, thus replying to the question "$x \in A$?". By employing this counterintuitive method, the machine has the capability to determine whether a real y that appears on the oracle belongs to a set A. In addition, such a machine can decide membership in A of an arbitrary real number z. Also, the characteristic function of A can be computed by assuming that A is the oracle. If the number z appears on the input tape, we just copy it on the oracle tape and query the oracle to see whether z belongs to A. The answer is clearly the value of $\chi_A(z)$. Obviously, there is no limit to the number of times the machine can seek advice from the oracle.

Suppose that p is an infinite-time Turing machine. When running p on input x and oracle A, the result of a halting computation will be written as $\varphi_p^A(x)$.

Definition 4.2.8 A function f is infinite-time A-computable if it can be computed as φ_p^A for some machine p.

Assume that A and B are two oracles; we will say that A is infinite-time computable from B, written $A \leq_\infty B$, if the characteristic function of A is infinite-time B-computable.[1] This definition is meaningful for any kind of oracle (i.e., a set of real numbers or an individual real number if a real number is considered as a subset of ω).

The relation $\leq_\infty$ is transitive and reflexive; thus, we can easily obtain the notion of infinite-time degrees: $A \equiv_\infty B$. This is an equivalence relation, and equivalence classes are denoted by $[A]_\infty$. In addition, for a real x, we have $x \equiv_\infty A_x$, where A_x is a set of finite approximations of x appended with zeros. Also, we write $A <_\infty B$ if $A \leq_\infty B$ and $A \not\equiv_\infty B$. Moreover, it is not difficult to define the corresponding notions of infinite-time semidecidability, clockability and writability for infinite-time oracle Turing machines.

Assume that A and B are two oracles. Then the expression $A \oplus B$ will be used to denote an oracle that codes, in some standard manner, the information contained in A and B. Obviously, $A \oplus B$ is the least upper bound of A and B with respect to $\leq_\infty$.

Given an oracle A, the strong jump of A, written $A^\blacktriangledown$, is defined as follows:

$$A^\blacktriangledown = H^A = \{(p,x) \mid \varphi_p^A(x)\!\downarrow\}.$$

Notice that $\varphi_p^A(x)\!\downarrow$ means that $\varphi_p^A(x)$ is convergent. The weak jump of A is the set

$$A^\triangledown = A \oplus h^A = A \oplus \{p \mid \varphi_p^A(0)\!\downarrow\}.$$

The set A is included in $A^\triangledown$ because some particularly complex sets of real numbers cannot be computed only from h^A. Now we are ready to present the main results concerning infinite-time oracle machines.

Theorem 4.2.20 $A <_\infty A^\triangledown <_\infty A^\blacktriangledown$.

Corollary 4.2.4 *The set $A^\blacktriangledown$ is not computable from $A \oplus z$ for any real z. In particular, $0^\blacktriangledown$ is not computable from any real.*

---

1. Clearly, this notion is an extension of *Turing reducibility*: A is *Turing reducible* to B, written $A \leq_T B$, if A is recursive in B.

Notice that 0^∇ and $0^\blacktriangledown$ are actually equivalent to h and H, respectively.

Let α be an ordinal number that is coded by some real z that is $A^\blacktriangledown$. The iterates $A^{\nabla(\alpha)}$ with respect to z are defined by induction on α such that $A^{\nabla(\alpha)} = A \oplus w_\alpha$ for some real w_α. The iterates start with $w_0 = 0$, so that $A^{\nabla(0)} = A \oplus 0$. At successor stages we want

$$A^{\nabla(\beta+1)} = (A^{\nabla(\beta)})^\nabla = (A \oplus w_\beta) \oplus h^{A^{\nabla(\beta)}},$$

so we demand that $w_{\beta+1} = w_\beta \oplus h^{A^{\nabla(\beta)}}$. At limit stages δ, we let $w_\delta = \bigoplus_{\beta<\delta} w_\beta$ and depend on z for the organization of the information.

Theorem 4.2.21 $A^{\nabla\blacktriangledown} \equiv A^\blacktriangledown$. *Indeed, for any ordinal α that is $A^\blacktriangledown$-writable,* $A^{\nabla(\alpha)\blacktriangledown} = A^\blacktriangledown$.

Theorem 4.2.22 Δ_2^1 *is closed under the jump operators ∇ and $\blacktriangledown$.*

Theorem 4.2.23 *The relation $x \leq_\infty y$ is semidecidable but not decidable.*

4.2.7   Post's Problem for Supertasks

Hamkins and Lewis[75] address the equivalent of Emil Leon Post's problem in the setting of infinite-time computing. But first, let us recall Post's original problem. If $A \leq_T B$ and $B \leq_T A$, then we write $A \equiv_T B$. The equivalence classes of $\equiv_T$ are called *Turing degrees* or T-degrees. A set A is *complete* if it is recursively enumerable and also for every set B that is recursively enumerable it holds that $B \leq_T A$. Post's problem asks whether there are recursively enumerable sets that are neither recursive nor complete. Here is the answer to the supertask analogue of Post's problem as stated in [75]:

Theorem 4.2.24 *Depending on the context, the supertask analogue of Post's problem has both positive and negative solutions. Specifically:*

(i) *In the context of the reals, there are no degrees strictly between 0 and 0^∇.*

(ii) *In the context of sets of reals, there are degrees strictly between 0 and 0^∇. Indeed, there are incomparable semidecidable degrees.*

4.3   Infinite-Time Automata

A finite automaton, or finite-state machine, is a conceptual computing device that has as input a string (i.e., a sequence of symbols that belong to some alphabet A) and produces no output at all other than an indication of whether the input is acceptable. A finite automaton has an input tape, which is divided into cells each of them holding one symbol of the input. A scanning head moves on the tape, reading the contents of each cell. A finite control changes the state of the automaton according to the current state and the symbol just read. Initially, the scanning head is placed at the leftmost cell and always moves to the right just after each read operation, and the finite control is set in a designated initial state. When the scanning head reaches the end of the input string, the finite automaton indicates the acceptance or rejection of the input string according to the state it has entered. Since we have extended the functionality of Turing machines so they may perform an infinite number of steps to achieve their computational tasks, it is quite reasonable to expect to be able to extend the functionality of any kind of automaton so it can perform an infinite number of steps to achieve a computational task. Indeed, J. Richard Büchi has introduced finite automata operating on infinite sequences. In addition, David E. Müller has defined deterministic automata on infinite words.

Grégory Lafitte [105] presents a two-way Wojciechowski automaton, or W^2-automaton, that can recognize a finite, infinite, or transfinite string in a transfinite number of steps. Formally, a Wojciechowski automaton is defined as follows.

Definition 4.3.1 A Wojciechowski automaton, or W-automaton, is a quintuple $(Q, \Sigma, \delta, \iota, F)$ with Σ a finite alphabet, Q the finite set of its states, $\delta \subseteq (2^Q \cup Q) \times \Sigma \times Q$ the transition relation, $i \in Q$ the initial state, and $F \subseteq (2^Q \cup Q)$ the finite set of its final states.

In discussing the operation of a Wojciechowski automaton, by *state* we mean an element of $2^Q \cup Q$.

A W^2-automaton is a W-automaton on a two-way countable tape. At a limit stage, the scanning head is placed automatically on top of the first cell. In addition, if at a previous successor stage the scanning head was on top of a cell for at least one stage, the symbol on this cell will change to $\natural$ if something else was printed on the cell before, and otherwise, it is replaced by $\flat$ if the symbol $\natural$ was printed on it. Practically, the symbol printed on the cell changes from $\natural$ to $\flat$ and vice versa.

Definition 4.3.2 A W^2-automaton is a quintuple $\mathscr{A} = (Q, \Sigma, \delta, i, F)$, where Σ is a set of distinct symbols called the *alphabet*, Q is a finite set of states, $\delta \subseteq (2^Q \cup Q) \times \Sigma \cup \{\flat, \natural\} \times W \times \{\leftarrow, \downarrow, \rightarrow\}$ is the transition relation, $i \in Q$ is the initial state, and $F \subseteq (2^Q \cup Q)$ is the finite set of final states.

Let Σ be a finite alphabet and let α be an ordinal number. Then all strings of length α will be called α-sequences. We now define continuous α-sequences, which are necessary for the discussion that follows:

Definition 4.3.3 An α-sequence φ on Q is continuous if for any successor ordinal β, we have $\varphi(\beta) \in Q$ and if for any limit ordinal β,

$$\varphi(\beta) = \Big\{ q \in Q \ \Big| \ \{\gamma < \beta | \varphi(\gamma) = q\} \text{ is cofinal to } \beta \Big\}.$$

A run with label $\sigma \in (\Sigma \cup \{\flat, \natural\})^{\omega\alpha}$, that is, $\sigma : \alpha \to (\omega \to (\Sigma \cup \{\flat, \natural\}))$, where α is an ordinal number, of a W^2-automaton $\mathcal{A} = (Q, \Sigma, \delta, i, F)$ is a continuous $(\alpha + 1)$-sequence $(\varphi_q, \varphi_{\text{pos}})$ on $2^Q \times \mathbb{N}$ such that $\varphi_q(0) = i$, $\varphi_{\text{pos}}(0) = 0$, $\sigma(0) \in \Sigma^\omega$ is the original content of the tape, and for any ordinal $\beta < \alpha$,

$$\Big(\varphi_q(\beta), \sigma(\beta)(\varphi_{\text{pos}}(\beta)), \varphi_q(\beta+1), \varrho(\varphi_{\text{pos}}(\beta+1) - \varphi_{\text{pos}}(\beta))\Big) \in \delta,$$

where $\varrho(1) = \to$, $\varrho(0) = \downarrow$, $\varrho(-1) = \leftarrow$, and $\sigma(\beta)$ specifies the contents of the tape at stage β. Also, φ_q and φ_{pos} return the state of the machine and the position of the scanning head at every stage.

W^2-automata are unexpectedly powerful conceptual computational devices. Indeed, the following result makes this precise.

Theorem 4.3.1 *Both finite- and infinite-time decidable languages can be accepted by W^2-automata.*

In other words, W^2-automata have the power of infinite-time Turing machines.

4.4   Building Infinite Machines

In the previous section we have presented a theory of machines that can perform an infinite number of steps to accomplish their computational tasks. However, unless it is possible to perform supertasks, the theory presented so far is merely a mathematical curiosity.[2] The possibility of creating such machines depends mainly on the properties of our universe. For instance, if time and space are continuous, in spite of quantum gravity expecting them to be granular, then in principle, it is possible to perform a supertask.[3] Similarly, in a Newtonian universe (i.e., a universe in which the laws of the Newtonian mechanics hold) space, time, and matter are

---

2. This is not quite true, since, for example, there are systems that operate virtually forever (e.g., operating systems), and so infinite-time Turing machines may have some unexpected applications.
3. See Chapter 8 for more regarding this issue.

continuous, and thus it is possible to build such machines. Indeed, E. Brian Davies [47] explores the possibility of building an infinite machine in such a universe. In the rest of this section I will briefly describe his construction.

Davies starts with the assumption that it is possible to construct a machine that contains an infinite number of parts with no lower limit on their sizes. However, it is necessary to give a detailed description of the machine to avoid paradoxes. Davies assumes that it is possible to construct a machine M_1 that contains a Babbage-type computer (i.e., a machine resembling Charles Babbage's *difference engine*) with a specified clock time c_1 and a memory of size m_1 bytes. It also contains a robotic factory that can produce a new version of the computer and of the factory (i.e., a new machine M_2). The machine M_2 is is not identical to M_1. First of all, M_2 has memory size that is twice the memory size of M_1, and its components are 16 times smaller than those of M_1. From these, one may deduce that the size (diameter) of M_2 is at most $s_2 = \frac{s_1}{8}$. We also assume that its clock time is $c_2 = \frac{c_1}{8}$. Practically, this means that signals do not need to travel any faster in M_2 than they do in M_1. In short, M_2 is smaller, faster, and more powerful than M_1. Clearly, the question regarding our ability to build such machines depends mainly on the progress of technology. Over the last two centuries, each generation of tools has been used to produce the next one, and in the course of time, tools have become steadily smaller, faster, and more accurate. In addition, most machine tools operate in a rather classical manner (i.e., quantum phenomena are not observable at all). The same remarks apply to computer design and performance. Thus according to Davies, there is no obvious inconsistency in making the previous assumption, and so we can safely continue with our construction.

The machine M_2 is capable of building M_3 and so on. In the end we have a series of machines where M_i is directly connected to M_{i-1} and M_{i+1}. The characteristics of each machine M_n are described by the following equations:

$$\forall n > 0 : c_n = \frac{c_{n-1}}{8}, \quad m_n = 2m_{n-1}, \quad s_n = \frac{s_{n-1}}{8}.$$

It is also possible to estimate the total size of all machines together. Indeed, their potential total size is at most

$$s_1 \sum_{n=0}^{\infty} 8^{-n} = \frac{8s_1}{7} < \infty.$$

Assume that $\mathcal{P}_n$ is a sequence of propositions whose solutions require steadily more computation as n increases. Also, assume that the length of the computation does not increase rapidly with n. The machine M_1 is given the general problem (i.e., the whole sequence $\mathcal{P}_n$) and operates as follows: it tries to solve the problem for $n = 1$; if it succeeds, it reports "yes" (e.g., by blowing a horn). Otherwise, it constructs M_2 and passes to it the entire problem together with the number $n = 2$. The second machine behaves similarly. At the ith stage the machine M_i tries to solve the problem for the case $n = i$, and if it succeeds, it informs M_{i-1}, which passes the message up the chain. If it fails, it constructs M_{i+1} and passes the problem down the chain. After a suitable finite length of time, M_1 either gets the good news that the problem has been solved or can deduce that it is not soluble for any n.

The machines have the capability to deduce whether a program will run forever on a Turing machine. Given the program, starting with the case $n = 1$, we run it on M_n until either it has stopped, the memory of M_n is full, or M_n has carried out 2^n steps. If at that time the program has not stopped, we pass the same program to M_{n+1}. If the program stops on any of the machines, then a report is sent back to M_1. In case M_1 has not received any report after a certain finite length of time, it can deduce that the program does not halt.

4.5 Metaphysical Foundations for Computation

Steinhart [193] attempted to define metaphysical foundations for computation capable of supporting both classical computers and hypercomputers. Using this formalism it is quite possible to directly compare machines and their computational power.

A logical space is filled with individuals that combine with properties. Both individuals and properties are sets. For the rest of the discussion $D = \{i_1, i_2, \ldots\}$ and $P = \{p_1, p_2, \ldots\}$ will denote sets of individuals and properties, respectively. Notice that both sets may be infinite. A property that combines with n individuals is dubbed an n-place property. In particular, properties that combine with many individuals are *relations*. As an example, let us consider the sets $D = \{A, B\}$ and $P = \{p, q, r\}$, where both p and q are one-place properties, and r is a two-place property (i.e., a relation).

Definition 4.5.1 A fact over individuals and properties is a list of the form $(p, i_1, \ldots, i_m)$, where p is an m-place property and $i_1, \ldots, i_m$ are individuals.

For instance, (r, A, B) and (p, A) are facts.

Definition 4.5.2 A *logical space* over individuals and properties is the set of all facts over these particular individuals and properties.

For example, the logical space F of D and P is the set

$$\{(p, A), (p, B), (q, A), (q, B), (r, A, B), (r, B, A)\}.$$

Definition 4.5.3 A *situation* over a logical space is any subset of the logical space.

We will denote by S the set of all situations over a logical space F. Clearly, S is the power set of F (i.e., $S = 2^F$).

Situations can be ordered in the obvious way. Thus, for any two situations $a, b \in S$, $a \leq b$ if and only if $a \subseteq b$. Depending on the nature of the situations it is possible to define additional ordering schemes.

Definition 4.5.4 A *series* is a function from an ordinal μ to some ordinary set V. In particular, a *series H of situations* over some set S of situations is simply a function $H : \mu \to S$. We say that the series H is *indexed* by μ.

If $(S, \leq)$ is a linear order, a series H of situations is

$$\text{constant} \Leftrightarrow (\forall n, m \in \mu)\Big(H(n) = H(m)\Big),$$

$$\text{increasing} \Leftrightarrow (\forall n, m \in \mu)\Big((n < m) \Leftrightarrow (H(n) \leq H(m))\Big),$$

$$\text{decreasing} \Leftrightarrow (\forall n, m \in \mu)\Big((n < m) \Leftrightarrow (H(m) \leq H(n))\Big).$$

A series H of situations that is not constant and neither increasing nor decreasing is termed *oscillating*. If a series H is increasing or decreasing, then it converges to U if and only if U is respectively the least upper bound or the greatest lower bound of H.

It is not totally unrealistic to assume that an algorithm is a well-defined computational rule on a domain (i.e., a function). And it is equally reasonable to assume that such a rule is a formula in the language of set theory. Thus, we will call any function instantiating such a rule an operator. In particular, any function $f : S \to S$ is a successor operator if there is a rule R such that $f(x) = y \Leftrightarrow R(x, y)$.

Definition 4.5.5 A series H is recursive for successor ordinals if there is a successor operator f such that for every ordinal λ less than μ, $H(\lambda + 1) = f(H(\lambda))$.

Let us denote by S^∞ the set of infinite series of situations over S. In addition, let $\langle H(\alpha)\rangle$ denote any infinite series in S^∞.

Definition 4.5.6 A (partial) function $l : S^\infty \to S$ is a *limit operator* if

(i) there is a rule R such that $R(\langle H(\alpha)\rangle, y) \Leftrightarrow l(\langle H(\alpha)\rangle) = y$, and

(ii) $\langle H(\alpha)\rangle$ somehow *converges* to y.

The set-theoretic least upper bound $\cup_{\alpha<\lambda}\langle H(\alpha)\rangle$ is an example of a limit operator.

Definition 4.5.7 Given a series H, if there is a limit operator l such that

$$\forall \lambda < \mu : H(\lambda) = l\left(\left\{H(\alpha) = h \middle| \alpha < \lambda\right\}\right),$$

then H is *continuous at limit ordinals*.

Definition 4.5.8 A series H is called *well behaved* if

(i) it is recursive for successor ordinals, and

(ii) it is continuous at limit ordinals.

Definition 4.5.9 A series H indexed by μ is *algorithmic* if

(i) H is well behaved, and

(ii) there is an $\alpha < \mu$ such that $H(\alpha)$ is a fixed point, that is, H is constant above α.

Any algorithm can be identified by an inductively defined property that is free in some variable H and is defined on an ordinal number α. In addition, the free variable H ranges over series of situations. The most general form of an algorithm defined this way is

$$(\forall n)\left((n < \alpha) \Rightarrow C(H, n)\right),$$

where $C(H, n)$ is the conjunction of three components in which neither H nor n is a bound variable. More specifically, these components specify the values of H for various types of ordinals. The *initial* component is used to specify the value of H for 0, the first ordinal. The *successor* component is used to specify the successor operators that can determine the value of H for ordinals that are less than α. The *limit* component is used to specify the limit operators that determine H for limit ordinals that are less than α. Let us now see how one can define an algorithm that computes the factorial of an integer m (where we define $\omega! = \omega$):

$$m! = \lambda H.(\forall n)\left((n \leq (\omega + 1)\right) \Rightarrow$$
$$\left(\left((n = 0) \Rightarrow \left(H(n) = 0\right)\right)\right.$$
$$\wedge \left((0 < n < \omega) \rightarrow \left(H(n) = H(n-1) \cdot m\right)\right)$$
$$\left.\wedge \left((n = \omega) \Rightarrow \left(H(n) = \omega\right)\right)\right).$$

Now it is quite reasonable to ask, "What is the relation between machines and algorithms?" The answer is very simple.

Definition 4..5.10 A machine is a series of situations that implement an algorithm.

Thus, one can specify a machine (e.g., Turing machine) as a series of situations that implements a particular algorithm.

Definition 4..5.11 An algorithm over some set S of situations is an inductively defined property of some series in S.

A *machine* is a series of situations that *implements* (realizes or models) an algorithm. Any series of sets that is well behaved and converges is an *algorithmic series of sets*. We are now ready to define logically possible machines.

Definition 4..5.12 A *logically possible machine* is any algorithmic series of sets.

To understand this definition, let us first note that finite machines are special cases of their infinite counterparts, and physically possible machines are special cases of metaphysically possible machines. Now, a metaphysically possible machine is just a special case of a logically possible machine. But is the concept of algorithmic series of sets so powerful that it transcends Turing computability? This question can be addressed by means of an example borrowed from set theory.

Assume that X and Y are two arbitrary sets. Then $X \precsim Y$ if and only if there is an injection $f : X \to Y$. If $X \precsim Y$, then there is an injection $g : X \to Z$, for some $Z \subseteq Y$. If X is an infinite set, the aleph function, written $\aleph(X)$, is the next cardinal greater than X. Formally, $\aleph(X) = \cap\{x | x \not\precsim X\}$. The first aleph is $\aleph_0 = \omega$, the next cardinal greater than $\aleph_0$ is $\aleph(\aleph_0)$, and the next cardinal greater than $\aleph(\aleph_0)$ is $\aleph(\aleph(\aleph_0))$, and so on. In general, $\aleph_{n+1} = \aleph(\aleph_n)$ when n is a successor ordinal, and

$$\aleph_\lambda = \bigcup_{\beta < \lambda} \aleph_\beta$$

when λ is a limit ordinal. Let us now define the superaleph series as follows:

$$\mu_0 = \aleph_0; \quad \mu_{n+1} = \aleph_{\mu_n}; \quad \vartheta = \bigcup\{\mu_n | n \in \omega\}.$$

The first few elements of the superaleph series are: $\aleph_0, \aleph_{\aleph_0}, \aleph_{\aleph_{\aleph_0}}, \ldots$. Let us now explain how we can generate the elements of the superaleph series. Suppose that have at our disposal an element ζ_i of the superaleph series. Then the next element, ζ_{i+1}, is obtained by replacing the zero in ζ_i with $\aleph_0$. For instance, by replacing the zero in $\aleph_{\aleph_{\aleph_0}}$ with $\aleph_0$ we get $\aleph_{\aleph_{\aleph_{\aleph_0}}}$, which is the next element of the superaleph series. The limit ϑ of the superaleph series is denoted by an endless series of subscripted $\aleph$'s, that is,

$$\vartheta = \aleph_{\aleph_{\aleph_{\cdot_{\cdot_{\cdot}}}}}.$$

Observe that $\aleph(\vartheta) = \aleph_\vartheta = \vartheta$. In other words, ϑ is a fixed point of the aleph function. This implies that if we start an interaction from $\aleph_0$ up to the superalephs, we will stop at ϑ. In general, the aleph series is algorithmic, since it is also well behaved. In addition, this is a proof that algorithmic series exceed Turing computability.

The theory presented so far can be used to classify any computing device, provided that interaction does not count as a new paradigm, which, of course, is not true. The theory can be used not only to classify machines, but minds as well, provided, of course, that minds are purely computational devices. Indeed, Steinhart [194] has examined this idea. However, there is no proof that all phenomena in nature are computational and that minds are some sort of computing device. Following Copeland, Steinhart calls himself a "wide mechanist" (i.e., a computationalist that rejects the Church-Turing thesis), and so it was quite natural for him to postulate the existence of *superminds*. Although, I agree with Steinhart and Copeland that minds have hypercomputational capabilities, I favor the idea that minds have both hypercomputational and *paracomputational* capabilities, that is, capabilities that cannot be classified as computational, and that is why I call them *hyperminds*. So Steinhart's theory can only partially classify hyperminds.

V. Interactive Computing

Traditionally, a computational task is considered successful only if it halts after some finite amount of time. However, if we insist on this simple requirement, most modern computer-based equipment will be considered as a failure. For example, a computer-controlled mechanical respiration support system cannot stop operating, or else the patient being supported by this system will die. In addition, operating systems and word processors are written to receive unbounded input over time and therefore do not halt. Also, a rover maneuvering on the surface of another planet should not stop operating before its projected life expectancy,[1] or else it will be considered a (partial) failure.

Apart from this, another aspect of modern computing is that many programs do not compute any function at all. For instance, one may wonder what function is computed by a web server or an FTP client? Quite naturally, one may respond to this question that any web server actually computes some bizarre, huge, unwieldy function. But by going one step further, one can assume that walls, chairs, and even fish tanks ompute such functions (and I will discuss these ideas later). However, one should note that a web server may crash because of a power failure, a random attack, or just because the system administrator shuts it down for maintenance. Since such events are usually not scheduled, one cannot possibly conclude that web severs actually compute something, unless one is a mystic. These and similar observations make it clear that the classical foundations of computer science are inadequate, because they fail to capture many characteristics of modern computer systems. One way out of this dilemma is to introduce interaction into our formal apparatus, and that is exactly the subject of this chapter—how interaction broadens the concept of computability.

5.1 Interactive Computing and Turing Machines

Let us start with a simple question: is the Turing model of computation sufficient to explain and describe modern computer systems? The answer

---

1. For a system with practically unlimited power supply, this is not really an issue.

is clearly no. The inadequacy of the classical model was briefly presented in the introductory chapter and the paragraph above; however, it is necessary to provide rigorous arguments in favor of the deficiency of this model in describing and explaining the functionality of modern computer systems. Clearly, the adoption of the Turing machine as a complete model for algorithms and general problem-solving lies at the heart of the problem. Most readers will agree with Lynn Andrea Stein's [192] remark that

> Computation is a function from its inputs to its outputs. It is made up of a sequence of functional steps that produce—at its end—some result that is the goal. This is what I was taught when I was trained as a computer scientist. It is a model that computer scientists by and large take for granted. It is something the members of the field share.

To be fair, Stein is not a proponent of this point of view. On the contrary, she is in line with Peter Wegner and Eugene Eberbach, who claim [217] that

> The T[uring]M[machine] model is too weak to describe properly the Internet, evolution or robotics, because it is a closed model... In the case of the Internet, the Web clients "jump" into the middle of interaction, without a knowledge of the server state and previous history of other clients. A dynamic set of inputs and outputs, parallel interaction of multiple clients and servers, a dynamic structure of the Internet communication links and nodes, is outside what a sequential, static and requiring full specification Turing machine can represent.

Of course, Wegner has expressed similar thoughts in other instances (e.g., see [218, 215]), but this is the most recent account of these ideas. Similar views are expressed in a milder tone by Jan van Leeuwen and Jiři Wiedermann [208]:

> The given examples of interactive and global computing indicate that the classical Turing machine paradigm should be revised (extended) in order to capture the forms of computation that one observes in the systems and networks in modern information technology.

In addition, the classical model artificially imposes limits to what can be done with modern computers. Here is what Stein has to say about this [192]:

> Increasingly, however, the traditional computational metaphor limits, rather than empowers, us today. It prevents us from confronting and working effectively with computation as it actually occurs. This is true both within computer science, which still clings fervently to the metaphor, and in other disciplines where

> dissatisfaction with the computational metaphor [i.e., the idea
> that the brain is like a computer] has in some cases caused an
> anticomputationalist backlash.

It is really debatable whether the anticomputationalist backlash was caused
by a dissatisfaction with the classical computational metaphor. On the contrary, computationalism asserts that *all* mental processes are mechanical in
their nature. In other words, according to computationalism, mental processes can be implemented by either computers or hypercomputers. And
precisely this is the reason for the anticomputationalist backlash. Apart
from this, the essence of the whole argument is that the traditional model
of computation is clearly inadequate for modern computer practice. For example, young students who are trained to program sequentially on systems
with a single processor, are not adequately prepared for the real world, in
which most modern programming tasks involve some kind of concurrency,
and in many cases one has to implement "algorithms" on machines with
more than one processor.

A typical counterargument to the previous rhetoric would be that all
parts of various interactive systems can be modeled by Turing machines.
However, a Turing machine always computes a result; but then, one should
be able to answer the following question raised by Stein: "What is it that
the world-wide web calculates?" In addition, one may ask what an Internet relay chat server computes. Naturally, one may raise similar questions
for many other instances in which modern computer equipment is in use
today. Our inability to give convincing answers to such questions is a clear
indication that the Turing machine is an outdated model of computation
that has a very limited role to play in modern-day computing.

Bertil Ekdahl [56] argues that interactive computing can be simulated
by oracle Turing machines. However, this argument is clearly a fallacy: The
oracle of a Turing machine contains quite specific information (e.g., the
characteristic function of a set) that is used in the course of the operation of the machine. Thus, one may say that an oracle machine is thereby
able to communicate with the external world. But a typical interactive system has bidirectional communication with the environment, which is not
the case for an oracle machine. Also, oracle machines have all the drawbacks of ordinary Turing machines that make then inadequate as models
of interactive systems (i.e., they expect their input at the beginning of the
computation and succeed in computing something only when they stop). In
addition, one should not forget that interaction is a primitive notion (e.g.,
the π-calculus, which was introduced by Robin Milner, Joachim Parrow,
and David Walker [133], was built around this primitive notion), just as
the notion of sequentially reading from and writing to a storage medium is
a primitive notion in which the Turing machine model rest.

Doug Lea [109] remarks that just as "the few constructs supporting sequential programming lead to a wide range of coding practices, idioms, and

design strategies, a few concurrency constructs go a long way in opening up new vistas in programming." Consequently, as Stein notes, if we discourage (or even prevent) students from adopting certain styles of thinking and understanding just because they deviate from the unrelenting sequentialism of the computational metaphor, students are not learning new coding practices, idioms, and design strategies, and eventually become ill prepared for today's software market.

If Turing machines are inadequate for describing modern computer systems, then we clearly need other formalisms that can deal with the various aspects of these systems. Indeed, there have been a number of calculi and/or conceptual devices that address these issues. In the rest of this chapter I am going to give an overview of some of them.

5.2   Interaction Machines

When Turing proposed his famous machine, he actually set the foundations of sequential computing. However, in the case of interactive computing, things proceeded in the opposite direction. First, programmers implemented interactive systems and practiced interactive programming, and only then did theoreticians start to formulate theories that dealt with certain aspects of interactive computing (for example, see [4, 129]). However, an integrated theory of interactive computing appeared only in 1998 when Wegner published his paper "Interactive foundations of computing" [216].

In this paper Wegner discusses the basic characteristics of *interaction machines* as well as their computational power. In addition, he presents "interaction grammars" that extend the Chomsky hierarchy of grammars.

An interaction machine is simply a Turing machine that is augmented with the capability of performing dynamic read and/or write actions that provide it with a way of directly interacting with the external world. This additional capability can be implemented by allowing interaction machines to be connected with their environment—more specifically, with a single or multiple input stream or via synchronous or asynchronous communication. From a practical point of view this means that there is no single definition of the structure of an interaction machine. Moreover, all interaction machines are open systems. The *observable* behavior of interaction machines is specified by *interaction histories*, which take the form of *streams* that are the interactive time-sensitive analogue of strings. Formally, if A is a set, then by a stream over A we mean an ordered pair $s = (a, s')$ where $a \in A$ and s' is another stream.[2] The following statement is a clear indication that the additional "hardware" is not just some kind of accessory.

---

2. Streams are objects that do not belong to the standard set-theoretic universe, but they do belong to the universe of non-well-founded sets (see [8] for details).

Proposition 5.2.1 *It is not possible to model interaction machines by Turing machines.* [216]

Interaction machines can be viewed as mappings over streams that take time into account. Such mappings cannot be classified as functions, since functions are timeless. In other words, interaction machines extend the theory of computability by introducing *computable nonfunctions* over histories. This nonfunctional facet of interaction machines applies also to other aspects of these machines. This can be demonstrated by a simple example: consider a rover maneuvering on the surface of another planet. Clearly, the rover is an interactive system that must respond to external stimuli. For instance, when it encounters a boulder it must change its course; when it is going down into a crater it must use its brakes to reduce its speed, while when it is going up a hillside it must boost its engines. In many cases, the software loaded into the rover's memory cannot handle totally unexpected situations, and so a new, updated software is uploaded to the rover. None of these actions can be predicted, and sometimes they are not among the actions one initially expects the rover to face. In other words, these actions cannot be described by a function, and thus one may say that they cannot be described algorithmically. From this example it is not difficult to see that the behavior of interaction machines cannot be described by Turing computable functions. An interesting and, to some degree, unexpected effect of interaction is that if we enhance algorithms with interactive behavior, we create systems that operate in a smart (not intelligent!) way, or in Wegner's own words, "[e]xtending algorithms with interaction transforms dumb algorithms into smart agents." The crux of the ideas presented so far have been summarized by Wegner in the form of a thesis.

Thesis 5.2.1 *Inductive computing: Algorithms (Turing machines) do not capture the intuitive notion of computing, since they cannot express interactive computing and intuitive computing includes interaction* [216].

Before we proceed with the presentation of interaction grammars, we will briefly recall the definitions of formal grammar and the Chomsky hierarchy of grammars, as well as their relationship to various forms of automata. Readers familiar with these notions can safely skip this material. Assume that Σ is an arbitrary set and that ε denotes the empty string. Then

$$\Sigma^* = \{\varepsilon\} \cup \Sigma \cup \Sigma \times \Sigma \cup \Sigma \times \Sigma \times \Sigma \cup \cdots .$$

is the set of all finite strings over Σ. Let us now recall the definition of a grammar.

Definition 5.2.1 A grammar is defined to be a quadruple $G = (V_N, V_T, S, \Phi)$ where V_T and V_N are disjoint sets of terminal and nonterminal (syntactic class) symbols, respectively; S, a distinguished element of V_N, is called the starting symbol. Φ is a finite nonempty relation from $(V_T \cup V_N)^* V_N (V_T \cup V_N)^*$ to $(V_T \cup V_N)^*$. In general, an element (α, β) is written as $\alpha \to \beta$ and is called a production or rewriting rule [204].

Grammars are classified as follows:

Unrestricted grammars There are no restrictions on the form of the production rules.

Context-sensitive grammars The relation Φ contains only productions of the form $\alpha \to \beta$, where $|\alpha| \le |\beta|$, and in general, $|\gamma|$ is the length of the string γ.

Context-free grammars The relation Φ contains only productions of the form $\alpha \to \beta$, where $|\alpha| = 1$ and $\alpha \in V_N$.

Regular grammars The relation Φ contains only productions of the form $\alpha \to \beta$, where $|\alpha| \le |\beta|$, $\alpha \in V_N$, and β has the form aB or a, where $a \in V_T$ and $B \in V_N$.

Syntactically complex languages can be defined by means of grammars. To each class of languages there is a class of automata (machines) that *accept* (i.e., they can answer the decision problem "$s \in L$?," where s is a string and L is a language) this class of languages, which are generated by the respective grammars. In particular, *finite automata* accept languages generated by regular grammars, *push-down automata* accept languages generated by context-free grammars, *linear bounded automata* accept languages generated by context-sensitive grammars, and *Turing machines* accept *recursive* languages, that is, a subclass of the class of languages generated by unrestricted grammars.

An interaction grammar is not used to recognize strings but rather streams defined above.

Definition 5.2.2 An interaction grammar IG is defined to be a quadruple (V_N, V_T, S, R), where V_N, V_T, and S have their "usual" meaning and R is a set of production rules. Given a production rule $\alpha \to \beta$, β may be formed using the "listening" operator . and the "nondeterministic choice" operator $+$.[3]

Generally speaking, the . operator waits for input, while the $+$ operator selects nondeterministically an event from a list of events when input arrives. Thus, an interactive grammar containing only the production rule

$$\text{BinDigit} \to (0 + 1).\text{BinDigit}$$

describes infinite streams, expressing reactive systems that react to a continuous (nonhalting) stream of zeros and ones over time.

---

3. Although it is not explicitly stated, one may use parentheses for clarity.

It is known that one can compose sequential processes and create a new process that has the combined effect of the two processes. Practically, this means that one can compose two Turing machines to create paired Turing machines that compute exactly what the two distinct machines compute. On the other hand, it is not possible to compose interaction machines in a similar way. However, we can combine interaction machines by means of the parallel composition operator, denoted by |. Thus, the behavior of $P|Q$ is "equal" to the behavior of P, the behavior of Q, and the interaction that takes place between P and Q. It is interesting to note that parallel composition is a commutative operation, that is, $A|B = B|A$.

Interactive identity machines are a special form of interaction machines that immediately output their input without transforming it. These machines can express richer behavior than Turing machines, because they trivially model Turing machines by simply echoing their behavior. Interactive identity machines can be used to model "echo intelligence" (a behavior that is best exemplified by the legendary Eliza program by Joseph Weizenbaum [221]).

5.3   Persistent Turing Machines

Persistent Turing machines, which were introduced by Dina Goldin [69], are extended Turing machines that can describe a limited form of interactive behavior. In particular, they can be employed to describe *sequential interactive computations* that are applied to a dynamic stream consisting of input/output pairs and have their state stored in some medium [70]. A persistent Turing machine is a Turing machine that operates on a number of different tapes. In addition, the contents of a distinguished tape, which is called the *persistent work tape* (or just work tape), are preserved between any two complete computational tasks. This distinguished tape plays the role of the permanent *memory* of the machine, and its contents specify the *state* of the machine before and after a computation. The states of a persistent Turing machine are represented by strings with no restriction on their length (i.e., they may even be infinite).

A persistent Turing machine $\mathscr{P}$ defines a partial recursive function $\varphi_{\mathscr{P}}: I \times W \to O \times W$, where I, O, and W denote its input, output, and work tape. To demonstrate how we can define this function, I will borrow an example from [69]. A telephone answering machine $\mathscr{A}$ is actually a persistent Turing machine that defines the following function:

$$\varphi_{\mathscr{A}}(\text{record } x, y) = (\text{ok}, yx),$$
$$\varphi_{\mathscr{A}}(\text{play back}, x) = (x, x),$$
$$\varphi_{\mathscr{A}}(\text{erase}, y) = (\text{done}, \varepsilon).$$

The answering machine can record, play back, and erase messages. In addition, the work tape of the answering machine contains a stream of recorded messages. Thus, $\varphi_{\mathscr{A}}$ fully describes the observable behavior of the answering machine. Notice that the contents of the work tape are only part of the definition of $\varphi_{\mathscr{A}}$ and by no means affect the behavior of $\mathscr{A}$.

Let us summarize: a persistent Turing machine $\mathscr{P}$ transforms an input stream $(i_1, i_2, \ldots)$ to an output stream $(o_1, o_2, \ldots)$ using a function $\varphi_{\mathscr{P}}$. Initially, the state of $\mathscr{P}$ is empty. In the course of its operation the state of $\mathscr{P}$ changes. For instance, in the case of our answering machine, a possible input stream may be

$$(\text{record } A, \text{record } BC, \text{erase}, \text{record } D, \text{record } E, \text{play back}, \ldots).$$

This input stream generates the output stream

$$(\text{ok}, \text{ok}, \text{done}, \text{ok}, \text{ok}, DE, \ldots),$$

while the state evolves as follows:

$$(\varepsilon, A, ABC, \varepsilon, D, DE, DE, \ldots).$$

Assume that I and O are the input and output streams of a persistent Turing machine $\mathscr{P}$. Then the *interaction stream* of $\mathscr{P}$ is a stream of pairs, where the first part of each pair comes from the input stream and the second part from the output stream. Thus, the interaction stream of our answering machine has the following form:

$$\Big((\text{record } A, \text{ok}), (\text{record } BC, \text{ok}), (\text{erase}, \text{done}), (\text{record } D, \text{ok}), \ldots\Big).$$

In order to compare two different conceptual computing devices, Goldin uses the notion of behavioral equivalence. Two conceptual computing devices are equivalent if they have the same behavior. In the case of string-manipulating devices (e.g., ordinary Turing machines), the collection of strings that are processed and generated by the device constitutes its behavior. For example, the behavior of a Turing machine is formed by the strings that are read and printed by its scanning head. More generally, the behavior of a conceptual computing device $\mathscr{D}$ can be modeled by its corresponding language $\mathcal{L}(\mathscr{D})$. For instance, for any persistent Turing machine $\mathscr{P}$, the set of all interaction streams makes up its language $\mathcal{L}(\mathscr{P})$. Since the language of a conceptual computing device models its behavior, one can say that two such devices $\mathscr{D}_1$ and $\mathscr{D}_2$ are equivalent if $\mathcal{L}(\mathscr{D}_1) = \mathcal{L}(\mathscr{D}_2)$.

A persistent Turing machine processes an arbitrary input stream that is generated by its environment. Clearly, this is not a realistic assumption, since the external environment cannot yield an arbitrary input stream (e.g., the winning numbers in a lottery drawing are usually in the range 1 to 48, and these numbers are the input for the lottery players). This remark has led Goldin to a general definition of equivalence in the following way.

Definition 5.3.1 Assume that C is a set of conceptual computing devices and B a function that returns the behavior of some machine. Then an environment O for C is a function $O : C \to \beta_O$ that is *consistent*, which means that

$$\forall \mathscr{M}_1, \mathscr{M}_2 \in C : B(\mathscr{M}_1) = B(\mathscr{M}_2) \Rightarrow O(\mathscr{M}_1) = O(\mathscr{M}_2).$$

The elements of β_O are called *feasible behaviors* (within the environment O). If $O(\mathscr{M}_1) \neq O(\mathscr{M}_2)$, then $\mathscr{M}_1$ and $\mathscr{M}_2$ are *distinguishable* in O; otherwise, they *appear equivalent* in O.

Given a set C of conceptual computing devices with behavior B, then any environment O for C can be used to partition C into equivalence classes. Each of these classes is called a *behavioral equivalence class*, since the members of each equivalence class appear equivalent in O. Based on this, it is possible to classify environments.

Definition 5.3.2 Given two environments O_1 and O_2, then O_1 is *richer* than O_2 if its behavioral equivalence classes are strictly finer that those of O_2.

Quite naturally, it is possible to define an infinite sequence Θ of finite persistent Turing machines' environments $\Theta = (O_1, O_2, \ldots)$, provided that for any k, $O_k(\mathscr{M})$ is the set of prefixes of interaction streams, of length less than or equal to k. It can be proved that for any such sequence, O_{k+1} is richer than O_k. The main result concerning environments is the following.

Theorem 5.3.1 *The environments in Θ induce an infinite expressiveness hierarchy of persistent Turing machine behaviors, with Turing machines at the bottom of the hierarchy* [69].

Goldin admits that the behavior of any persistent Turing machine is not rich enough to describe an arbitrary interactive system. However, as mentioned above, these machines can be used to describe any sequential interactive computation. This observation has been formulated in [70] as follows.

Thesis 5.3.1 *Any sequential interactive computation can be performed by a persistent Turing machine.*

On the other hand, the behavior of a Turing machine is at the bottom of the expressiveness hierarchy, which simply implies that Turing machines are an inadequate model of computation for modern computer equipment.

5.4 Site and Internet Machines

Site and Internet machines were introduced by van Leeuwen and Wiedermann [209] to model individual machines, possibly connected with other machines, and a network of site machines. More specifically, a site machine models a normal personal computer that is equipped with a hard disk having potentially unlimited capacity. A site machine can communicate with its environment by sending and receiving messages via a number of ports. One may think of a site machine as a random-access machine that can use sockets to communicate with its environment. The messages that a site machine may receive or send consist of symbols from a finite alphabet Σ. The special symbol $\tau \in \Sigma$ is used to designate the end of some communication. One may think that τ is something like the ASCII EOT (End Of Transmission) character that signals the end of the current transmission.

Typically, the hardware and/or software of a site machine can be changed by an external operator called an *agent*. The agent is part of the environment and communicates with a site machine via its ports. As in real life, when the configuration of the machine changes (e.g., when it is being maintained by the agent), either the machine is temporarily switched off or its communication with the environment is temporarily blocked. Since site machines are equipped with a permanent memory, no data is lost during hardware or software upgrades. When the upgrade process is finished, the machine will be able to resume its operation and consequently, its communication with the environment. It is quite possible to define a function γ that returns a description of the hardware or software upgrade that is taking place at time t. If no such operation is taking place, one may assume that γ returns an empty string. Generally speaking, the function γ is *noncomputable* (in the classical sense of the word) and its values are not a priori known. These remarks are justified because one cannot foresee the actions of any agent. In other words, one cannot tell beforehand what might go wrong with a computer system. If we could actually compute such a function, then the notion of a computable future would be no exaggeration!

A site machine performs a computation by transforming an infinite multiplex input stream into a similar output stream. More specifically, if a site machine has n input ports and m output ports, it processes a stream of n-tuples to produce a stream of m-tuples. In other words, a site machine computes mappings Φ of the form $(\Sigma^n)^\infty \to (\Sigma^m)^\infty$. Note that if A is an alphabet, then A^ω denotes the set of infinite strings over the alphabet A. Also, $A^\infty = A^* \cup A^\omega$, which is the set of finite and infinite strings over the alphabet A.

Clearly, a site machine is not a basic conceptual computing device. Thus, if one wants to study the computational power of site machines, it is necessary to design a conceptual computing device that mimics the behavior of a site machine. Most attempts to define new conceptual computing devices are based on the Turing machine. In general, this approach is based on the conservative idea that the Turing model is simple and valid, so all extensions should be based on it. Thus, we are going to construct a new conceptual device that is basically a Turing machine augmented with a number of new features. More specifically, our new extended Turing machine will be equipped with three new features: *advice, interaction,* and *infinity of operation.*

Any candidate mechanism that models the change of software or hardware must satisfy the following two requirements:

(i) changes should be independent of the current input read by the machine up to the moment of the actual change, and

(ii) changes should not be large.

These requirements can be met once we demand that the description of new hardware or software depend only on the moment t it actually happens. In addition, the size of the description has to be "at most polynomial in t" (i.e., it has to be reasonably short).

Oracles can be used to enter new, external information into the machine. However, "ordinary" oracles are too "loose" for our case, and so van Leeuwen and Wiedermann have opted to use *advice functions.* Turing machines with advice were studied by Karp and Lipton [94]. Assume that $S \subset B$, where $B = \{0, 1\}^*$. In addition, suppose that $h : \mathbb{N} \to B$. Next, we define the set

$$S : h = \left\{ wx \ \middle| \ \Big(x \in S\Big) \wedge \Big(w = h(|x|)\Big) \right\}.$$

Recall that $|x|$ denotes the length of the bit string x. Let S be any collection of subsets of B. Also, let $\mathcal{F}$ be any collection of functions from the set of natural numbers to the set of natural numbers. Then

$$S / \mathcal{F} = \left\{ S \ \middle| \ (\exists h)\Big((\lambda n.|h(n)| \in \mathcal{F}) \wedge (S : h \in S)\Big) \right\}.$$

The intuitive meaning of $S / \mathcal{F}$ is that it is the collection of subsets of B that can be accepted by S with $\mathcal{F}$ "advice." In this book we will be concerned only with the class P/poly. Notice that the P/poly class of languages is characterized by a Turing machine that receives advice whose length is polynomially bounded and computes in deterministic polynomial time. By substituting the set $\{0, 1\}$ with Σ, one may get similar definitions and results.

In order to make a Turing machine with advice able to interact with its environment, we must equip it with a (finite) number of input and output ports. In addition, in order to accommodate infinite computation, one may consider the modus operandi of infinite-time Turing machines. Having roughly specified how advice, interaction, and infinity of operation can be accommodated in a single conceptual computing device, we need to give a description of how the resulting machine will operate. Initially, the tapes of the machine are assumed to be filled with blanks. In addition, the machine's operation depends on some controlling device. At each step, the machine reads the symbols that appear in its input ports and writes some symbols to its output ports. What the machine will do next depends on what it has read, what lies under its scanning heads, and the instruction being executed. Also, at any time t the machine can consult its advice only for values of $t_1 \leq t$. Machines that have these characteristics are termed *interactive Turing machines with advice*.

Theorem 5.4.1 *For every site machine there exists an interactive Turing machine with advice $\mathscr{A}$ that has the same computational power. In addition, for every interactive Turing machine with advice there exists a site machine that has the same computational power.*

The following theorem makes precise the equivalence stated in the previous theorem.

Theorem 5.4.2 *Assume that $\Phi:(\Sigma^n)^\infty \to (\Sigma^m)^\infty$, $n, m > 0$, is a function. Then the following statements are equivalent:*

(i) The function Φ can be computed by a site machine.

(ii) The function Φ can be computed by an interactive Turing machine with advice.

The Internet is the international computer network of networks that connects government, academic, and business institutions. Every machine that is part of the Internet has its own address. Internet machines are a model of the Internet. As such, an Internet machine consists of a number of different site machines. All machines that make up an Internet machine have their own unique addresses. As in the case of a simple network, we need to know which machines are active at any given moment. Thus, we define a function α that returns the list of addresses of those machines that are active at time t. In addition, we can safely assume that for all t, the size of the list $\alpha(t)$ is polynomially bounded.[4] Also, we assume that the site machines making up an Internet machine operate asynchronously and communicate by exchanging messages.

Typically, an IP packet is a chunk of data transferred over the Internet using the standard Internet protocol. Each packet begins with a header containing the address of the sender, the address of the receiver, and general system control information. Similarly, the header of any message that site machines exchange contains the address of both the sender and the receiver. Naturally, it is unnecessary to include any system control information, since we are defining a conceptual device in the broad sense of the term. In the real world, it is impossible to predict the amount of time it takes for a message to arrive at a destination machine from the moment it

---

4. A function $f(n)$ is polynomially bounded if $f(n) = O(n^k)$ for some constant k. Practically, this means that there are positive constants c and l such that $f(n) \leq cn^k$ for all $n \geq l$. The values of c and l must be fixed for the function f and must not depend on n.

has been sent, not to mention the possibility that the message never gets delivered. This implies that the time it takes for a message emitted by a site machine to reach its destination should not be predictable. However, one can give an estimate of this time. Thus, at any given moment t, for any two site machines $i,j \in \alpha(t)$, one can define a function β that will "compute" the estimated delivery time. For messages that are addressed to some machine $k \notin \alpha(t)$, the sending machine will receive an error message just after the message has been sent. Clearly, not all machines are directly connected and thus the message is actually sent from a machine that resides in the proximity of where the non-existing machine is supposed to be. Messages that have the same (existing) recipient enter a queue if they arrive at same time, and consequently, they will be processed accordingly. At any time t and for any machine $i \in \alpha(t)$, the function γ returns a (formal) description of the hardware or software upgrade that might take place at t on machine i.

Functions α, β, and γ fully specify the operation of a given Internet machine. Generally speaking, these functions are noncomputable and their return values are "computed" by consulting a number of finite tables.

It is not hard to see that Internet machines compute mappings that are similar to those that can be computed by site machines. However, since an Internet machine consists of a number of site machines that may have different numbers of input and output ports, this obviously affects the mappings that can be computed by a given Internet machine. Without getting into the technical details, one can prove that for every Internet machine there exists an interactive Turing machine with advice that *sequentially* realizes the same computation as the Internet machine. Clearly, the opposite also holds true.

Site and Internet machines are conceptual computing devices that are supposed to model our personal computers and the Internet, respectively. Both these conceptual computing devices seem to transcend the capabilities of the Turing machine. They seem to transcend even the capabilities of interaction machines. In spite of the fact that it has not been directly demonstrated how these machines can tackle classically unsolvable problems, we still classify them provisionally as hypermachines, since they seem to transcend the capabilities of Turing machines.

5.5 Other Approaches

If we assume that the Church–Turing thesis is indeed valid, then for every effectively computable function f there is a λ-term and vice versa. Let us now hypothesize that there exists a calculus that is built around a notion more "fundamental" than the corresponding notion on which the λ-calculus is built. Also, assume that this new calculus is general enough so one can simulate the λ-calculus within it, but at the same time, it is impossible to simulate this new calculus within the λ-calculus. Clearly, this hypothetical new calculus is more expressive than the λ-calculus. In addition, it would be interesting to see whether classically noncomputable functions become "computable" in this new framework, provided that we are able to define an equivalent model of computation. The very existence of such a calculus, and its accompanying model of computation, would affect the validity of the Church–Turing thesis. Naturally, a direct consequence would be a "broadening" of the thesis.[5] The most important question is whether such a calculus actually exists.

The π-calculus [132] is a process algebra that is built around the primitive notion of interaction. The calculus is particularly well suited for the description of systems in which *mobility*[6] plays a central role. In addition, the π-calculus has as a special case the λ-calculus [130]. In other words, for every λ-term there is an "equivalent" π-calculus process expression, but not vice versa. Moreover, if there are two λ-terms that are equated using λ-calculus means, their translations can be distinguished in the π-calculus, which makes the π-calculus strictly more expressive than the λ-calculus [19].

Let us now see how we can translate a λ-term into the π-calculus. Since this translation is purely syntactic, we need to briefly review the syntax of both calculi. The set of π-calculus process expressions is defined by the following abstract syntax:

$$P ::= \Sigma_{i \in I} \pi_i.P_i \ \Big| \ P_1|P_2 \ \Big| \ \text{new } \alpha \ P \ \Big| \ !P \ .$$

If $I = \emptyset$, then $\Sigma_{i \in I} \pi_i.P_i = \mathbf{0}$, which is the null process that does nothing. In addition, π_i denotes an *action prefix* that represents either sending or receiving a message, or making a silent transition:

$$\pi ::= x(y) \ \Big| \ \bar{x}\langle y \rangle \ \Big| \ \tau \ .$$

The expression $\Sigma_{i \in I} \pi_i.P_i$ behaves just like one of the P_i's, depending on what messages are communicated to the composite process; the expression $P_1|P_2$ denotes that both processes are concurrently active; the expression new α P means that the use of the message α is restricted to the process P; and the expression $!P$ means that there are infinitely many concurrently active copies of P.

The set of λ-terms is defined by the following abstract syntax:

$$M ::= x \ \Big| \ \lambda x.M \ \Big| \ MN \ .$$

We are now ready to present the translation of any λ-term into the π-calculus.

---

5. This is true, as evidenced by the fact that the authors of the various models of interactive computation presented in this chapter have reformulated the Church–Turing thesis.
6. The term "mobility" here means among others things that processes may move in a virtual space of linked processes or that processes move in a physical space of computing sites.

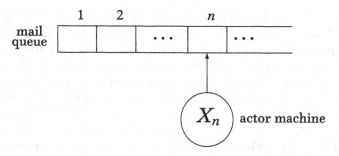

Figure 5.1: An abstract representation of an actor.

Definition 5.5.1 Assume that M is an arbitrary λ-term. Then its translation $[\![M]\!]$ into the π-calculus is an abstraction defined inductively as follows:

$$[\![x]\!](u) \stackrel{\text{def}}{=} \bar{x}\langle u \rangle,$$

$$[\![\lambda x.M]\!](u) \stackrel{\text{def}}{=} u(xv).[\![M]\!]\langle v \rangle,$$

$$[\![(MN)]\!](u) \stackrel{\text{def}}{=} \text{new } v\Big([\![M]\!]\langle v \rangle \mid \text{new } x(\bar{v}\langle xu \rangle \mid \,!x[\![N]\!])\Big).$$

Notice that in the last equation, x is a bound name in N. Also, $[\![M]\!](u)$ denotes that $[\![M]\!]$ is actually an abstraction that is applied to an argument list u.

The π-calculus is not really a model of computation; it is rather a mathematical theory with which one can describe the functionality of computational models or systems. A theory that is closer to what one may call a true model of interactive computation is the *actors* model of concurrent computation created by Carl Hewitt, Henry Baker, and Gul Agha [4]. The actors model is an untyped theory that is a generalization of the λ-calculus. Actors communicate with each other by sending messages. Incoming communication is mapped to a triple that consists of:

 (i) a finite set of messages sent to other actors,

 (ii) a new behavior that is a function of the communication accepted (and thus the response to the next communication depends on it), and

(iii) a finite set of newly created actors.

Each actor has its own mail address and its own mail queue, with no limit on the number of messages it can hold. Notice that the behavior of an actor is determined by the relationships among the events that are caused by it. Also, it is rather important to note that an actor is defined by its behavior and not by its physical representation. Figure 5.1 depicts an abstract representation of an actor. The information contained in the actor machine determines the behavior of the actor; thus, it can be sensitive to history.

Actors are a model of computation that is more powerful than the classical model of computation. For instance, it is not difficult to simulate arbitrary sequential processes (e.g., Turing machines) or purely functional systems based on the λ-calculus by a suitable actor system, but it is not possible to simulate an actor system by a system of sequential processes. The reason why the converse is not possible is the ability of any actor to create other actors. And this is one of the reasons the π-calculus is more expressive than the λ-calculus: by using the replication operator, !, one can specify the generation of an unbounded number of copies of a given process.

VI. Hyperminds

Dexter Jettster: ...Those analysis droids only focus on symbols. Huh! I should think that you Jedi would have more respect for the difference between knowledge and...wisdom!

Obi-Wan Kenobi: Well, if droids could think there'd be none of us here, would there?

From a dialog in the movie *Star Wars Episode II: The Attack of the Clones*, produced and directed by George Lucas.

Is the mind just a computing device, or is it something more? This and similar questions have prompted a number of thinkers and researchers to propose various theories that aim to falsify the general belief that the mind is actually a computing device. In this direction, one may argue that computers are actually "mental prostheses or orthoses, not stand-alone minds" [198]. Indeed, it is not an overstatement to say that computers dully execute commands and deliver results that only a conscious mind can interpret. Obviously, it is not an exaggeration to say that this *naive* remark forms a basis for more rigorous arguments against computationalism, such as the Chinese room argument. Interestingly enough, cognitive science (i.e., "the interdisciplinary study of mind and intelligence, embracing philosophy, psychology, artificial intelligence, neuroscience, linguistics, and anthropology" [201]) began by assuming that the human mind is indeed a Turing machine. Because of its impact on modern thinking, any voice against the kernel of cognitive science is faced with great skepticism.

This chapter is a short presentation of various attacks against computationalism. First, there is a presentation of various arguments based on results from mathematical logic, such as Gödel's incompleteness theorems. Then we present a number of purely philosophical arguments against the idea that the mind is a Turing machine. In addition, there is a more elaborate discussion of the Chinese room argument and related issues. Next, there is a discussion of the mind from a neurobiological point of view, and we conclude with a discussion of the cognitive aspects of the human mind.

6.1   Mathematics and the Mind

6.1.1   The Pure Gödelian Argument

John Lucas was probably the first to use Gödel's famous incompleteness results to attack computationalism.[1] The essence of his argument [116] is that since *machines* are "concrete instantiations of a formal system," they should not be able to prove a particular proposition that a mind can clearly see to hold true. Thus, minds are not machines. It is rather interesting to note that Paul Benacerraf examined Lucas's argument and concluded that: "If I am a Turing machine, then I am barred by my very nature from obeying Socrates profound philosophic injunction: KNOW THYSELF" [13]. As a side effect, Benacerraf concluded [13] that

> Psychology as we know it is therefore impossible. For, if we are not at best Turing machines, then it is impossible, and if we are, then there are certain things we cannot know about ourselves or any others with the same output as ourselves. I won't take sides.

Lucas's argument was expounded by Roger Penrose in *The Emperor's New Mind* [150] and its sequel *Shadows of the Mind* [151]. In accordance with Lucas, Penrose believes that minds are not machines, and in addition, he believes that computers cannot simulate brain processes. The summary of Penrose's argument that follows is based on Searle's summary that appears in Chapter 4 of [175]:

(i) Classically, the halting problem, which is a specific version of Gödel's incompleteness theorem, cannot be solved. Thus, this can be used to show that our conscious behavior is not computable. In particular, Penrose considers some nonstopping computational processes that cannot be shown to be nonstopping by purely computational methods, but at the same time we can see that the processes are nonstopping.

(ii) The operation of a *neuron* can be simulated by computer. Thus, the behavior of neurons is computable. This implies that neurons cannot be used to explain consciousness, since consciousness has noncomputable features.

---

1. Actually, as Lucas admits in the first page of [116], the purpose of his work was to attack *mechanism* (i.e., the doctrine that all natural phenomena are explicable by material causes and mechanical principles), which one might say is a forerunner of computationalism.

(iii) A theory of consciousness should be based on noncomputable phenomena that might take place at the level of microtubules in neurons. But in order to understand these phenomena we need a new physics.

Although many thinkers and researchers are convinced that a computational model of the mind is extremely implausible, still they are not convinced by Penrose's argument. For instance, Solomon Feferman [61] shows that there are flaws in Penrose's argument. Interestingly enough, Penrose was "happy to agree with all the technical criticisms and corrections that Feferman refers to in his section discussing" his "treatment of the logical facts" [153]. Feferman also points out that it is misleading to assume that the equivalence between formal systems and Turing machines can be used to derive a general methodology for proving theorems. After all, mathematicians arrive at proofs "through a marvellous combination of heuristic reasoning, insight and inspiration (building, of course, on prior knowledge and experience)" [61]. Another attack on the Gödelian argument has been put forth by Selmer Bringsjord and Michael Zenzen [26].

From the discussion above, it should be clear that Penrose not only rejects "strong AI," but also "weak AI." Quite naturally, he believes that no computer program can have the qualities of *awareness* and *understanding*. Obviously, it is one thing to believe that no computer program can possess these qualities, and another to believe that no machine can possess these qualities. Humans, which may be viewed as biological machines, have both qualities and thus trivially refute the idea that no machine can have awareness and understanding. However, John McCarthy, in his attack against Penrose's ideas [124], supports the idea that computer programs can have awareness and understanding. More specifically, he advocates [123] that interrupts,[2] which are supported by many popular programming languages, might form the basis for the implementation of self-awareness in computer programs. Clearly, we have a situation in which a hardware device sends some unintelligent message that is processed by a computer program, which is dully executed by a CPU. In addition, a conscious biological machine (e.g., Peter) assigns meaning to all of these, and just because of this assignment, the computer program might be self-aware! Although I believe that one day there will be conscious machines, built atop a very different yet to be discovered machine architecture, the current machine architecture is not, at best, a promising direction. And of course, this may explain why space probes landing on other planets rarely survive more than their expected "life" span.

The debate over the Gödelian argument is quite active and recently Michael Redhead [164] presented a simplified version of that argument, presented in the framework of the system Q (a form of arithmetic), which

---

2. Roughly, an interrupt is a signal created and sent to the CPU, which is caused by some action taken by a hardware device. For example, pressing certain key combinations can cause hardware interrupts.

has the following axioms (recall that $S(x) = x + 1$):

$$(y = 0) \vee (\exists x)\left(y = S(x)\right),$$
$$0 \neq S(x),$$
$$S(x) = S(y) \Rightarrow x = y,$$
$$x + 0 = x,$$
$$x + S(y) = S(x + y),$$
$$x \cdot 0 = 0,$$
$$x \cdot S(y) = (x \cdot y) + x.$$

Observe that in this set of axioms there is no provision for proof by mathematical induction. Now consider the following statement:

$$\text{for all } n, m \in \mathbb{N} \text{ there exists a proof that } m \times n = n \times m. \qquad \text{(A)}$$

First, notice that we cannot switch the order of the quantifiers to get

$$\text{there exists a proof that for all } n, m \in \mathbb{N} : m \times n = n \times m. \qquad \text{(B)}$$

The reason for this deficiency is the lack of an induction axiom. Notice also that the proof of (A) depends on the specific numbers n and m that are chosen, and the length of the proof will increase as the numbers get bigger and bigger. But it should be clear that the length of the proof is finite. On the other hand, the proof of (B) is by no means finite, since it must cover every possible case. It is interesting that we can argue that

$$\text{for all } n, m \in \mathbb{N} : m \times n = n \times m. \qquad \text{(C)}$$

is actually true in system Q. Since the axioms and the theorems of system Q are *analytically* true (i.e., they express defining properties of the natural numbers), we may replace (A) by

$$\text{for all } n, m \in \mathbb{N} \text{ it is true that } m \times n = n \times m. \qquad \text{(D)}$$

But (D) is strictly equivalent to

$$\text{it is true that for all } n, m \in \mathbb{N} : m \times n = n \times m. \qquad \text{(E)}$$

The essence of this statement is that the commutative law of multiplication is true. Notice that truth commutes with the universal quantifier, whereas provability does not. This argument can also be viewed as a first step at showing that system Q is incomplete, since we have found a sentence that we agree is true but not provable in Q. Of course, this is not the only such sentence. For example, other such sentences are the associative laws of addition and multiplication. Since Q is not a recursive theory, one may say that human mathematical reasoning is stronger than any nonrecursive theory. Figuratively speaking, human mathematical reasoning beats Turing machines.

Dale Jacquette [90] has proposed a variant of the Turing test in which the interrogator asks questions about the truth values of Gödel sentences and their negations. Since I do not expect all readers to be familiar with the Turing test, I will briefly explain it.

The Turing test was proposed by Turing [207] as a means to tackle the question whether machines can actually think. The test has the form of a game called the "imitation game." In this game, we have a person, a machine, and an interrogator, who is in a room separated from the person and the machine. The aim of the game is to allow the interrogator to ask questions to both the person and the machine and to determine from their responses which one is the person and which one is the machine. The interrogator knows the person and the machine by labels "X" and "Y," respectively, and at the end of the game she says either "X is a person and Y is a machine" or "X is a machine and Y is a person." The interrogator is allowed to put questions to the person and the machine thus:

Will X please tell me the length of her hair?

(For a detailed discussion of the Turing test and related issues, see [144].)

According to Jacquette, the mind[3] may use an nonprogrammable nonalgorithmic procedure to judge whether some Gödel sentence is true. The procedure can be characterized as an "intensional conditional in the imperative mood" [90, p. 5]:

(P)   If S says that S is unprovable [relative to some recursively based logic], then answer (print): "S is true."

Jacquette claims that his is a nonalgorithmic implementable procedure, which can be interpreted as the claim that no programming language can be used to implement this procedure. However, this procedure is realizable by a mind simply because a mind understands the meaning of Gödel sentences and, most importantly, the meaning of the negation of Gödel sentences. This crucial information is used by the mind to decide when a sentence S says that it is unprovable. Interestingly enough, if the interrogator decides to explain that $S = \neg\,\mathrm{Thm}(n)$ and $\mathrm{Gn}(\neg\,\mathrm{Thm}(n)) = n$ (recall that $\mathrm{Gn}(A)$ denotes the Gödel number of any well-formed formula A), then both minds and machines can deduce that S is formally undecidable. However, if the interrogator has opted to choose predicates other than $\neg\,\mathrm{Thm}$ to represent unprovability, this information will become useless. Also, one might observe that the appearance of the external negation symbol in $\neg\,\mathrm{Thm}$

---

3. Clearly, only a mind that has mastered the complexities of mathematical logic can sit next to a machine and play this version of the imitation game. Thus, for the rest of this discussion, the word mind will not just mean any ordinary mind, but a mind well versed in mathematical logic.

could be used to distinguish Gödel sentences from their negations by first translating "problematic" constructions into prenex form, which are then checked for occurrences of an outermost negation symbol. But even this approach will not have the expected results, since, for example, one may replace ¬Thm with NoThm with the expected semantic meaning. Thus, if both Gödel sentence formulations are tried out by the interrogator, the machine that employs the prenex trick will inevitably confuse Gödel sentences of the first formulation with negations of Gödel sentences in the second formulation.

The crux of Jacquette's argument against mechanism is that the mind's procedure is at the same time intensional and nonalgorithmic. A mind has no problem understanding any Gödel sentence as well as its negation. Thus, it can determine when a sentence says of itself that it is either unprovable or provable. In addition, Jacquette claims that a mind's intensionality and understanding of a sentence's meaning cannot really be simulated by a machine. This means that a machine cannot really fool the interrogator, since she can ask about the truth values of alternatively formulated Gödel sentences and their negations, thus forcing the machine into making mistakes.

Storrs McCall has put forth another argument against computationalism, initially in [121] and later on in [122]. This argument is based on the assumption that Turing machines *know* only what they can *prove* from a set of axioms and a set of well-defined rules of inference. Based on this, McCall tried to show that no Turing machine can know whether the Gödel sentence G of the form, "This statement is unprovable," is true. In a nutshell, the reason why this makes sense is that the truth value of G depends on the consistency of *Peano arithmetic*. Notice that Peano arithmetic, or just PA, is the theory of natural numbers defined by the five Peano axioms (named after the Italian mathematician Giuseppe Peano, who proposed them in 1889):

(i) $0 \in \mathbb{N}$ (zero is a natural number);

(ii) for each $x \in \mathbb{N}$, there exists exactly one $S(x) \in \mathbb{N}$, called the successor of x;

(iii) $S(x) \neq 0$ (zero is not the successor of any natural number);

(iv) $(S(x) = S(y)) \Rightarrow (x = y)$; and

(v) (induction schema) if φ is an arithmetic property such that 0 has this property and if $\varphi(x)$ implies $\varphi(S(x))$ for every x, then every number has the property φ.

Since it is not known whether PA is consistent, it is possible to argue about G by cases:

A₁. If PA is consistent, then G is not provable in PA.

A_2. If PA is consistent, then $\neg G$ is not provable in PA.

McCall assumes that whatever statement holds,[4] truth and provability diverge because if PA is consistent, then G is true and unprovable; but if it is inconsistent, then G is provable and false. Thus, PA contains nontheorems that are true or theorems that are false. According to McCall, the importance of this observation is that humans can distinguish the two entities, but Turing machines fail to do so. Let us assume that statement A_1 holds. In addition, the predicate $\text{Prov}(\text{Gn}(A))$ will denote that A is provable (or that A is not a theorem). Now, first note that $G \equiv \neg\,\text{Prov}(\text{Gn}(G))$. If by $\text{Cons}(\text{PA})$ we symbolize the statement "PA is consistent," then statement A_1 can be written formally as follows:

$$\text{Cons}(\text{PA}) \Rightarrow \neg\,\text{Prov}(\text{Gn}(G)).$$

Equivalently, statement A_1 can be written as

$$\text{Cons}(\text{PA}) \Rightarrow G.$$

McCall assumes that this is a theorem that can be proved. However, this may not be correct, since the proof has to be in PA itself and not in the metatheory. Let us now consider the formal version of A_2:

$$\text{Cons}(\text{PA}) \Rightarrow \neg\,\text{Prov}(\text{Gn}(\neg G)).$$

According to McCall, it can be shown that this statement is true (see [121] for details). However, one cannot have a formal proof of the "theoremhood" of this statement, and according to McCall, "there are good reasons to believe that [the formal version of statement A_2] is in fact unprovable in PA." The final result is that a Turing machine programmed to enumerate theorems in PA will almost certainly never include the statement above in the set of PA theorems. This, in turn, implies that there is a difference between human and machine thinking. Indeed, no computer program can model all of human reasoning.

Ignoring for the moment the remarks made by Tennant, one would not expect someone to find any flaws in this argument. However, Panu Raatikainen [162] has shown that there is a flaw in McCall's argument. In particular, Raatikainen has derived the formal equivalent of A_1, which implies that machines can make the distinction between true and derivable sentences. More specifically, by assuming $\text{Cons}(\text{PA})$, one may get[5]

$$\frac{\text{Cons}(\text{PA}) \quad \text{Cons}(\text{PA}) \Rightarrow G}{G} \Rightarrow \mathcal{E}\;\cdot$$

---

4. As Neil Tennant [199] observes, the reasons for claiming that the first sentence is true (it can be proved within PA) are very different from the reasons for claiming that the second sentence is true (even if it is true, it is not provable within PA).

5. Assume that $\circledast$ is a logical operator. Then the symbols $\circledast\mathcal{E}$ and $\circledast\mathcal{I}$ denote an elimination rule for $\circledast$ and an introduction rule for $\circledast$, respectively.

As was noted previously, $\neg\,\text{Prov}(\text{Gn}(G)) \equiv G$, which can be written as

$$(\neg\,\text{Prov}(\text{Gn}(G))) \Rightarrow G) \wedge (G \Rightarrow \neg\,\text{Prov}(\text{Gn}(G))).$$

This, in turn, is used as a premise in the following deduction:

$$\frac{(\neg\,\text{Prov}(\text{Gn}(G))) \Rightarrow G) \wedge (G \Rightarrow \neg\,\text{Prov}(\text{Gn}(G)))}{G \Rightarrow \neg\,\text{Prov}(\text{Gn}(G))}\ \wedge 2\mathcal{E}\cdot$$

Since G holds, we get

$$\frac{G \quad G \Rightarrow \neg\,\text{Prov}(\text{Gn}(G))}{\neg\,\text{Prov}(\text{Gn}(G))}\ \Rightarrow\mathcal{E}\cdot$$

There is a small problem here: G cannot be proved inside PA. If we now apply $\wedge\mathcal{I}$, we get

$$\frac{G \quad \neg\,\text{Prov}(\text{Gn}(G))}{G \wedge \neg\,\text{Prov}(\text{Gn}(G))}\ \wedge\mathcal{I}\cdot$$

And finally, by applying $\Rightarrow\mathcal{I}$ we get

$$[\text{Cons}(\text{PA})]$$
$$\vdots$$
$$\frac{G \wedge \neg\,\text{Prov}(\text{Gn}(G))}{\text{Cons}(\text{PA}) \Rightarrow (G \wedge \neg\,\text{Prov}(\text{Gn}(G)))}\ \Rightarrow\mathcal{I}\cdot$$

The conclusion is just the formal counterpart of A_1. Raatikainen finishes his paper by saying that although McCall's argument is not valid, this does not mean that computationalism is actually correct.

Bringsjord and his colleagues at the Rensselaer Artificial Intelligence and Reasoning (RAIR) Laboratory [25] reported their Gödelian argument for minds whose computational capabilities transcend the capabilities of the Turing machine. The members of the RAIR lab were involved in an effort to devise a (partial) solution to the busy beaver problem, and their efforts led to the formulation of their argument. Before going on, it is necessary to explain what this problem is about. The description of the problem that follows is from the busy beaver section of RAIR's lab web page:[6]

> Consider a binary-alphabet Turing Machine which is given an infinite, blank tape as input. If this machine halts, we define its productivity as the number of 1's left on the tape after the machine is run to completion. If it does not halt, the machine is given a productivity value of zero. Now consider all of the binary-alphabet Turing Machines that have n states. The machine in this set which has the highest productivity is called a Busy Beaver, and its productivity is the result of the Busy Beaver function $\Sigma(n)$. Alternatively, the productivity score can be defined as the number of transitions made before halting.

6. http://www.cs.rpi.edu/~kelleo/busybeaver/.

For reasons of brevity, the solution will not be discussed. Interested readers should point their web browsers to RAIR's busy-beaver web page for details.

The argument's goal is to refute computationalism, when it is understood as the supporting theory of the thesis that people are computers, which, in turn, are realizations of Turing machines. Assuming that p ranges over persons and m over Turing machines, this thesis can be stated as follows:

$$\forall p \exists m \; p \frown m, \qquad (\mathscr{C})$$

where $\frown$ is pronounced "are." This means that $p \frown m$ can be interpreted as p *instantiates* (or *realizes*) m. Assume that each person is a realization of some Turing machine. If a measure of the mental capabilities of any person is equal to the measure of the complexity of a Turing machine (e.g., the number of states plus the number of transitions used), then all people are Turing machines whose measure of complexity is at or below some threshold. More specifically, if we assume that C is a function that has a Turing machine as argument and returns a number that characterizes its complexity, then the idea just presented can be written formally as follows:

$$\forall p \exists m \; (p \frown m \wedge C(m) \le k), \qquad (\mathscr{C}')$$

where $k \in \mathbb{N}$ is the threshold. The goal of Bringsjord's team was to devise an argument (not a proof) to refute the thesis that people are computers. The argument goes as follows:

- There are persons who have managed to determine the productivity of the initial segment of Turing machines (e.g., such persons are members of the RAIR lab; see [25] for details):

$$\exists p \Big(D(p, \Sigma(1)) \wedge \cdots \wedge D(p, \Sigma(6)) \Big). \qquad (1)$$

- There is a natural number at and beyond which Turing machines with measure of complexity less than or equal to k fail to determine productivity:

$$\exists n \, \forall m \Big(C(m) \le k \Rightarrow \neg D(m, \Sigma(n)) \wedge \neg D(m, \Sigma(n + 1)) \wedge \cdots \Big). \qquad (2)$$

- If a person can determine the productivity for n, then this same person can determine the productivity for $n + 1$:

$$\forall n \, \forall p \Big(D(p, \Sigma(n)) \Rightarrow D(p, \Sigma(n + 1)) \Big). \qquad (3)$$

- Assume that computationalism, as expressed by $(\mathscr{C}')$, actually holds. Also, suppose that p^*, who is an arbitrary person, determines the initial segment of the busy-beaver problem, that is,

$$D(p^*, \Sigma(1)) \wedge \cdots \wedge D(p^*, \Sigma(n)). \qquad (3')$$

Since $(\mathcal{C}')$ holds for any person, it must hold true for p^*, that is,

$$\exists m \left(p^* \frown m \wedge C(m) \leq k \right). \tag{4}$$

Let us randomly choose an m^* and an n^* such that

$$\left(p^* \frown m^* \wedge C(m^*) \leq k \right) \tag{5}$$

and such that

$$\forall m \left(C(m) \leq k \Rightarrow \neg D(m, \Sigma(n^*)) \wedge \neg D(m, \Sigma(n^* + 1)) \wedge \cdots \right). \tag{6}$$

Clearly, (6) holds for m^*:

$$\left(C(m^*) \leq k \Rightarrow \neg D(m^*, \Sigma(n^*)) \wedge \neg D(m^*, \Sigma(n^* + 1)) \wedge \cdots \right). \tag{7}$$

From (5) and (7) we can deduce

$$\neg D(m^*, \Sigma(n^*)) \wedge \neg D(m^*, \Sigma(n^* + 1)) \wedge \neg D(m^*, \Sigma(n^* + 2)) \wedge \cdots .$$

By identity elimination and induction using (3), (5), and (3'), we can infer $\forall n \, D(m^*, \Sigma(n))$, which is a contradiction. From this it follows that since humans are information processors with capabilities lying somewhere in the arithmetic hierarchy and if humans are ordinary Turing machines they have a certain fixed size k, humans are hyper-computers.

Clearly, no one expects such an argument to win critical acclaim without any objection. On the contrary, there are issues that even Bringsjord et al. have spotted. For example, for skeptics, premise (3) practically implies that sooner or later people will be able to solve any problem. First of all, Bringsjord et al. respond by saying that what they claim does not mean that given enough time, anything is possible. They note that there are problems that even infinite-time Turing machines cannot solve, and such problems cannot be solved by any human. The essence of their argument is that if humanity "gets to n in the Σ problem, it can get to $n + 1$." And this is exactly the difference between Turing machines and humans: Turing machines cannot solve the problem for $n+1$ if they have successfully solved the problem for n; while it is also true that there is a limit to what humans can do, it is just above the limit of what machines can achieve.

Stewart Shapiro [179] has given an interesting account of the battle between computationalists and the Lucas-Penrose side over the Gödelian argument. Shapiro starts by exploring the meaning of the words "machine" and "human" in the context of this battle. Generally speaking, one may assume that when computationalists speak of machines they actually mean Turing machines, and when the Lucas-Penrose side speaks of humans they actually mean creatures that have unlimited lifetimes, attention spans and energy, as well as unlimited resources at their disposal. In addition, another crucial assumption concerning these idealized human beings is that they do not make any mistakes! Both parties assume that there exists a set K consisting of "all and only the analogues of arithmetic theorems, sentences in the language of first-order arithmetic that can be known with unassailable, mathematical certainty" [179, p. 277]. This set is called the set of *knowable* arithmetic sentences. Since each element of K can be identified with its Gödel number, one may assume that $K \subset \mathbb{N}$. Computationalists, quite expectedly, take it for granted that the Church-Turing thesis is valid and thus assume that K is recursively enumerable. Of course, the Lucas–Penrose side does not agree with this conclusion and argues that that there are procedures employed by humans that cannot be simulated by a Turing machine. Interestingly, its seems that hypercomputation has no place in this battle: computationalists completely deny it and the Lucas–Penrose side assumes that noncomputable processes are necessarily nonmechanical. Obviously, in the eyes of a proponent of hypercomputation both views are wrong: since the Church-Turing thesis is not valid, K is not recursively enumerable, while there are processes that transcend the Church-Turing barrier and that are purely mechanical. In spite of this, let us continue with Shapiro's analysis.

If T is the set of truths of first-order arithmetic, then by assumption $K \subseteq T$. However, let us suppose that $K = T$. Assume that Φ is an arithmetic proposition. Then either $\Phi \in T$ or $(\neg \Phi) \in T$. If $\Phi \in T$, then $\Phi \in K$ and so Φ is knowable. Otherwise, $(\neg \Phi) \in T$ and $(\neg \Phi) \in K$ and so it is knowable in principle that Φ is false. Let us recapitulate: if in the language of first-order arithmetic $T = K$, then for every arithmetic proposition Φ, an idealized human can determine whether Φ is true or false; that is, every arithmetic proposition can be *decided* by an idealized human being. Now, by Tarski's theorem on truth in arithmetic, no program can output a correct true or false value for every statement of number theory, which implies that T is not recursively enumerable. Thus, if $T = K$ and every arithmetic truth can be proved by an idealized human being, the set K is not recursively enumerable and the computationalists are wrong.

In order to defend their own belief, computationalists demand that $T \neq K$. Assume that $\Phi \in T$ and $\Phi \notin K$. Then Φ is an *unknowable* truth. This implies that both Φ and $\neg \Phi$ are *absolutely undecidable*, and so even an idealized human being cannot decide whether Φ is true or false. In other words, if what computationalists believe is true, there are absolutely undecidable arithmetic propositions.

In conclusion, this battle will be over once we know whether $T = K$. However, computationalists can easily avoid losing this battle, since "[they] are having trouble coming up with a reasonable mechanistic thesis for Lucas and Penrose to attack" [179, p. 300]. However, it seems that the whole battle is like trying to convince Alfred Square, resident of the two-dimensional Edwin A. Abbott's Flatland [2], that there is a three-dimensional world. Clearly, this is almost impossible unless Alfred is able to enter the three-dimensional world in order to realize that his world is just part of this brave new world!

6.1.2 The Argument from Infinitary Logic

Another mathematically oriented argument, which is based on the isolation and exploitation of mathematical reasoning, is the argument from infinitary logic. Mathematical reasoning seems to be infinitary in nature and, consequently, one may argue that it is also irreducible to language usage. However, this seems to be a side issue irrelevant to the present discussion. The argument from infinitary logic aims at showing that the infinitary nature of mathematical reasoning is in general part of what makes a mind a hypermind. Our presentation is based on the exposition of the argument that is included in [26].

In order to apprehend the argument, it is necessary to be familiar with infinitary logic. The brief, rough exposition that follows is based on [11]. Assume that μ and λ are two infinite cardinals such that $\lambda \leq \mu$ and that $\mathcal{L}$ is a fixed first-order language. Also, suppose that Φ is a set of formulas of $\mathcal{L}$ such that card(Φ) < μ. Then $\bigwedge \Phi$ and $\bigvee \Phi$ will denote infinite conjunctions and disjunctions with card(Φ) conjuncts or disjuncts, respectively. In addition, if X is a set of individual variables such that card(X) < λ and φ is an $\mathcal{L}$-formula, then $\exists X \varphi$ and $\forall X \varphi$ are formulas. Moreover, if φ and ψ are $\mathcal{L}$-formulas, then $\varphi \wedge \psi$ and $\neg \varphi$ are formulas. More generally, all $\mathcal{L}$-formulas are formulas. A language having these characteristics is an infinitary language, denoted by $\mathcal{L}_{(\mu,\lambda)}$. In particular, the language $\mathcal{L}_{(\omega_1,\omega)}$, where ω_1 denotes the set of countable ordinals, is one that allows countably infinite conjunctions but only finite quantifications. Now we can proceed with the argument from infinitary reasoning as presented in [26]:

(i) All reasoning is computable.

(ii) For every case of reasoning R there exists a Turing machine (or any equally powerful device) M such that some computation C of M is such that $R = C$ [from (i)].

(iii) For every computation C of every Turing machine M there is an equivalent deduction D in some instantiation of $\mathcal{L}_I$ (i.e., first-order logic).

(iv) For every case of reasoning R there exists a deduction D in some instantiation of $\mathcal{L}_I$ such that $R = D$ [from (ii), (iii); universal elimination, hypothetical syllogism, and universal introduction].

(v) There exists a case of reasoning R^*, namely reasoning with $\mathcal{L}_{(\omega_1,\omega)}$, that is such that for every deduction D in some instantiation of the first-order logic $\mathcal{L}_I$, $R^* \neq D$.

(vi) It is not the case that all reasoning is *computable* [*reductio ad absurdum*; (iv), (v) contradictory].

The designers of this argument claim that it is valid because the inferences are formally correct. In addition, they discuss a number of objections to this argument. The first objection is that this argument is not really *convincing*. Their response to this objection is simple: it is one thing to have a convincing argument and another thing to have a *sound* argument. Furthermore, it is important to notice that the history of science is full of *unconvincing* but sound theories, such as the theory that the Earth moves around the Sun.

Another objection concerns reasoning in and about $\mathcal{L}_{(\omega_1,\omega)}$ that is simply manipulation of finite expressions that are clearly computable, such as the following expression borrowed from [26, p. 108]:

$$\bigvee_{n<\omega} \exists x_1 \cdots \exists x_n \forall y (y = x_1 \vee \cdots \vee y = x_n).$$

The essence of the response to this objection is that although Hilbert noticed that proofs are presented as finite strings on finite sheets of paper and consequently put forward the ideas we presented in the introductory chapter, Gödel managed to abolish Hilbert's ideas. In addition, Gödel proved that "human mathematical reasoning is *not* always limited to Hilbertian reasoning: some form of infinitistic reasoning must be employed for some proofs of formulas about $\mathbb{N}$" [26, p. 109].

6.1.3 The Modal Argument

According to Selmer Bringsjord and Konstantine Arkoudas [23], there are basically two methods for attacking computationalism when starting from mathematical results in the realm of incompleteness. The first method is the one described in the previous section, while the second method is the one that will be presented in this section. The proof that minds are not Turing machines is a two-stage process. First, it is necessary to make suitable idealizations of minds and machines, and then one must prove a formally valid modal argument.

Like Shapiro, Bringsjord and Arkoudas believe that idealized computers can be identified with ordinary Turing machines. Unlike Shapiro's idealized humans with unlimited capacities, the idealized humans of Bringsjord and Arkoudas take input and yield output that reflects decisions based on the inputs taken. Also, they assume that (part) of the human mind is actually an information-processing device.

Let us consider the following decision problem: Given a Turing machine $\mathcal{M}_0$ and an input string w, does $\mathcal{M}_0$ halt on input w? It has been proved that there is no algorithm (i.e., no Turing machine) that can decide this problem. Assume that $D(\mathcal{M}, \mathcal{M}', i)$ is a predicate that stands for the sentence, "Turing machine $\mathcal{M}$ determines whether Turing machine $\mathcal{M}'$ halts on input i." Using this predicate we can formally specify the undecidability of the problem above in quantified modal logic as follows:

$$\forall \mathcal{M} \exists i \neg \Diamond D(\mathcal{M}, \mathcal{M}_0, i). \tag{M1}$$

Notice that the modality $\Diamond$ is associated to logical or mathematical possibility, that is, $\Diamond \varphi$ if and only if it is logically or mathematically possible that φ. Assume that $M(x)$ stands for "x is a Turing machine," $P(x)$ for "x is a person," and $I(x)$ for "x is input for a Turing machine." Then (M1) can be written as follows

$$\exists x \Big(M(x) \wedge \forall y \Big(M(y) \rightarrow \exists u \big(I(u) \wedge \neg \Diamond D(y, x, u) \big) \Big) \Big).$$

For the sake of argument let us assume that persons are indeed Turing machines, or, more accurately, that persons are physically realized Turing machines. This assumption can be specified in the following way:

$$\forall P \exists \mathcal{M} \; P \frown \mathcal{M}. \tag{M2}$$

From (M1) and (M2) we deduce that

$$\forall P \exists i \neg \Diamond D(P, \mathcal{M}_0, i). \tag{M3}$$

Bringsjord and Arkoudas conclude that since there are persons, (M3) is inconsistent with

$$\forall P \forall i \Diamond D(P, \mathcal{M}_0, i). \tag{M4}$$

And so if we can prove (M4), we have an indirect proof of $\neg$(M1), which means that computationalism is false.

The crucial question is whether (M4) is actually true. Before going on, it is necessary to clarify that the "modal argument is not inseparably linked to a particular formal derivation or a particular proof theory." This means that one may present this argument even in first-order logic. However, the authors have presented their argument in this manner because they happen to be comfortable with it. Clearly, this book is about hypercomputation, and so far we have presented a good number of conceptual devices that transcend the capabilities of the Turing machine that are eventually realizable. Assume that $\mathcal{H}$ stands for any hypermachine. Then it follows that

$$\forall \mathcal{H} \forall i \Diamond D(\mathcal{H}, \mathcal{M}_0, i). \tag{M5}$$

If we are inclined to assume that a person may be a hypermachine and not just a Turing machine, we can formally express this as follows:

$$\left(\forall \mathcal{H} \forall i \Diamond D(\mathcal{H}, \mathcal{M}_0, i)\right) \rightarrow \left(\forall P \forall i \Diamond D(P, \mathcal{M}_0, i)\right). \tag{M6}$$

Proposition (M4) follows by *modus ponens* from (M5) and (M6).

No argument remains unchallenged, and this argument is no exception. In the remainder of this section I will present two objections to the modal argument as well as the responses offered by the designers of the argument.

If one assumes that computationalism is the belief that people are physical computers, then one may hope to refute the modal argument. In particular, if we assume that C ranges over embodied computers, then the formal expression describing computationalism takes the following form:

$$\forall P \exists C \ P \frown C. \tag{M2$'$}$$

Based on this, proposition (M1) must be replaced with

$$\forall C \exists i \neg \Diamond D(C, \mathcal{M}_0, i). \tag{M1$'$}$$

But this proposition is false, since there is some machine C_0 (e.g., an oracle Turing machine, a trial-and-error machine) that can solve the halting problem for $\mathcal{M}_0$. Computationalism is the doctrine that advocates that persons are just symbol processing "machines" and not hypermachines, which implies that (M1$'$) cannot possibly be true.

Let us now discuss the second objection, which is based on the common belief that modern physical computers running some program P are physically instantiated Turing machines. Obviously, at this point we should pretend that there is no *empirical* evidence for the view that modern digital computers are not Turing machines. Suppose that $\mathcal{B}$ ranges over modern digital computers running some program P. Then proposition (M2) takes the following form:

$$\forall \mathcal{B} \exists \mathcal{M} \ \mathcal{B} \frown \mathcal{M}. \tag{M2$''$}$$

It follows from (M1) and (M2$''$) that

$$\forall \mathcal{B} \exists i \neg \Diamond D(\mathcal{B}, \mathcal{M}_0, i). \tag{M3$''$}$$

But this proposition is inconsistent with

$$\forall \mathcal{B} \forall i \Diamond D(\mathcal{B}, \mathcal{M}_0, i). \tag{M4$''$}$$

This means that digital computers running some program are not computers! The problem is that proposition (M4$''$) is true only if every digital computer is actually a hypercomputer, while on the other hand, proposition (M3$''$) is true only if modern digital computers are instantiations of Turing machines.

6.2   Philosophy and the Mind

The mind as an object of philosophical inquiry has been a very attractive subject of study for several thousand years. Almost every philosopher has had something to say about the mind, which in many cases has affected people's lives in quite unexpected ways. In particular, various prejudices and folk beliefs have deeply affected the formation of philosophical doctrines, which, in turn, reflect these prejudices and beliefs. For instance, as Searle notes in [176], Cartesian dualism gave the material world to scientists and the mental world to theologians. Thus the new scientific discoveries of the time posed no threat to traditional religion. Although the philosophy of the mind is a very interesting subject, we will concentrate on arguments against computationalism. The reader with a general interest in the subject should consult any textbook on the philosophy of mind.

6.2.1   Arguments Against Computationalism

Let us now present a number of important arguments against computationalism. The presentation of these arguments is highly influenced by Searle's presentation in [176].

The term *qualia* (singular: quale) refers to the ways things seem to us. In particular, qualia describe the qualitative character of conscious experiences. To make things clear, imagine that you and a friend are staring at a landscape at sunset. The way it looks to you—the particular, personal, subjective visual quality of the landscape—is the quale of your visual experience at the moment. Perhaps, that is why no color model (i.e., a mechanism by which we can describe the color formation process in a predictable way) can accurately describe colors. Since qualia really exist and computationalism does not take them into account, one may conclude that computationalism is false. Note that we assume here that computationalism and *functionalism* are being conflated. Functionalism, which is a doctrine quite similar to computationalism, argues that what it takes to be a mind is independent of its physical realization.

Thomas Nagel [139] argues that although one may have perfect knowledge of a bat's neurophysiology, she will not be able to say what it is like to be a bat. Even if she could by gradual degrees be transformed into a bat, she could not imagine the way she would feel when, eventually, she would be metamorphosed into a bat. The argument is based on the observation that bats have a sensory apparatus considerably different from ours, and it aims to show that having complete knowledge of everything that goes on inside the body of an animal is still insufficient to explain consciousness. Yujin Nagasawa [137] has put forth an interesting objection to Nagel's argument. More specifically, Nagasawa claims that if we have a vivid imagination or a sophisticated simulation system, there is no problem for us to know what it is like to be bat without being a bat like creature. However, an immediate response is that one cannot really say how it feels like to "enjoy" smoking a cigarette when one has never smoked one. Imagination is simply not enough!

A similar argument is the one that Frank Jackson published in [89]. Assume that it is possible to create a dome inside of which everything is black and white. Maria grows up in this dome and she is educated by watching distant-learning programs on a black-and-white television set and by reading black-and-white books and magazines. In this way Maria learns everything other pupils learn about the physical world that surrounds us. Thus, she knows there are objects that are red, but she has never seen any red object in her life. Now, if Maria knows everything she should know, she should have no problem recognizing the red Ferrari in a full-color photo of sport cars. But this is not true, since the very moment she sees the red Ferrari in the photo, she will learn what it is like to sense red. In a nutshell, knowledge is not enough to know what it is like to sense colors.

Another argument against computationalism has been put forward by Ned Block. This argument is considered by many as an immediate antecedent to the Chinese room argument. Block's argument goes like this: Assume that the brain of a typical human being consists of around 1.5 billion neurons.[7] Also, assume that each Chinese citizen plays the role of a neuron. For instance, neuron firing can be *simulated* by the act of calling another person using a cellular phone. This "artificial" brain lacks mental states (e.g., one cannot claim that it "feels" wrath), and thus it cannot be classified as a real brain. A similar argument was advanced by Searle [174]. This argument has been dubbed the "Chinese gym" argument, while Block's argument is known as the "Chinese nation" argument. Searle's argument goes like this. Imagine that there is a hall containing many monolingual English-speaking men. These men would carry out the same operations as the neurons of a connectionist architecture (i.e., neural networks) that models the brain process that take place on the brain of the human in the Chinese room argument. No one in the gym speaks any Chinese, and there is no way to imagine that the system considered as a single entity, understands Chinese. Yet the system gives the impression that it understands Chinese.

---

7. Actually, the brain of an adult human has more than 100 billion neurons [181], but the core of Block's argument is that the entire population of China will implement the functions of neurons in the brain. Thus, we cannot actually use the real figure for the presentation of the argument.

6.2.2   The Chinese Room Argument Revisited

In 2004, the Chinese room argument (CRA) turned 25 years old, but age is not slowing the CRA down. It is still a subject of debate as well as a source of inspiration for members of the scientific community. And the recent collection of selected papers on the CRA [159], which was edited by John Preston and Mark Bishop, as well as Jerome Wakefield's recent paper on the CRA [214], which was the most viewed paper on the "Minds and Machines" web site in 2003, are clear proofs of this. Apart from its popularity, the real question is whether the CRA is still valid. And that is exactly the subject of this section.

An interesting idea concerning the validity of the CRA was put forth by Bruce MacLennan [118], who rightly claims that if one accepts the CRA in the digital setting, then one should also accept it in the analog setting, and conversely, if one does not accept it in the digital setting, then one should not accept it in the analog setting. Here the term "analog setting" refers to analog computation (see Chapter 9). MacLennan does not believe in the validity of the CRA. He has proposed the "granny room argument," that is, the analogue of the CRA in an analog computing setting, in order to refute the CRA based on his view that one has to accept or reject the applicability of the CRA in both the digital and analog settings. In the granny room there is a person who is exposed to a continuous visual image and produces a continuous auditory output. By making use of various analog computational aids the person in the room "implements the analog computation by performing a complicated, ritualized sensorimotor procedure." When the system sees an image of MacLennan's grandmother it will respond, "Hi, Granny!" MacLennan believes that his argument refutes the CRA, but the truth is that this argument does not actually do so. In fact, one may question the point of substituting symbol recognition with face recognition. Assume that the person inside the room has photos for each face that can possibly appear, and depending on the face seen, she produces what MacLennan calls a *(continuous) auditory image*. For example, when she sees face A, she has to say, "Hello, Stella!" Practically, this argument does not differ from the classical "digital" version of the CRA. The point is that facial recognition is no different from symbol recognition, and thus the CRA remains immune from attack even in the "analog" setting.

Jerome C. Wakefield [214] presents some interesting ideas concerning the CRA. In particular, he criticizes the formulation of the CRA as presented by Searle in [175, pp 11-12]:

i.   Programs are entirely syntactic.

ii. Minds have a semantics.

iii. Syntax is not the same as, nor by itself sufficient for, semantics.

∴   Programs are not minds.

According to Wakefield, this syllogism is problematic because the third premise is a "straightforward denial of computationalism," since "the no-semantics-from-syntax intuition is precisely what strong AI proponents are challenging with their computationalistic theory of content." However, we feel that it is necessary to see first what Searle has to say in [175] about the third step:

> [T]he general principle that the Chinese Room thought experiment illustrates: merely manipulating formal symbols is not in and of itself constitutive of having semantic contents, nor is it sufficient by itself to guarantee the presence of semantic contents. It does not matter how well the system can imitate the behavior of someone who really does understand, nor how complex the symbol manipulations are; you cannot milk semantics out of syntactical processes alone.

To claim that 2 is a set is clearly counterintuitive. In addition, depending on which sets one identifies with the natural numbers, there are many other things that are equally counterintuitive (e.g., $2 \in 3$). However, the existence of such counterintuitive results does not mean that the reduction of numbers to sets is problematic. Similarly, one cannot claim that since there some counterintuitive results in the thought experiment associated with the CRA, one can object to the claim that certain computer states are beliefs, which, in a nutshell, is the essentialist objection to the CRA. Wakefield claims that this is a valid objection to the CRA and argues that the CRA can be reinterpreted in such a way as to make it immune to the essentialist attack. In particular, if we explain the meaning of the CRA in an indeterminate way, the new argument still poses a challenge to computationalism and strong AI. This new formulation of the CRA has been dubbed the *Chinese Room Indeterminacy Argument*, or just CRIA.[8] Wakefield's CRIA goes as follows [214]:

i.   There are determinate meanings of thoughts and intentions-in-action. In addition, a thought about a syntactic shape is different from any thoughts that possess the semantic content that is expressed by the syntactic shapes.

ii.   Any syntactic fact underdetermines, and at the same time leaves indeterminate, the contents of thoughts and intentions-in-action.

∴   The content of thoughts and intentions-in-action cannot be constituted by syntactic facts.

And as Wakefield notes, "[t]his indeterminacy argument provides the needed support for Searle's crucial third premise."

---

8. An argument is called *indeterminate* when it is open to multiple incompatible interpretations consistent with all the possible evidence.

If one could have demonstrated that syntax is indeed the same as semantics, then she would have managed to refute the CRA. And the easiest way to achieve this goal would be to show or at least to provide evidence that some computer program understands. By following this line of thinking, Herbert Alexander Simon and Stuart A. Eisenstadt [184] describe three programs they believe provide evidence that computer programs can understand and thus falsify the CRA. For instance, they present a program called ZBIE that *simulates* human language learning. The program has as inputs sentences in any natural language and description lists that represent simple scenes (e.g., "The boy pulls on the oar under the lash."). After some time, the program acquires a vocabulary of words related to the scenes it has as input and a vocabulary of relational structures. In addition, using sentences in two languages as inputs, instead of sentences and scenes, ZBIE can learn to translate from one language to another. However, there are some issues with these "astonishing" capabilities. First, notice that even modern specialized programs fail to provide meaningful translations. For instance, the author used a mechanical language translator to translate the sentence above to Greek and the resulting text back to English only to get back the completely different sentence, "the boy pulls in the oar under the whip." And of course, if a modern professional tool does this kind of work, what should one expect from a tool of the early 1970s? On the other hand, when someone learns a new word, she tries to associate this new word with her own experiences so as to grasp its real meaning. For example, when a juvenile learns the word "orgasm," she will not really understand the real meaning of the word until the day she first experiences an orgasm. So syntax is simply not enough to understand what an orgasm is. In other words, Jaak Panksepp's question, "Could you compute me an orgasm?" has a negative answer. More generally, it is meaningless to say that a computer program understands just because some talented computer programmer has figured out a number of cases that make a computer program appear as if it really understands. A clever set of rewriting rules cannot possibly be equated with understanding.

6.3   Neurobiology and the Mind

The brain is part of the central nervous system and includes all the higher nervous centers. It is also the center of the nervous system, and the seat of consciousness and volition. As such, it is of great importance to neurobiologists. Until recently, most biologists employed *reductionism* (i.e., the idea that the nature of complex things can always be explained by simpler or more fundamental things) to explain biological phenomena (e.g., the discovery of the structural and chemical basis of living processes is a result of the application of reductionism to biology). However, it is quite surprising, particularly for nonspecialists, that biologists are gradually abandoning reductionism in favor of *emergence*, which is roughly the idea that some properties of a system are irreducible. Indeed, as Marc Van Regenmortel notes [210]:

> Complex systems are defined as systems that possess emergent properties and which, therefore, cannot be explained by the properties of their component parts. Since the constituents of a complex system interact in a non-linear manner, the behaviour of the system cannot be analysed by classical mathematical methods that do not incorporate cooperativity and non-additive effects.

And he concludes by stating that "reductionism is not the panacea for understanding the mind." Interestingly enough, biological naturalism is an explanation of the so-called *mind–body problem* (i.e., "How can a decision in my soul cause a movement of a physical object in the world such as my body?" [176, p. 17]) that is based on exactly these principles. More specifically, biological naturalism is based on the following theses [176, pp. 113–114]:

(i) Conscious states, with their subjective, first-person ontology, are real phenomena in the real world. It is impossible to do an eliminative reduction of consciousness in order to show that it is just an illusion. In addition, it is not possible to reduce consciousness to its neurobiological basis, because such a third-person reduction would leave out the first-person ontology of consciousness.

(ii) Conscious states are entirely caused by lower-level neurobiological processes in the brain. Conscious states are thus *causally reducible* to neurobiological processes. However, they have absolutely no life of their own independent of the neurobiology. Causally speaking, they are not something "over and above" neurobiological processes.

(iii) Conscious states are realized in the brain as features of the brain system, and thus exist at a level higher than that of neurons and synapses. Individual neurons are not conscious, but portions of the brain system composed of neurons are conscious.

(iv) Because conscious states are real features of the real world, they function causally. For instance, the reader's conscious thirst causes him or her to drink water.

As a direct consequence, one can surely simulate in principle the functioning either of parts of the brain or of the whole brain in a computer. However, it is impossible for the computer simulation to become conscious. In order to make things clear, let us give a somewhat trivial argument. Many people are aware that water is the chemical compound H_2O and that ethanol is the chemical compound CH_3CH_2OH. Each water molecule consists of atoms, which, in turn, consist of electrons, neutrons and protons. And of course the same applies to the ethanol molecules. The question is, since both water and ethanol consist of exactly the same basic building blocks, why do they taste different, and more generally, why do they have different properties? Certainly, the answer is that their molecules consist of different numbers of electrons, neutrons, and protons and that these elementary particles are arranged in different ways. So it is not enough to know the constituents of a compound to have a complete image of its properties. Analogously, one may say that it is not enough to study the properties of neurons and how they are connected in order to (fully) understand the brain and its operations.

If we suppose that the computational theory of the mind is indeed true, then we should expect that the brain operates in a discrete manner. Indeed, according to "modern" computationalism, the brain operates in discrete manner in a discrete universe. However, to the disappointment of many computationalists, Michael Spivey and his colleagues Marc Grosjean and Günther Knoblich [188] reported that there is compelling evidence that language comprehension is a continuous process. In their experiment, Spivey and his colleagues had at their disposal forty-two volunteers, who were Cornell University undergraduate students who took psychology courses. Each volunteer was presented with color images of two objects on a screen, and a prerecorded audio file instructed them to click one of the images with a mouse. One of the objects had the role of a distractor object and the other the role of a target object. When the students were instructed to click one of the two objects and the names of the objects did not sound alike, such as apple and jacket, the trajectories of their mouse movements were straight and direct to the objects they were instructed to click on. On the other hand, when the students were instructed to click on an "apple" and were presented with two objects with similar sounding names (e.g., "apple" and "maple"), they were slower to click on the correct object, and in addition, their mouse trajectories were much more curved.

This experiment provided powerful support for models of continuous comprehension of acoustic-phonetic input during spoken-word recognition. In addition, the data gathered from this experiment provide support to the claim that the continuous temporal dynamics of motor output reflect continuous temporal dynamics of lexical activation in the brain. In other words, one may say that cognition does not operate by entering and leaving states (e.g., like a state machine or automaton) but rather can have values in between (e.g., it may be partially in one state or another) and eventually stabilizes to a unique interpretation, which, for example, can be the recognition of a certain word.

Panksepp is the father of the emerging field of *affective neuroscience*, which supports the idea that affective and cognitive mental processes are distinct. A summary of "recent conceptual and empirical advances in understanding basic affective process of the mammalian brain and how we might distinguish affective from cognitive processes" was presented in [146]. The following short presentation of affective neuroscience is based on this paper.

It is a common belief, shared particularly among nonscientists, that emotional processes have both *cognitive* and *affective* attributes. In addition, these attributes rank highest among a number of other attributes emotional processes may have. However, because of the difficulty unambiguously distinguishing the two attributes in the laboratory, many scientists have begun to question the utility of this distinction. In spite of this skepticism, Panksepp believes that this very distinction may prove helpful in deciphering the neurobiological nature of the basic affective quality of conscious actuality. Panksepp advances this idea because affective feelings are, not completely but to a considerable degree, distinct neurobiological processes from an anatomical and a neurochemical point of view. Also, this distinction is evident to a similar degree with respect to peripheral bodily interactions. Emotional and motivational feelings "push" organisms to make cognitive choices (e.g., to find food when hungry, water when thirsty, companionship when lonely). If this idea is indeed true, then it is necessary to develop special techniques to understand affective organic processes in neural terms, which, in turn, may provide a solid basis for the construction of a coherent science of the mind. As a side effect of such a development, new psychiatric therapeutics will be advanced. Interestingly, the foundation on top of which emotional and motivational processes are built is analog in nature. In addition, this foundation is to a large degree the result of evolutionary process. Let us now see why Panksepp advocates the distinction between affects and cognitions.

First of all, emotional states are inherently characterized by valence. In other words, they are characterized by either aversive or attractive feelings that do not accompany pure cognitions. It is not entirely unreasonable to suppose that various basic emotional and motivational responses and the accompanying types of valence have their origin in inherently evolutionarily controlled states of the nervous system. These mental abilities of the brain are not built just from the perceptions of external events and the cognition that follows. Instead, they have an intrinsic structure of their own. However, emotions are not just disturbances of the physical setting in which they occur. In addition, they help control the way we perceive the world around us.

Although many forms of brain damage severely impair cognitions, still emotional responses and many basic affective tendencies are not affected. This dictum is based on the fact that early decortication (i.e., removal of the outer covering of the brain) of neonatal rats affects the ability of these animals to learn while their emotional and motivational behaviors remain almost intact. Ralph Adolphs, Daniel Tranel, and Antonio Damasio [3] reported the results of their study to test the hypothesis that the recognition of emotions is probably "composed" in different brain regions, which depends on the nature of the stimuli that have caused these emotions. Adolphs et al. studied a person who had suffered extensive bilateral brain lesions, and their findings support the dictum above. These and similar observations have led Panksepp to conclude that, *"Cognitions are largely cortical while affects are largely subcortical."*

It is an everyday observation that children are very emotionally alive, which suggests that "affective competence *is* elaborated more by earlier maturing medial brain systems than more rostrally and laterally situated cognitive systems" [146, p. 10]. These remarks affirm that affects are more likely to be evolutionary "givens." The higher cortico-cognitive processes that keep in check emotionality appear gradually as the organisms mature.

Processes that resemble discrete computational processes may generate cognitions, while neurochemical processes that resemble analog computational processes may be responsible for the generation of affects. A direct consequence of this observation is that in the case of long-term emotional learning, the conditioning of holistic "state" responses plays an important role, while in the case of cognitive learning, the temporal resolution of formal operations and propositions plays an important role. Probably, this is the reason why it is hard to activate cognitions by directly stimulating the brain, while this does not hold true for affects.

Cognitions do not generate facial or bodily expressions and do not have any effect on the tone of our voice, while emotions generate such expressions and changes in tone. Although the importance of facial expressions in the study of emotional feelings has not remained unchallenged, still it is clear that these emotional actions can cause congruent feelings. And in cases in which someone has suffered cortical damage, full emotional expressions cannot be generated by cognitive means, while they can be aroused by spontaneous emotional states.

Over the past 15 or more years, various studies have revealed emotional asymmetry and asymmetries in motor output (for instance, see [46, 78, 91, 185]). There are two general theories of emotional asymmetry: the right-hemisphere hypothesis and the valence hypothesis. According to the right-hemisphere hypothesis, the right hemisphere is the center of all forms of emotional expression and perception. On the other hand, the valence hypothesis posits that emotional valence deeply affects hemispheric asymmetry for expression and perception of emotions. More specifically, the right hemisphere is dominant for negative emotions and the left hemisphere is dominant for positive emotions. Both hypotheses have received empirical support.

It is an unfortunate fact that our way of thinking and perceiving the world around us is constrained by prevailing cultural and scientific assumptions. And this is why affective issues have been confronted with great skepticism. However, this attitude is changing, and a growing number of researchers now recognize the importance of affects. One of the main reasons for this turnaround is that by understanding what affects really are, we may hope to understand what consciousness really is.

6.4   Cognition and the Mind

The arguments and ideas presented in this section have appeared in periodicals whose scope is marginally related to the philosophy of mind.

In Section 3.1.2 we presented a model of the mind based on the assumption that the mind is a trial-and-error machine. Here we follow a different path by assuming that the mind is a machine that has semantic content.

People are definitely not computers, but people are definitely (some sort of) *machines*, since they can calculate, memorize, etc. And naturally the question is, What kind of machines are people? James H. Fetzer presents some interesting ideas on this matter in [62]. A sign is a generalization of the concept of a symbol. Charles Sanders Peirce divides signs into three categories: *icons*, *indices*, and *symbols*. Here is how Peirce explains the difference among these three categories:[9]

> There are three kinds of signs. Firstly, there are *likenesses*, or icons; which serve to convey ideas of the things they represent simply by imitating them. Secondly, there are *indications*, or indices; which show something about things, on account of their being physically connected with them. Such is a guidepost, which points down the road to be taken, or a relative pronoun, which is placed just after the name of the thing intended to be denoted, or a vocative exclamation, as "Hi! there," which acts upon the nerves of the person addressed and forces his attention. Thirdly, there are *symbols*, or general signs, which have become associated with their meanings by usage. Such are most words, and phrases, and speeches, and books, and libraries.

One may say that an icon is a thing that resembles that for which it stands, an index is a cause or an effect of that for which it stands, and a symbol is merely habitually or conventionally associated with that for which it stands. Based on this division, Fetzer suggests that there should be at least three kinds of minds. More specifically, Type I minds that can process icons, Type II minds that can process icons and indices, and Type III minds that can process icons, indices, and symbols. Although Fetzer stopped here, we can go on and introduce Type IV minds as minds that manipulate only indices and Type V minds as minds that manipulate only symbols. However, computers process symbols according to their form and not the meaning

---

9. The excerpt is from Peirce's paper entitled *What Is a Sign?* which is available online from http://www.iupui.edu/~peirce/ep/ep2/ep2book/ch02/ep2ch2.htm.

that may be associated to them by usage. On the other hand, a mind capable of processing symbols, while aware of the meaning associated with their "meaning," is clearly different from a Type V mind. Let us call these minds Type VI minds. It seems that the sci-fi androids are Type VI minds, but I will not argue about this idea.

A Type III mind is actually a *semiotic* system; while a modern computing system (i.e., a Type V "mind") is a symbolic system. There are two differences between semiotic and symbolic systems. First, a symbolic system is able to process syntax (i.e., it is able to manipulate meaningless marks), while a semiotic system is able to process signs that are meaningful for this system. Second, a symbolic system manipulates marks by executing some computational procedure, but a semiotic system manipulates signs by noncomputational procedures. Human thought processes cannot be described by symbol systems, but they can be described by semiotic systems. Another important difference between semiotic and symbolic systems is that in the case of semiotic systems there is a "grounding" relationship between signs and what they stand for, while in the case of symbolic systems, such a relation does not exist.

These observations have led Fetzer to propose that the mind is actually a semiotic engine. As such, the mind processes information in a nonalgorithmic way.

Quite recently, Chris Eliasmith discovered a major flaw in functionalism and reported it in [57]. Recall that the Turing machine is a conceptual device, and as such, its properties are independent of any particular realization. In addition, it is easy to characterize a Turing machine from its input, the state of the machine, and the program being executed. Functionalists believe that what makes something a mental state depends on its function in the cognitive system of which it is a part. More specifically, mental states are functional relations between sensory stimulations (input), behavior (state of the machine), and their mental states (the program being executed). Thus, cognitive functions can be completely characterized by high-level descriptions abstracted from their implementation. Also, "two systems are functionally isomorphic if *there is a correspondence between the states of one and the states of the other that preserves functional relations*" [161]. This implies that any system isomorphic to a mind is a mind. Assume that there are two functionally isomorphic systems having different implementations. Then these will have the same mental states (if any). This is the thesis of multiple or universal realizability (i.e., the fallacious claim that anything can be described as implementing a computer program), which Eliasmith refutes in [57].

The argument against the multiple realizability thesis is based on the idea that two computing devices that are equivalent (or isomorphic if you prefer this term) are not equal. In particular, machine equivalence provides little information regarding the way a machine actually computes something, and it is this way that is cognitively relevant. For instance, although a modern CISC machine is equivalent to a RISC machine, in the sense that one can compile and execute exactly the same programs on both machines, a RISC machine is faster (e.g., consider operating systems, such as OpenSolaris and GNU/Linux, that are available for both architectures and think about their performance). Clearly, if we compile the same program under the same operating system running on two different architectures the resulting binary files will be completely different. Obviously, both binaries will produce the same results, but one will be executed much faster than the other. The reason for this difference in performance is due to the simplicity of the RISC architecture or to the complexity of the CISC architecture. Clearly, this means that the implementation, contrary to the functional belief, really matters. In other words, a system that is functionally isomorphic to a mind is not necessarily a mind.

By having as a starting point "the cognitive study of science," Roland Giere [64] shows that only "distributed cognition" can be employed to understand cognition as it occurs in modern science. Giere uses an example to demonstrate the validity of his ideas. In particular, he considers the large hadron collider of the European Center for Nuclear Research (known as CERN), which is coupled with a very large detector called ATLAS. The ATLAS project involves many scientists, technicians, and support personnel and aims to obtain direct experimental evidence of the existence of the Higgs boson.[10] Since there is no reason to explain all the details involved, it suffices to say that the experiment involves the acceleration of certain elementary particles to very high energies and their subsequent collision in the detector. Depending on what goes on in the detector, one may decide whether the Higgs boson actually exists.

When finished, the ATLAS project will produce some knowledge, which is actually a cognitive product. Thus, one may view the ATLAS project as a cognitive process. Clearly, one may wonder about the nature of scientific cognition starting with this particular example. As expected, the "standard" answer to this problem is that a *cognitive agent*, which is a human or artificial *individual*, acquires a *symbolic representation* that is *computationally* processed according to a set of syntactic rules. This answer is problematic for a number of reasons. First of all, it is not clear who or what this cognitive agent is. A typical answer to this question is that the cognitive agent is the person who interprets the final output. There are two problems with this response. First, if we assume that such a person indeed exists, then this person "operates" by manipulating and thus is incapable of understanding anything. Second, there is actually no such person, since the final output is the result of a complex interaction among people with different kinds of expertise who consult sophisticated equipment. Thus, we cannot find a single person who has the required property.

A partial solution to these problems emerges if we consider the notion

10. The Higgs boson is a hypothetical particle whose very existence would validate the "standard" mechanism by which particles acquire mass.

of *collective cognition*. In this setting, we assume that each individual participating in the project is actually a computational system. We may therefore say that the final output is the conjunction of the outputs produced by each individual. Clearly, this solution insists that humans are computers and as such is simply unacceptable. Apart from that, it does not take into consideration the artifacts that play a crucial role in the project.

A better idea is to use the notion of *distributed cognition* (i.e., a cognitive system that is collective but includes not only persons but also instruments and other artifacts as parts of the cognitive system). In this new setting, scientists, technicians, machines, sensors, etc., interact harmoniously to achieve a final result. Obviously, this does not mean that machines and sensors are conscious. Instead, when the cognitive system is viewed as a whole, one may easily say that it is a computational system. But does it make sense to say that the ATLAS project is actually a computational project?

The whole project is not computational at all. First of all, when elementary particles interact, no symbolic representation is transformed by syntactic-like operations. And since computation is identified with the transformation of symbolic representations by syntax-manipulation operations, one easily deduces that elementary-particle interaction is not a computational process. Unfortunately, not everybody shares this idea. For instance, there are those who believe that even the whole universe is a gigantic computer that computes its next state. However, such beliefs are based on unjustified assumptions (see Section 8.5 for a more detailed discussion of these issues). But it is equally interesting to say that it is the beauty of computation in general and the "desire for a single, overarching explanation for everything" that has compelled many thinkers and researchers to support the idea that the universe is a computer. Nevertheless, the project is partially computational in the sense that there are computers that do actually compute. Thus, Project ATLAS is a hybrid system. There are some further questions related to the very nature of knowledge, but a proper treatment of such questions falls outside the scope of this book.

VII. Computing Real Numbers

As was mentioned in the introduction of this book, a typical Turing machine can compute real numbers. However, not all real numbers are computable in the classical sense of the word. For instance, if we consider the universal Turing machine U and the countably infinite set of tapes that may be used by it, then we can define a real number R_U as follows:

$$\text{the } n\text{th digit of } R_U = \begin{cases} 1 & \text{if } U \text{ halts on the } n\text{th tape,} \\ 0 & \text{if } U \text{ does not halt on the } n\text{th tape.} \end{cases}$$

Clearly, the number R_U is not Turing computable. Thus, any conceptual or real computing device that would allow one to compute such a number would be automatically classified as a hypermachine. In other words, real number computation is a promising research area in the field of hypercomputation.

In this chapter, we briefly outline Type-2 machines and their accompanying theory of effectivity. Strictly speaking, Type-2 machines are not hypermachines, but some of their extensions can be classified as hypermachines. And this is the raison d'être of including this short introduction to Type-2 computability theory. Next, we present an extension of the theory of Type-2 machines, which is followed by a short discussion of the so-called BSS-machines and a presentation of a model of feasible real-number random-access machines.

7.1 Type-2 Theory of Effectivity

The Type-2 theory of effectivity is an extension of classical computability and complexity theories developed by Klaus Weihrauch and his colleagues. The Type-2 theory of effectivity is a theory of computable analysis. Notice that since in this book we are mainly concerned with computability, we will not discuss the part of the theory extending complexity theory. The discussion that follows is based on Weihrauch's recent book [219].

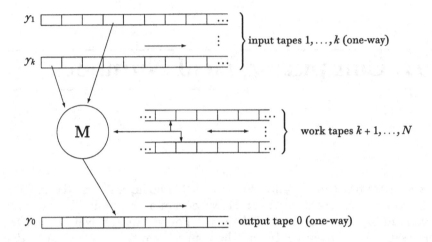

Figure 7.1: A Type-2 machine in action.

7.1.1   Type-2 Machines

A Type-2 machine is basically a Turing machine equipped with more than one input tape, a number of working tapes, and one output tape. Each tape has its own scanning head for reading and writing symbols on it. In general, the symbols that can be printed on the various tapes are not drawn from identical alphabets. In particular, the symbols that may be printed on the output tape and on any input tape belong to the set Σ, while the symbols that may be printed on the work tapes belong to the set Γ. By definition, $\Sigma \cup \{\flat\} \subseteq \Gamma$, where $\flat$ is a special symbol that is not an element of Σ. In addition, it is necessary to state that a Type-2 machine may process both finite and infinite input strings, which gives it additional expressive power compared to an ordinary Turing machine. Figure 7.1 depicts a typical Type-2 machine.

Assume that k is an integer greater than zero. Then a type specification is a tuple $(Y_1, \ldots, Y_k, Y_0)$, where $Y_i \in \{\Sigma^*, \Sigma^\omega\}$. A type specification actually denotes the *type* of a function $f : Y_1 \times \cdots \times Y_k \to Y_0$ computable by a Type-2 machine. In other words, a type specification is a template specifying the form of its arguments and its return value. A program is a flowchart operating on the output tape and the various input tapes. The stock of commands that can be used to make a program for a Type-2 machine follows:

- the "HALT" command with its obvious meaning,

- the "i:left" command that moves the scanning head on tape i one cell to the left,

- the "i:right" command that moves the scanning head on tape i one cell to the right,

- the "*i*:write(*a*)" command that writes the symbol $a \in \Gamma$ on the cell being scanned by the scanning head of *i*, and

- the "*i*:if(*a*)" command that checks whether *a* is the symbol that is being scanned by the scanning head that sits atop tape *i*.

Notice that the commands "*i*:left" and "*i*:write(*a*)" are not allowed on an input tape *i*, while on the output tape only sequences "o:write(*a*);o:right" are allowed. We are ready to give a formal definition of Type-2 machines [219].

Definition 7.1.1 A Type-2 machine M is a Turing machine with k one-way, read-only input tapes together with a type specification $(Y_1, \ldots, Y_k, Y_0)$ with $Y_i \in \{\Sigma^*, \Sigma^\omega\}$, giving the type for each input tape and the one-way output tape.

Previously, it was speculated that Type-2 machines are more expressive than Turing machines just because they can handle infinite strings. However, this speculation is not enough to characterize a Type-2 machine as a hypermachine. On the other hand, it is interesting to consider the class of strings that can be recognized by a Type-2 machine and the class of real numbers that can be computed by this conceptual computing device, since it can handle infinite-length strings. The first question will be addressed in the rest of this subsection, while the second question will be addressed in the remainder of this section.

Suppose that $\mathscr{M}$ is a Type-2 machine that can compute a function f having the following type specification:

$$(Y_1, Y_2, \ldots, Y_k, Y_0).$$

This particular device handles k-tuples (i.e., $(a_1, \ldots, a_k)$, where $a_i \in Y_i$). Each element of the k-tuple is printed on the corresponding input tape (i.e., the first element is printed on the first input tape, the second element on the second input tape, etc.). More specifically, the symbols making up each element of the k-tuple, which can be either finite or infinite, are printed on consecutive cells, starting from the cell that is next to the cell on which the scanning head rests. In addition, all other cells should be empty and this is denoted by printing the special symbol $\bar{b}$ on all other cells. Also, all other tapes have to be completely blank (i.e., the symbol $\bar{b}$ will be printed on each cell of each tape). Assume that $f(a_1, \ldots, a_k) = a_0$, where $a_0 \in \Sigma^*$ (i.e., $Y_0 = \Sigma^*$). Then the machine $\mathscr{M}$, after processing its input, will print the string a_0 on the output tape in a finite amount of time and halt. However, if $a_0 \in \Sigma^\omega$ (i.e., $Y_0 = \Sigma^\omega$), then $\mathscr{M}$ will be printing the symbols making up the a_0 on the output tape ad infinitum. In other words, a string function $f : Y_1 \times \cdots \times Y_k \to Y_0$ is computable by a Type-2 machine $\mathscr{M}$ if for each argument $(a_1, \ldots, a_k)$, the machine prints on its working tape the string $f(a_1, \ldots, a_k)$. When $f(a_1, \ldots, a_k)$ is undefined, then the machine never ceases operation, and at the same time it will print only finitely many symbols on the output tape. It is worth mentioning that a typical Type-2 machine does not take into consideration partial results in the way that infinite-time Turing machines do. Thus, Type-2 machines differ fundamentally from infinite-time Turing machines. Clearly, it should not be difficult to define a new conceptual computing device that is structurally equivalent to a Type-2 machine, but operates in transfinite time. In this case, it would be interesting to see whether these machines are more powerful than infinite-time Turing machines.

From the discussion so far, it follows that Type-2 machines can compute strings falling into the following categories:

(i) All strings $w \in \Sigma^*$ are computable.

(ii) An infinite string $s \in \Sigma^\omega$ is computable if and only if the constant function $f : \{( )\} \to \Sigma^\omega$, $f( ) = s$, is computable.

(iii) Any k-tuple $(a_1, a_2, \ldots, a_k)$, $a_i \in \Sigma^\infty$, is computable if and only if each component a_i is computable.

If string functions are Type-2 computable, then there should be a way to characterize the computability of the composition of computable functions. Indeed, the following result provides such a characterization:

Theorem 7.1.1 *Suppose that $k, n \in \mathbb{N}$ and $X_1, \ldots, X_k, Y_1, \ldots, Y_n, Z \in \{\Sigma^*, \Sigma^\omega\}$, and that for all $i = 1, \ldots, n$,*

$$g_i : X_1 \times \cdots \times X_k \to Y_i \quad and \quad f : Y_1 \times \cdots \times Y_n \to Z,$$

are computable functions. Then the composition

$$f \circ (g_1, \ldots, g_n) : X_1 \times \cdots \times X_k \to Z$$

is computable if $Z = \Sigma^\omega$ or $Y_i = \Sigma^*$ for all i.

A set $A \subseteq \Sigma^*$ is *recursive* or *decidable* if its characteristic function is computable. Also, a set is called *recursively enumerable* if it is the domain of a computable function $f : \Sigma^* \to \Sigma^*$.

Definition 7.1.2 Assume that $X \subseteq Z \subseteq Y = Y_1 \times \cdots \times Y_k$, where $k \geq 1$ and, as usual, $Y_i \in \{\Sigma^*, \Sigma^\omega\}$. Then

(i) the set X will be *recursively enumerable open in Z* if $X = \text{dom}(f) \cap Z$, where $f : Y \to \Sigma^*$ is a computable function, and

(ii) the set X is *decidable in Z* if X and $Z \setminus X$ are recursively enumerable in Z.

In case $Z = Y$, it is not necessary to include the "in Z" part of the terminology.

The following theorem characterizes decidable sets.

Theorem 7.1.2 *A set X is decidable in Z if and only if there exists a computable function $f : Y \to \Sigma^*$ such that $f(z) = 1$ if $z \in X$ and $f(z) = 0$ if $z \in Z \setminus X$.*

7.1.2   Computable Topologies

It is not really difficult to see that computability on Σ^* and Σ^ω can actually be reduced to computability on 2^* and 2^ω, respectively. More specifically, suppose that

$$\Sigma = \{a_1, a_2, \ldots, a_n\}$$

is an alphabet; then a possible encoding of the symbols a_i is the following:

$$a_i \mapsto \underbrace{1 \ldots 1}_{i-1} 0, \text{ for all } i < n, \text{ and } a_n \mapsto \underbrace{1 \ldots 1}_{n}.$$

More generally, given a set M it is not difficult to define functions that map finite or infinite strings to elements of the set M. In particular, the surjective functions $\nu : \Sigma^* \to M$ and $\delta : \Sigma^\omega \to M$ are called a *notation* and a *representation* of M, respectively. Notations and representations are collectively known as *naming systems*. The fact that a naming system is a surjective function implies that for every element of M there is a *name*. In addition, it should be clear that any element of M may have more than one name.

For the sets $\mathbb{N}$, $\mathbb{Z}$, and $\mathbb{Q}$ we define the following "standard" notations:

(i) The binary notation $\nu_{\mathbb{N}} : 2^* \to \mathbb{N}$ of the natural numbers is defined by $\mathrm{dom}(\nu_{\mathbb{N}}) = \{0\} \cup 1\{0,1\}^*$ and $\nu_{\mathbb{N}}(a_k \ldots a_0) = \sum_{i=0}^{k} a_i \cdot 2^i$, where $a_i \in 2$.

(ii) The integer notation $\nu_{\mathbb{Z}} : \Sigma^* \to \mathbb{Z}$ of integer numbers is defined by $\mathrm{dom}(\nu_{\mathbb{Z}}) = \{0\} \cup 1\{0,1\}^* \cup -1\{0,1\}^*$, $\nu_{\mathbb{Z}}(w) = \nu_{\mathbb{N}}(w)$, $\nu_{\mathbb{Z}}(-w) = -\nu_{\mathbb{N}}(w)$, for all $w \in \mathrm{dom}(\nu_{\mathbb{N}}) \setminus \{0\}$, and $\nu_{\mathbb{Z}}(0) = 0$.

(iii) The rational notation $\nu_{\mathbb{Q}} : \Sigma^* \to \mathbb{Q}$ of rational numbers is defined by $\mathrm{dom}(\nu_{\mathbb{Q}}) = \{u + \text{"/"} + v \mid u \in \mathrm{dom}(\nu_{\mathbb{Z}}), v \in \mathrm{dom}(\nu_{\mathbb{N}}), \nu_{\mathbb{N}}(v) \neq 0\}$ and $\nu_{\mathbb{Q}}(u + \text{"/"} + v) = \nu_{\mathbb{Z}}(u) \,/\, \nu_{\mathbb{N}}(v)$, where $+$ is the string concatenation operator.

At this point we should warn readers that what follows demands familiarity with basic topological notions. Thus, readers not familiar with basic topology are advised to consult either an introductory book on topology or the précis of topology included in Section D.3.

Assume that $\gamma : Y \to M$ is a naming system. Also, suppose that $x \in M$ and $X \subseteq M$. Then

(i) x is called γ-computable if $x = \gamma(y)$ for some computable $y \in Y$.

(ii) X is called γ-open, or γ-decidable if $\gamma^{-1}[X]$ is open or decidable in dom(γ).

The set τ_γ of the γ-open subsets of M is called the *final* topology of γ on M. Let us now define *effective* and *computable* topological spaces.

Definition 7.1.3 Assume that M is a nonempty set and $\sigma \subseteq 2^M$ is a countable set of subsets of M such that

$$x = y \quad \text{if} \quad \{A \in \sigma \mid x \in A\} = \{A \in \sigma \mid y \in A\},$$

and $v : \Sigma^* \to \sigma$ is a notation of σ. Then the triple $\mathbf{S} = (M, \sigma, v)$ is an effective topological space.

We will denote by τ_S the topology on M generated by the subbase σ.

Definition 7.1.4 Let $\mathbf{S} = (M, \sigma, v)$ be an effective topological space. Then if the set

$$\left\{ (u, v) \;\middle|\; \Big(u, v \in \text{dom}(v)\Big) \wedge \Big(v(u) = v(v)\Big) \right\}$$

is recursively enumerable, then the topological space $\mathbf{S}$ is computable.

Effective topological spaces are associated with representations. Indeed, the following definition makes precise this association.

Definition 7.1.5 Assume that $\mathbf{S} = (M, \sigma, v)$ is an effective topological space. Then its standard representation $\delta_S : \Sigma^\omega \to M$ is defined by means of the following sentence:

$$(\forall w \in \Sigma^*)(\forall x \in M)(\forall p \in \Sigma^\omega)$$

$$\left(\left[\Big(\big(p \in \text{dom}(\delta_S)\big) \wedge \big(\iota(w) \lhd p\big) \Big) \Rightarrow \Big(w \in \text{dom}(v)\Big) \right] \right.$$

$$\left. \wedge \left[\Big(\delta_S(p) = x\Big) \Leftrightarrow \Big(\{A \in \sigma \mid x \in A\} = \{v(w) \mid \iota(w) \lhd p\}\Big) \right] \right).$$

Note that for any two strings u and x we write $u \lhd x$ if u is a substring of x, and the function $\iota : \Sigma^* \to \Sigma^*$ is defined as follows:

$$\iota(a_1 a_2 \ldots a_n) = 110a_10a_2 \ldots 0a_n011,$$

for all $n \in \mathbb{N} \setminus \{0\}$ and $a_1, a_2, \ldots, a_n \in \Sigma$.

7.1.3 Type-2 Computability of Real Numbers

Any real number x is represented by a convergent sequence of closed rational intervals $(I_0, I_1, I_2, \ldots)$ with rational endpoints (i.e., if $I_j = [a, b]$, then $a < b$ and $a, b \in \mathbb{Q}$) such that $I_{n+1} \subseteq I_n$, for all $n \in \mathbb{N}$, and $\{x\} = \cap_{n \in \mathbb{N}} I_n$. Suppose that σ is an infinite string encoding the sequence $(I_0, I_1, \ldots)$. Then σ is a name of x. Thus, the real number x is computable if and only if σ is computable by a Type-2 machine. Clearly, in order to have a full theory, we need to specify how to encode a sequence of rational intervals into a string.

In general, a sequence of open rational intervals can be identified with a sequence of open balls.

Definition 7.1.6 Let $n \in \mathbb{N}$. Then the set

$$Cb^{(n)} = \{B(a, r) \mid a \in \mathbb{Q}^n, r \in \mathbb{Q}, r > 0\}$$

is the set of open rational balls of dimension n, where

$$B(a, r) = \{x \in \mathbb{R}^n \mid d(x, a) < r\}.$$

Notice that for any $x, y \in \mathbb{R}^n$ their maximum distance is

$$d(x, y) = \|x - y\|,$$

where $\|x\|$ denotes the maximum norm of x defined as follows.

Definition 7.1.7 Let $n \in \mathbb{N}$. Then for $(a_1, \ldots, a_n) \in \mathbb{R}^n$, the maximum norm of this tuple is defined as follows:

$$\|(a_1, \ldots, a_n)\| = \max\{|a_1|, \ldots, |a_n|\}.$$

The notation I^n of the set $Cb^{(n)}$ is defined as follows:

$$I^n(\iota(v_1) \ldots \iota(v_n)\iota(w)) = B((\overline{v_1}, \ldots, \overline{v_n}), \overline{w}),$$

where $\overline{x} = \nu_{\mathbb{Q}}(x)$. Notice that $I^1(\iota(u)\iota(v))$ is the open interval $(\overline{u} - \overline{v}, \overline{u} + \overline{v})$. Let us now proceed with the definition of three special computable topological spaces:

(i) $\mathbf{S}_= = (\mathbb{R}, Cb^{(1)}, I^1)$,

(ii) $\mathbf{S}_< = (\mathbb{R}, \sigma_<, \nu_<)$, where $\nu_<(w) = (\overline{w}, \infty)$, and

(iii) $\mathbf{S}_> = (\mathbb{R}, \sigma_>, \nu_>)$, where $\nu_>(w) = (-\infty, \overline{w})$.

The standard representations of these computable topological spaces are denoted by $\varrho = \delta_{\mathbf{S}_=}$, $\varrho_< = \delta_{\mathbf{S}_<}$, and $\varrho_> = \delta_{\mathbf{S}_>}$. In addition, the sets $\sigma_<$ and $\sigma_>$ are defined implicitly.

The following result characterizes the final topologies of the representations presented above.

Lemma 7.1.1 *The real line topology $\tau_{\mathbb{R}}$ (i.e., the set of all open subsets of $\mathbb{R}$) is the final topology of ϱ. Similarly,*

$$\tau_{\varrho_<} = \{(x, \infty) \mid x \in \mathbb{R}\}$$

and

$$\tau_{\varrho_>} = \{(-\infty, x) \mid x \in \mathbb{R}\}$$

are the final topologies of $\varrho_<$ and $\varrho_>$, respectively.

As has been pointed out already, not all real numbers are computable, and clearly the characterization presented above is not the only one. For instance, the reader may recall that on page 7 we presented Turing-computable real numbers. Since the theory of Type-2 computability has been designed as an extension of Turing computability that does not actually go beyond the Church–Turing barrier, it follows that it should be equivalent to Turing computability of real numbers. And this should be valid for a number of similar approaches. Indeed, the following result makes this equivalence explicit.

Lemma 7.1.2 *Let $x \in \mathbb{R}$. Then the following statements are equivalent:*

(i) *x is ϱ-computable.*

(ii) *x is computable in the sense of Definition 1.2.1.*

(iii) *There is a computable function $g : \mathbb{N} \to \Sigma^*$ such that*

$$(\forall n \in \mathbb{N})\left(|x - (\nu_Q \circ g)(n)| \leq 2^{-n}\right).$$

(iv) *There is a computable function $f : \mathbb{N} \to \mathbb{N}$ such that*

$$(\forall n \in \mathbb{N})\left(\left||x| - \frac{f(n)}{n+1}\right| < \frac{1}{n+1}\right).$$

(v) *There are computable functions $s, a, b, e : \mathbb{N} \to \mathbb{N}$ with*

$$\left|x - (-1)^{s(k)}\frac{a(k)}{b(k)}\right| \leq 2^{-N}, \text{ if } k \geq e(N), \text{ for all } k, N \in \mathbb{N}.$$

7.1.4   The Arithmetic Hierarchy of Real Numbers

Closely related to ϱ-computability is the notion of *left-computability* and *right-computability*. More specifically, a real number x is called left-computable or right-computable if it is $\varrho_<$-computable or $\varrho_>$-computable, respectively. It is not difficult to show that if a real number x is left-computable, then $-x$ is right-computable. Also, x is computable if and only if it is both left- and right-computable.

Proposition 7.1.1 *Let $x \in \mathbb{R}$. Then x is left- or right-computable if and only if there exists a computable function $f : \mathbb{N} \to \mathbb{Q}$ such that $x = \sup_i f(i)$ or $x = \inf_i f(i)$, respectively.*

Let us denote by Σ_1 the set of all left-computable numbers and by Π_1 the set of all right-computable numbers. Then $\Delta_1 = \Sigma_1 \cap \Pi_1$ is the set of all computable numbers. These sets form the basis of the arithmetic hierarchy of real numbers, which was constructed by Xizhong Zheng and Weihrauch [232]. Let us now proceed with the presentation of this hierarchy.

Before we actually present the way we can construct the sets of the hierarchy, we need a few auxiliary definitions. For $\mathbb{Q}$, the set of rational numbers, we define the function $\mu_{\mathbb{Q}} : \mathbb{N} \to \mathbb{Q}$ by $\mu_{\mathbb{Q}}(\langle i, j, k \rangle) = (i - j) / (k + 1)$.[1] A function $f : \mathbb{N}^n \to \mathbb{Q}$ is called A-recursive if there is an A-recursive function $g : \mathbb{N}^n \to \mathbb{N}$ such that $f(i_1, \ldots, i_n) = \mu_{\mathbb{Q}} \circ g(i_1, \ldots, i_n)$. The set of all total A-recursive functions from $\mathbb{N}^n$, $n \in \mathbb{N}$, to $\mathbb{Q}$ is denoted by $\Gamma_{\mathbb{Q}}^A$.

The sets Σ_0, Π_0, and Δ_0 are all equal and contain all the computable real numbers. For $n > 0$,

$$\Sigma_n = \left\{ x \in \mathbb{R} : (\exists f \in \Gamma_{\mathbb{Q}}) x = \sup_{i_1} \inf_{i_2} \sup_{i_3} \ldots \Theta_{i_n} f(i_1, \ldots, i_n) \right\},$$

$$\Pi_n = \left\{ x \in \mathbb{R} : (\exists f \in \Gamma_{\mathbb{Q}}) x = \inf_{i_1} \sup_{i_2} \inf_{i_3} \ldots \overline{\Theta}_{i_n} f(i_1, \ldots, i_n) \right\},$$

$$\Delta_n = \Sigma_n \cap \Pi_n,$$

where Θ_{i_n} denotes $\sup_{i_n}$ if n is odd, and $\inf_{i_n}$ if n is even; conversely, $\overline{\Theta}_{i_n}$ denotes $\inf_{i_n}$ if n is odd, and $\sup_{i_n}$ if n is odd.

7.1.5   Computable Real Functions

Assume that $f : \mathbb{R} \to \mathbb{R}$ is a real function. We say that f is computable if there is a Type-2 machine that takes a ϱ-name of a real number $x \in \mathrm{dom}(f)$ as input and produces as output the ϱ-name of a real number y, which is the value of $f(x)$. Clearly, functions with n arguments can be computed by a Type-2 machine with n input tapes. The following statement is the main result of the Type-2 theory of effectivity.

Theorem 7.1.3 *Every ϱ-computable real function is continuous with respect to the real-line topology $\tau_{\mathbb{R}}$.*

---

1. $\langle i, j \rangle = \frac{1}{2}(i + j)(i + j + 1) + j$ is the Cantor pairing function. For all $i, j, k \in \mathbb{N}$ it holds that $\langle i, j, k \rangle = \langle i, \langle j, k \rangle \rangle$.

It is interesting to note that a number of functions that can be easily defined are not ϱ-computable, since they are not continuous. Although this restriction can be removed, we will not discuss this issue here. The interested reader should consult Weihrauch's monograph [219]. Let us now see which real functions are computable:

(i) $(x_1, \ldots, x_n) \mapsto c$, where $c \in \mathbb{R}$ is computable real number,

(ii) $(x_1, \ldots, x_n) \mapsto x_i$, where $1 \leq i \leq n$,

(iii) $x \mapsto -x$,

(iv) $(x_1, x_2) \mapsto x_1 + x_2$,

(v) $(x_1, x_2) \mapsto x_1 \cdot x_2$,

(vi) $x \mapsto 1 \mathbin{/} x$ for $x \neq 0$,

(vii) $(x_1, x_2) \mapsto \min(x_1, x_2)$,

(viii) $(x_1, x_2) \mapsto \max(x_1, x_2)$,

(ix) $x \mapsto |x|$,

(x) $(i, x) \mapsto x^i$, for all $i \in \mathbb{N}$ and all $x \in \mathbb{R}$; by convention $0^0 = 1$,

(xi) every polynomial in n variables with computable coefficients.

If we have two computable real functions, then their composition is also a computable function. In addition, there are a number of derived function operations that yield computable functions when fed with computable functions. In particular, if $f, g : \mathbb{R}^n \to \mathbb{R}$ are computable functions, then $x \mapsto a \cdot f(x)$ (if the real number a is computable), $x \mapsto f(x) + g(x)$, $x \mapsto f(x) \cdot g(x)$, $x \mapsto \max\{f(x), g(x)\}$, $x \mapsto \min\{f(x), g(x)\}$, and $x \mapsto 1 \mathbin{/} f(x)$ are computable functions.

Previously, it was stated that only continuous functions are computable. However, Martin Ziegler [233, 235] shows how it is possible to overcome this restriction and make computable noncontinuous functions. The key to Ziegler's solution is nondeterminism: any nondeterministic Turing machine can be simulated by a deterministic one since the choices are finitely many, but in the case of a Type-2 machine it is impossible to simulate a nondeterministic machine by a deterministic one, since both machines deal with infinite strings.

Definition 7.1.8 Assume that A and B are two uncountable sets whose representations are $\alpha : \Sigma^\omega \to A$ and $\beta : \Sigma^\omega \to B$, respectively. Also, assume that $f : A \to B$ is a function. Then f is *nondeterministically $(\alpha \to \beta)$-computable* if there is some nondeterministic one-way machine with the following characteristics:

- it has as input an α-name (i.e., given $a \in A$, there is an α-name x such that $\alpha(x) = a$), and

- it computes and consequently outputs a β-name for $b = f(a)$.

As in the deterministic case, in the nondeterministic case the composition of two computable functions is a computable function.

Lemma 7.1.3 *Suppose that the function* $f : A \to B$ *is nondeterministically* $(\alpha \to \beta)$-*computable and the function* $g : B \to C$ *is nondeterministically* $(\beta \to \gamma)$-*computable, then their composition* $g \circ f : A \to C$ *is non-deterministically* $(\alpha \to \gamma)$-*computable.*

7.2 Indeterministic Multihead Type-2 Machines

A typical Type-2 machine manipulates strings consisting of symbols drawn from arbitrary alphabets, which are representations of real numbers. However, as we have already noted above, this representation is not unique (i.e., more than one string may be the name of a real number). Clearly, this implies that the various properties of the numbers represented may not be evident. On the other hand, it is quite desirable to be able to define the computability of real functions by considering an embedding of real numbers into the set of infinite strings on which a Type-2 machine operates. This approach has been considered by Hideki Tsuiki [205]. In particular, Tsuiki presents an embedding that is called *Gray code* embedding, which is yet another binary expansion of real numbers. Using this method, any real number x is represented as an infinite string of ones and zeros interspersed with at most one $\perp$ symbol (in this case pronounced *indefiniteness*). However, a sequential access machine cannot manipulate strings containing the $\perp$ symbol. A way out is to have two scanning heads on a single tape and to allow indeterministic behavior. The resulting machines are called, quite naturally, *indeterministic multihead Type-2* machines.

Binary reflected Gray code, or simply Gray code, is a binary encoding of natural numbers. It is easy to get the Gray code of a number once we have at our disposal the ordinary binary representation of the number. In particular, if s is a list containing the digits of the binary representation of a natural number n, then we can define a Haskell function that does the job as follows:[2]

```
convert s = map xor (zip s (0:s))
```

---

2. Haskell is a standardized purely functional programming language featuring static typing, higher-order functions, polymorphism, type classes, and monadic effects, which was named after the logician Haskell Brooks Curry (see http://www.haskell.org for more information).

The function xor implementing the "eXclusive OR" operator can be defined in the following way:

$$xor\ (0,\ 0) = 0$$
$$xor\ (0,\ 1) = 1$$
$$xor\ (1,\ 0) = 1$$
$$xor\ (1,\ 1) = 0$$

Since a real number is an infinite list of binary digits, one can apply the function defined above to get the Gray code of a real number. To overcome the problem of multiple sequences representing the same number, the modified Gray code expansion has been defined.

Definition 7.2.1 The *Gray code embedding* of $\mathscr{I} = (0, 1)$ is an injective function $G : \mathscr{I} \rightarrow \Sigma^{\omega}_{\perp,1}$, where $\Sigma^{\omega}_{\perp,1}$ is the set of infinite strings over Σ in which the indefiniteness symbol may appear at most one time.[3] More specifically, the function G maps a real number x belonging to $\mathscr{I}$ to an infinite sequence $a_0 a_1 \dots$ using the following rule: if there is an odd number m such that $m \times 2^{-i} - 2^{-(i+1)} < x < m \times 2^{-i} + 2^{-(i+1)}$, then $a_i = 1$; if there is an even m such that the previous relation holds, then $a_i = 0$; and if $x = m \times 2^{-i} - 2^{-(i+1)}$ for some integer m, then $a_i = \perp$.

Definition 7.2.2 Assume that Σ and Γ are the input/output alphabet and the work-tape alphabet, respectively. Notice that $\bar{b} \in \Gamma$. An indeterministic multihead Type-2 machine with k inputs consists of

(i) k input tapes $I_1, I_2, \dots, I_k$ and one output tape O, and each tape has two scanning heads $H_1(T)$ and $H_2(T)$;

(ii) several work tapes, each tape having one scanning head;

(iii) a finite set of states $Q = \{q_0, q_1, \dots, q_m\}$, where q_0 is the initial state;

(iv) computational rules having the following form:

$$q, i_i(c_i), \dots, i_r(c_r), w_1(d_1), \dots, w_s(d_s)$$
$$\Rightarrow q', o(c), w_1'(d_1'), \dots, w_t'(d_t'), M_1(w_1''), \dots, M_u(w_u''),$$

where $q, q' \in Q$, i_j denote scanning heads of different input tapes, o is a scanning head of the output tape, w_j, w_j', and w_j'' denote scanning heads of work tapes, $c_j, c \in \Sigma$, $1 \leq j \leq r$, $d_j, d_j' \in \Gamma$, and M_l, $1 \leq l \leq u$ is either the symbol $+$ or the symbol $-$. It is important to say that each part of a rule is optional, and thus we may even have empty rules. When the machine is in state q and the scanning heads i_j and w_e sit atop cells on which the symbols c_j and d_e are printed, then the

---

3. In general, $\Sigma^{\omega}_{\perp,n}$, $n \in \mathbb{N}$, denotes the set of infinite strings drawn from the alphabet Σ, which may contain at most n copies of the indefinite symbol $\perp$.

machine enters state q' and prints the symbols c and d'_j on the cells where the scanning heads o and w'_j have stopped. Also, the scanning heads w''_j will move to the right or left depending on the value of M_j (a plus means move to the left and a minus move to the right); the scanning heads i_j and o will change their position according to the following rule. If either i_j or o is the first of the two scanning heads, then it takes the place of the second scanning head and the second one moves to the next cell (i.e., to the right); otherwise, the position of the first scanning head remains the same and the second scanning head moves to the cell next to the first one.

We add that initially the output tape is filled with $\perp$'s and the work tapes with $\flat$'s, the scanning heads of the work tapes rest above the first cell, and the two scanning heads of the input/output tapes are placed above the first and the second cells, respectively. At each step of the computation an applicable rule is chosen. When more than one rule can be chosen, a rule is chosen in a random way.

Indeterministic multihead Type-2 machines compute correspondences.[4]

Definition 7.2.3 An indeterministic multihead machine with k inputs *realizes* a correspondence $F : (\Sigma^\omega_{\perp,1})^k \rightrightarrows \Sigma^\omega_{\perp,1}$ if when the input tapes are filled with symbols $(p_1,\ldots,p_k) \in \mathrm{dom}(F)$, all computational paths yield infinite outputs, and the set of outputs is a subset of $F(p_1,\ldots,p_k)$. So F is indeterministic multihead computable if it is realizable by some indeterministic multihead Type-2 machine.

The previous definition can be adapted to cover correspondences of the form $F : Y_1 \times \cdots \times Y_k \rightrightarrows Y_0$, where $Y_i \in \{\Sigma^*, \Sigma^\omega_{\perp,1}\}$. Naturally, the next question is, what functions are actually computable?

In the case of Type-2 machines, computable functions are necessarily continuous. Thus, this may lead one to the conclusion that something similar must hold true for this case. Indeed, computable functions are those that are continuous, not in the real-line topology but in the Scott topology (see Section D.3) induced from the poset $(\{\perp, 0, 1\}, \leq)$, where $\perp < 0 < 1$.

Although the theory discussed so far concerns the open unit interval $\mathscr{I}$, it is not difficult to extend the theory to cover the whole real line $\mathscr{R}$.

7.3 BSS-Machines

BSS-machines are a model of real-number computation named for their inventors Lenore Blum, Michael Shub, and Stephen Smale. The theory

---

4. A *correspondence* from a set A to a set B is a triple $f = (A, B, R_f)$ such that $R_f \subseteq A \times B$. A correspondence f from A to B is denoted by $f : A \rightrightarrows B$. Correspondences are also known as multivalued functions or relations.

of BSS-machines is described in [16], which is coauthored by the inventors of BSS-machines and Felipe Cucker. The main difference between BSS-machines and most of the other models of computation presented so far is the fact that BSS-machines manipulate the numbers themselves and not some representation of them. Figuratively speaking, we may say that a BBS-machine is a sort of Turing machine in which real numbers are read from, and/or written to, cells. In what follows we will discuss finite-dimensional machines over a field, (general) machines over a field, and parallel machines.

7.3.1   Finite-Dimensional Machines

In its simplest form, a BSS-machine can be thought of as a formalization of a flow chart. Instead of giving a formal definition of this simple BSS-machine, it is better first to introduce the various concepts by means of an example.

An approximation of a Julia set can be drawn on a computer monitor using the so-called *pixel game*. Roughly, a computer program scans each pixel of a computer screen, and when a pixel with coordinates (x, y) corresponding to the complex number $x + iy$ belongs to a particular prisoner-set approximation, it is painted black (see [149, p. 798] and Figure 7.2 (a) for more details). Figure 7.2 (b) depicts a general flowchart machine M "implementing" the pixel game. Let us first assume that c has a specific value (e.g., 4). Machine M has four nodes (the boxes), each of a different kind. The topmost node is an input node, which is followed by a computation node, a branch node, and an output node. In addition, the halting set of M consists of all $z \in \mathbb{C}$ that when fed to the machine do not make it loop forever (here $\mathbb{C}$ is the set of complex numbers).

Let Ω_M be the halting set of M. Then the input–output map Φ is defined on Ω_M with values in $\mathbb{C}$, that is, $\Phi : \Omega_M \to \mathbb{C}$. The flowchart M is a machine over the real numbers because the branching depends on a comparison between real numbers. Thus, one may view M as a machine that transforms a pair of real numbers to another pair of real numbers. Thus, one may say that Φ is defined on $\mathbb{R}^2$ and its values are in $\mathbb{R}^2$, that is, $\Phi : \mathbb{R}^2 \to \mathbb{R}^2$. In addition, we may consider that the "input space," "state space," and "output space" of M are each the set $\mathbb{R}^2$. In general, after making such "changes" to a flowchart machine we get a machine that is a *finite-dimensional machine* over a ring or a field (see section D.2).

Definition 7.3.1 A *finite-dimensional machine M* over a ring R, without divisors of zero, consists of a finite directed connected graph that has four different types of nodes: *input, computation, branch,* and *output*. The only input node has no incoming edges and only one outgoing edge. All other node types may have more than one incoming edge; while computation

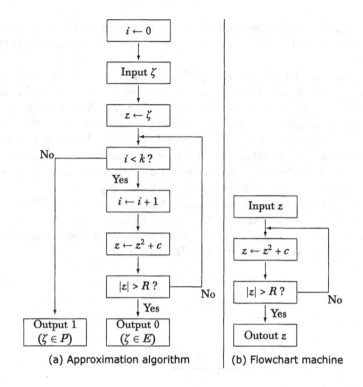

$$i \leftarrow 0$$

$$\text{Input } \zeta$$

$$z \leftarrow \zeta$$

No

$$i < k \, ?$$

Yes

$$i \leftarrow i + 1$$

$$z \leftarrow z^2 + c$$

$$|z| > R \, ?$$

No

Yes

Output 1
$(\zeta \in P)$

Output 0
$(\zeta \in E)$

(a) Approximation algorithm

$$\text{Input } z$$

$$z \leftarrow z^2 + c$$

$$|z| > R \, ?$$

No

Yes

Outout z

(b) Flowchart machine

Figure 7.2: A Julia set approximation algorithm and the corresponding flowchart machine.

nodes have only one outgoing edge, branch nodes have exactly two (a *Yes* edge and a *No* edge), and output nodes have no outgoing edges. The machine has three spaces: the *input space* $\mathcal{I}_M = R^n$, the *state space* $\mathcal{S}_M = R^m$, and the *output space* $\mathcal{O}_M = R^l$, where $m, n, l \in \mathbb{N}$. Maps of these spaces as well as *next node* assignments are associated with each node of the graph. In particular,

(i) a linear map $I : \mathcal{I}_M \to \mathcal{S}_M$ and a unique next node are associated with the input node;

(ii) a polynomial (or rational if R is a field) map $g_\eta : \mathcal{S}_M \to \mathcal{S}_M$ and unique next node β_η are associated with each computation node η;

(iii) a linear map $O : \mathcal{S}_M \to \mathcal{O}_M$ is associated with each output node.

[Recall that a polynomial (or rational) map $g : R^m \to R^m$ is given by m polynomials (or rational functions) $g_i : R^m \to R$, $i = 1, \ldots, m$. If R is a field, we assume that each g_i equals $p_i \, / \, q_i$, where p_i and q_i are polynomials.]

Previously, we stated that a BSS-machine manipulates real numbers, which implies that the machine must be able to insert these numbers into memory cells. Each machine is equipped with exactly m such cells. In particular, if a machine is in state $x = (x_1, \ldots, x_m) \in R^m$, then each x_i is a register with address i.

If we assume that R is a ring, M a machine over R, $\mathcal{N} = \{1, \ldots, N\}$ the set of nodes of M, and $\mathcal{S}$ the state space of M, then $\mathcal{N} \times \mathcal{S}$ is the *full space* of M, and H is a function from $\mathcal{N} \times \mathcal{S}$ to $\mathcal{N} \times \mathcal{S}$ that maps each pair (η, x) to the *next* pair (η', x'). The mapping is determined by the graph of M and its associated maps. The function H is called the *natural computing endomorphism*. This function is very important in the development of the theory of simple BSS-machines, since it is used to define basic notions such as the halting set Ω_M and the input-output map Φ_M.

Suppose that $x \in \mathcal{I}_M$ is some input and $\mathcal{S} \ni x^0 = I(x)$. Then the initial point $z^0 = (1, x^0)$ generates the the computation $z^0, z^1, \ldots, z^k, \ldots$. In other words, the computation generated by z^0 is identical to the orbit of z^0 generated by repeated application of H, that is,

$$z^0 = (1, x^0),$$
$$z^1 = H(z^0),$$
$$\vdots$$
$$z^k = \underbrace{H(H(H(H(\cdots z^0 \cdots))))}_{k-\text{times}}.$$

In order to make clear the notion of an orbit, let us recall that one can identify the Mandelbrot set with the recurrent equation

$$z_{n+1} = z_n^2 + z, \quad n = 0, 1, 2, \ldots,$$

where $z_0 = 0$. This particular sequence of points z_i is an orbit for each value z. In particular, z belongs to the Mandelbrot set if and only if its orbit does not tend to infinity.

Assume that the function $\pi_\mathcal{N} : \mathcal{N} \times \mathcal{S} \to \mathcal{N}$ is the projection of the full state space onto $\mathcal{N}$. Then the sequence of nodes $1, \eta^1, \ldots, \eta^k, \ldots$, where $\eta^k = \pi_\mathcal{N}(z^k)$, is the *computation path* γ_x *traversed* on input x.

A computation halts if there is a time T such that $z^T = (N, u)$ for some $u \in \mathcal{S}$. In this case, the finite sequence $z^0, \ldots, z^T$ is a halting computation. In addition, the finite sequence $1, \eta^1, \ldots, \eta^T$ of nodes is a halting path traversed by x. The halting time $T_M(x)$ is defined by

$$T_M(x) = \min\left\{ T_i \,|\, z^{T_i} = (N, u_i) \right\},$$

and from this we define

$$\Phi_M(x) = O(x^{T_M(x)}) \in \mathcal{O}_M.$$

If M does not halt on input x, and consequently, there is no such $T_M(x)$, then $\Phi_M(x)$ is undefined and we assume that $T_M(x) = \infty$. The halting set of M is defined to be the set of all inputs on which M halts, that is,

$$\Omega_M = \{x \in \mathcal{I}_M \mid T_M(x) < \infty\}.$$

Now that we have defined the basic notions associated with BSS-machines, let us see when a set is decidable.

Definition 7.3.2 A set $S \subset R^n$ is *decidable over R* if its characteristic function is computable over R; otherwise, it is called *undecidable over R*.

An interesting related question that has been put forth by Roger Penrose is whether the Mandelbrot set is decidable. Clearly, this question is strange, since decidability is closely associated with computability, and in addition, one can very easily write a computer program in almost every computer programming language to draw (approximations to) the Mandelbrot set. Quite surprisingly, it has been proved that the Mandelbrot set is undecidable.

Theorem 7.3.1 *The Mandelbrot set is not decidable over* $\mathbb{R}$ [16, p. 55].

Peter Hertling [81] presents some interesting results concerning the computability of the Mandelbrot set.

7.3.2   Machines over a Commutative Ring

Assume that R is a ring that is commutative under multiplication and has a unit element. Then we define the space R^∞ as follows:

$$R^\infty = \bigcup_{n \geq 0} R^n.$$

The space R^0 is the zero-dimensional module with just one point 0. Also, R^n, for $n > 0$, is the standard n-dimensional module over R. The space R_∞ is the *bi-infinite direct sum* space over R. This set consists of tuples of the form

$$(\ldots, x_{-2}, x_{-1}, x_0 \bullet x_1, x_2, x_3, \ldots),$$

where $x_i \in R$ for all $i \in \mathbb{Z}$, $x_k = 0$ if the absolute value of k is sufficiently large, and $\bullet$ is a distinguished marker between x_0 and x_1. The space R_∞ is equipped with two natural shift operations: the shift left operation σ_l and the shift right operator σ_r. These operations are defined as follows:

$$\sigma_l(x)_i = x_{i+1}, \qquad \sigma_r(x)_i = x_{i-1}.$$

The shift left operation shifts each element of the sequence x one coordinate to the left; shift right is the inverse operation. Let us now define machines over R.

Definition 7.3.3 A machine M over R is a finite-dimensional machine that has in addition a set Σ_M of *shift* nodes with associated maps. Also, R^∞ is both its input and output space (i.e., $\mathcal{I}_M = R^\infty$ and $\mathcal{O}_M = R^\infty$), and R_∞ is its state space (i.e., $\mathcal{S}_M = R_\infty$).

A shift node is basically a computation node that might have several incoming edges and one outgoing edge. Each shift node η is associated with a map $g_\eta \in \{\sigma_l, \sigma_r\}$.

It is not difficult to define a probabilistic version of machines over a ring. Indeed, all we need is an additional type of node and a mechanism to implement it.

Definition 7.3.4 A probabilistic machine M over R is a machine over R with an additional type of node, which is called *probabilistic*. Such nodes have two next nodes and no associated maps. When a computation reaches a probabilistic node, a "lottery is drawn" to choose the next node: the lottery draws one of two numbers, which correspond to the next nodes.

Let us now see what it means for a set to be decidable by a probabilistic machine over a ring.

Definition 7.3.5 Assume that $S \subseteq R^\infty$. Then the *error probability* of a probabilistic machine M with respect to S is the function $e_M : R^\infty \to \mathbb{R}$ defined by

$$e_M(x) = \Pr(M \text{ accepts } x \text{ and } x \notin S) + \Pr(M \text{ rejects } x \text{ and } x \in S),$$

where $\Pr(E)$ denotes the probability associated with event E.

7.3.3   Parallel Machines

A good number of problems have solutions that are inherently parallel. This simply means that they can be solved by machines with more than one processor. To put it simply, a parallel BSS-machine is a machine that has two or more processors that operate in a *synchronous* manner. Thus, in order to define parallel machines we need first to define processors.

Definition 7.3.6 A *processor* M is a finite directed, connected graph that has nodes of the following types: input, output, integral branch, real branch, computation, communication, shift, and halt. In addition, a processor has a state space $\mathcal{S}_M = \mathbb{Z}^k \times \mathbb{R}_\infty$, $k \in \mathbb{N}$, and a linear projection $\pi_M : \mathbb{Z}^k \to \mathbb{Z}$. By convention, $\mathbb{Z}^k$ and $\mathbb{R}_\infty$ are denoted by $\mathcal{S}_M^{\mathbb{Z}}$ and $\mathcal{S}_M^{\mathbb{R}}$, respectively.

As in the case of ordinary machines, each node of a processor is associated with maps and next nodes. In particular, the unique input node has no incoming edges and only one outgoing edge; the unique output node and any halt node have no outgoing edges. All other nodes may have several incoming edges and one outgoing edge, except the branch nodes, which have two outgoing edges. The maps that are associated each node type are described below:

(i) A computation node η has an associated map $(z,y) \mapsto (g_{\mathbb{Z},\eta}(z), g_{\mathbb{R},\eta}(y))$, where $g_{\mathbb{Z},\eta}$ is an integer polynomial and $g_{\mathbb{R},\eta}$ is a rational map.

(ii) An integral branch node has an associated polynomial function h_η: $\mathbb{Z}^\eta \to \mathbb{Z}$. The next nodes β_η^- and β_η^+ are associated with h_η's negative and nonnegative values, respectively. Similarly, a real branch node has an associated rational function $h_\eta : \mathbb{R}_\infty \to \mathbb{R}$, and the corresponding next nodes are associated with the corresponding values of h_η.

(iii) A shift node η is associated with a map $g_\eta : S_M^{\mathbb{R}} \to S_M^{\mathbb{R}}$.

(iv) A halt node has no next node and does not alter the current state.

Now we are ready to define parallel machines.

Definition 7.3.7 A *parallel machine* P is a sequence of identical processors M_i that comes with an associated activation function $p : \mathbb{N} \to \mathbb{N}$, an input space $\mathcal{I}_P = \mathbb{R}^\infty$, an output space $\mathcal{O}_P = \mathbb{R}^\infty$, and a state space $S_P = \cup_{h=1}^\infty (S_M)^h$. In addition, the input node is associated with a map $I_P : \mathcal{I}_P \to S_P$ and the output node has an associated function $O_P : S_P \to \mathcal{O}_P$.

7.4 Real-Number Random-Access Machines

As noted on page 15, a random-access machine is an alternative, more computer-oriented, formulation of the classical model of computation. This remark has prompted researchers in the area of real-number computation to try to define the analogues of random-access machines in this expanded framework. Clearly, a BSS-machine is a form of real-number random-access machine. Since it is not directly derived from the random-access machine model, however, we have decided not to discuss it alongside real random-access machines.

Vasco Brattka and Peter Hertling [22] have presented a *feasible* random-access machine without the drawbacks of other related approaches to the *design* of real random-access machines. In particular, this model takes into account the fact that common *representations* of real numbers are infinite in length (e.g., they may have an infinite number of digits),[5] and has been

---

5. In general, this is not true. For instance, Yaroslav Sergeyev [177] presents a way to represent real numbers with finite means.

Name	Notation	Cost	Comment
Assignment of constants	$n_i := m$	1	$m \in \mathbb{N}$
	$r_i := q$	1	$q \in \mathbb{Q}$
Simple copy command	$n_i := n_j$	$\ell(n_j)$	
	$r_i := r_j$	$\ell(r_j)$	
Mixed copy command	$r_i := n_j$	$\ell(n_j)$	
	$n_i := \lfloor r_j \rfloor_{n_k}$	$\ell(r_j, n_k)$	
Natural arithm. operat.	$n_i := n_j \otimes n_k$	$\ell(n_j, n_k)$	$\otimes \in \{+, \div, *, /, \%\}$
Real arithm. operations	$r_i := r_j \otimes r_k$	$\ell(r_j, r_k)$	$\otimes \in \{+, -, *\}$
	$r_i := r_j / r_k$	$\ell(r_j, 1/r_k)$	
Comparison operations	$n_i = n_j$	$\ell(n_i, n_j)$	
	$n_1 < n_j$	$\ell(n_i, n_j)$	
	$r_i <_{n_k} r_j$	$\ell(r_i, r_j, n_k)$	

Table 7.1: Operations and their costs, where ℓ is the maximum of the lengths of the binary representations of the integer part of its arguments, % is the modulus operator, and $\lfloor x \rfloor_k$ is the finite-precision staircase operation.

designed to provide a meaningful comparison operator. But first, we need a few auxiliary definitions.

The finite-precision staircase operation is defined as follows:

$$\lfloor x \rfloor_k \stackrel{\text{def}}{=} \left\{ n \in \mathbb{N} \mid n - \frac{1}{k+1} < x < n+1 \right\} \cup \left\{ 0 \mid x < 0 \right\}, \quad \forall x \in \mathbb{R}.$$

The result of the finite-precision staircase operation is not always unique. Thus, computations may become indeterministic. Also, the operator $\dot{-}$ is defined as follows:

$$x \dot{-} y = \begin{cases} x - y & \text{if } x \geq y, \\ 0 & \text{if } x \leq y. \end{cases}$$

We are now ready to define these new conceptual machines.

Definition 7.4.1 A *real-number random-access machine* is a triple $M = (X, Y, F)$, where X and Y denote the *input* space and *output* space, respectively, and F is a finite *flowchart* whose nodes are labeled by a finite set $Q \subseteq \mathbb{N}$ that necessarily contains zero, which is reserved as a label for the *initial node*. The input and output spaces are finite products of the sets $\mathbb{N}$ and $\mathbb{R}$. Each node of F is associated with an operation from Table 7.1 and a finite list of successor nodes. When the operation is a comparison, there are two successor nodes. In addition, the *final* node has no successor node. In all other cases, a node has exactly one successor node.

It should be noted that most of the operators of Table 7.1 can be defined in terms of the most "elementary" ones. For example, here is how one can define the real-number comparison operator:

$$(r_i <_{n_k} r_j) = \left(\lfloor 1 + r_i - r_j \rfloor_{n_k} = 0 \right).$$

Let us now describe how a computation proceeds. Like a BSS-machine, the machine begins its operation from the start node, while the input is stored in the respective input registers. It then follows a computation path that is specified by F. Since for one input there may be several computational paths, the outcome of some computation cannot be predicted. Thus, it is possible that identical input data may yield quite different output data. Division by zero crashes the machine and so it yields no output. When a final state is reached, the computation stops and the result of the computation is stored in the output registers.

7.5 Recursion Theory on the Real Numbers

The arithmetic hierarchy presented in Section 7.1.4 is not the only way to classify real numbers and functions according to their "incomputability." Indeed, Christopher Moore [136] has defined recursive functions on the real numbers in the spirit of the corresponding definitions for natural numbers (see Section 2.2). These numbers and functions are computable by conceptual analog machines operating in continuous time (see Chapter 9 for an overview of analog (hyper-)computation).

As in the case for natural numbers, we first need to define our function builders in order to define the notion of recursive function. The function builders are completely analogous to their classical counterparts. In particular, provided that f and g are already defined, we define the following function builders:

(i) *Composition*:

$$h(x_1, \ldots, x_n) = f(g(x_1, \ldots, x_n)).$$

(ii) *Differential recursion*:

$$h(x_1, \ldots, x_n, 0) = f(x_1, \ldots, x_n),$$

$$\frac{\partial}{\partial y} h(x_1, \ldots, x_n, y) = g(x_1, \ldots, x_n, y, h(x_1, \ldots, x_n, y)).$$

These two equations imply that $h = f$ when $y = 0$; otherwise, the partial derivative of h with respect to y depends on $h, y,$ and $x_1, \ldots, x_n$. The previous equations can be presented more compactly in the following form:

$$h(x_1, \ldots, x_n, y) = f(x_1, \ldots, x_n) + \int_0^y g(x_1, \ldots, x_n, y', h(x_1, \ldots, x_n, y')) dy'.$$

Notice that h is defined only when a finite and unique solution of the previous integral equation exists.

(iii) μ-recursion:

$$h(x_1,\ldots,x_n) = \mu_y f(x_1,\ldots,x_n,y) = \inf\{\, y \mid f(x_1,\ldots,x_n,y) = 0\}.$$

Based on these definitions, we define $\mathbb{R}$-recursion.

Definition 7.5.1 A function $h : \mathbb{R}^n \to \mathbb{R}^m$ is termed $\mathbb{R}$-recursive if it can be generated from the constants 0 and 1 with the function builders defined above.

A number of common functions are $\mathbb{R}$-recursive. Indeed, it can be proved that the following functions are $\mathbb{R}$-recursive:

 (i) addition: $f(x,y) = x + y$;

 (ii) multiplication: $f(x,y) = xy$;

 (iii) reciprocal: $f(x) = 1 \,/\, x$;

 (iv) division: $f(x,y) = x \,/\, y$;

 (v) exponentiation: $f(x) = e^x$;

 (vi) natural logarithm: $f(x) = \ln x$;

(vii) power function: $f(x,y) = x^y$;

(viii) trigonometric functions: $\sin x$, $\cos x$, and $\tan x$;

 (ix) modulus function: $x \bmod y$;

 (x) Kronecker's δ-function: $\delta(x) = 1$ if $x = 0$ and 0 otherwise;

 (xi) the function returning the absolute value: $|x|$;

(xii) the step function: $\Theta(x) = 1$ if $x \geq 0$ and 0 if $x < 0$;

(xiii) constants: -1, e, and π.

Clearly, the constants -1, e, and π are not functions, but they are computable in the sense of the following definition.

Definition 7.5.2 Suppose that x is a real number such that $x = g(0)$, where g is a $\mathbb{R}$-recursive function. Then x is a $\mathbb{R}$-recursive number.

Obviously, when x equals $g(y)$, it is also $\mathbb{R}$-recursive provided that both g and y are $\mathbb{R}$-recursive, since if $y = h(0)$ for some $\mathbb{R}$-recursive h, then $x = g(h(0))$, and so x is $\mathbb{R}$-recursive by closure under composition.

The set $\mathscr{K}$ of all $\mathbb{R}$-recursive numbers includes at least the rational numbers (i.e., $\mathbb{Q} \subset \mathscr{K}$, and since $\mathbb{Z} \subset \mathbb{Q}$, it follows that $\mathbb{Z} \subset \mathscr{K}$) and the algebraic numbers (i.e., numbers that are roots of some polynomial equation $a_n x^n + a_{n-1} x^{n-1} + \cdots + a_1 x + a_0 = 0$, where $a_i \in \mathbb{Z}$).

Assume that $s(x_1, \ldots, x_m)$ is an $\mathbb{R}$-recursive mathematical expression. Then we define its μ-number with respect to x_i, denoted by $M_{x_i}(s)$, as follows:

- $M_x(0) = M_x(1) = M_x(-1) = 0$,

- $M_x(h(g_1, g_2, \ldots)) = \max_i \left\{ M_{x_i}(h) + M_x(g_i) \right\}$,

- $M_x \left(h = f + \int_0^y g(x_1, \ldots, x_n, y', h) dy' \right) = \max \left\{ M_x(f), M_x(g), M_h(g) \right\}$,

- $M_y \left(h = f + \int_0^y g(x_1, \ldots, x_n, y', h) dy' \right) = \max \left\{ M_{y'}(g), M_h(g) \right\}$,

- $M_x(\mu_y f(x_1, \ldots, x_n, y)) = \max \left\{ M_x(f), M_y(f) \right\} + 1$.

To put it simply, $M_x(s)$ is the depth of nested μ's surrounding x in s. For any $\mathbb{R}$-recursive function h we define $M(h) = \max_i M_{x_i}(s)$ for all expressions s that define h. The μ-hierarchy is built from the sets $M_i = \{h|\ M(h) \le i\}$, and the set of all $\mathbb{R}$-recursive functions is the union $\cup_i M_i$. The following result makes clear the relationship between the arithmetic hierarchy and the μ-hierarchy.

Proposition 7.5.1 *It holds that $\Delta_i^0 \subset M_{2i}$ and $\Pi_i^0 \subset M_{2i+1}$ for all $i > 0$.*

Similar results also hold for the analytical hierarchy.

Proposition 7.5.2 *It holds that $\Delta_i^1 \subset M_{3+4i}$ and $\Pi_i^1 \subset M_{3+4i}$ for all $i > 0$.*

A corollary of Proposition 7.5.1 is that $\mathscr{K}$ contains many real numbers that are not Turing-computable. In addition, it follows from the previous result that the hyperarithmetic sets as well as all arithmetic sets are contained in M_7.

When a function is part of a step of a ladder of some computational hierarchy, this simply means that it can be computed by a class of (real or merely conceptual) computing devices. Functions that are $\mathbb{R}$-recursive can be computed by Claude Elwood Shannon's General Purpose Analog Computer (GPAC), which is a mathematical model of the differential analyzer that was invented by Vannevar Bush in 1927 (see Section 9.2). Moore

believes that there are a number of issues that make the GPAC an imprac-
tical model of computation. First of all, he assumes that time is granular,
and this is something that prohibits the GPAC from doing accurate cal-
culations. However, Moore's assumption is countered by recent scientific
evidence (for instance, see the discussion at the end of Section 8.3). Another problem is that quantum effects and noise may interfere with the
machine's operation. Although it is not a trivial task to tackle these problems, still they do not make the realization of the GPAC impossible. It is
important to state that the existence of the GPAC would pose a threat to
the validity of the Church-Turing thesis.

VIII. Relativistic and Quantum Hypercomputation

The theory of infinite-time Turing machines is practically useless unless it is possible to perform a supertask. If we can find ways to perform supertasks, we have in our hands a *real* tool to study a particular form of hypercomputation. In this chapter, I present a number of approaches to the problem of hypercomputation via supertasks as well as a short discussion of the physical limits of computation. In addition, I describe quantum adiabatic computing, a special form of quantum computation that is claimed to lead to hypercomputation.

8.1 Supertasks in Relativistic Spacetimes

John Earman [54] has given an account of the feasibility of supertasks in the framework of the general theory of relativity. In particular, he presents a number of spacetimes (see Definition D.5.2) that provide ways for carrying out supertasks, or more precisely, the functional equivalents of supertasks. Generally speaking, we have two parties that operate in such a spacetime. The first party has available an infinite amount of time, while the second party can use only a finite amount of time and is so situated that its past light cone[1] contains the entire world line[2] of the first party. Since the first party has no time limits, it can, for instance, check the digits of the number π to see whether they are random and communicate the result to the second party. Clearly, this is a supertask. Now, the second party should be able to know whether the digits of π are random in a finite amount of time, but it has a price to pay: to surrender to the effects of unbounded forces that will definitely end its life. Certainly, there are ways to overcome

---

1. A light cone is a double cone centered at each event E in spacetime. The future light cone consists of all the paths of light that begin at E and travel into the future, while the past light cone consists of all the paths of light that stop at E and come from the past.
2. The world line of an object is the sequence of spacetime events corresponding to the history of the object. World lines are timelike curves in spacetime.

such "difficulties" by exploiting spacetimes with unusual properties. Let us now examine these exotic spacetimes and problems associated with them.

Even those whose exposure to relativity is from popular science believe that supertasks are physically impossible, mainly because there is a limit to the speed with which things can move in the universe. However, the same theory that sets an upper limit on the speed of information transmission is based on the assumption that time is relative to the observer. This feature of any relativistic spacetime can be exploited in certain spacetimes to achieve time dilation in order to perform supertasks. Indeed, Itamar Pitowsky was the first thinker to set up a thought experiment in order to demonstrate how we can perform supertasks [155].

Suppose that there are no restrictions on the size of the computation space and so only time is of importance. Assume that Angelene is a mathematician obsessed with Ludwig Josef Johann Wittgenstein's problem: are there three consecutive 7's in the decimal expansion of π? In order to find the answer to this question, she travels to a satellite orbiting the Earth. The satellite has such a powerful engine that its instantaneous tangential velocity is $v(t) = c\sqrt{1 - e^{-2t}}$, where t is time in Earth's frame and c is the speed of light. In addition, the engine keeps the satellite in a fixed orbit. Let us denote by τ the satellite's local time; then $d\tau = e^{-t}dt$. Since $\int_0^\infty e^{-t}dt = 1$, we have that when one second passes on the satellite, an infinite amount of time has passed on Earth. While Angelene orbits the planet on the satellite, her students and colleagues are examining the decimal expansion of π to see whether it has three consecutive 7's. When these people get old, they ask their students and young colleagues to continue their work, and so on. If three consecutive 7's are encountered in the decimal expansion of π, the good news is transmitted to the satellite. Angelene has just one second to hit the brakes and return safely home. If no message arrives within one second, then Angelene will disintegrate, knowing that there are no three consecutive 7's in the decimal expansion of π. Formally, the previous story can be described as follows.

Definition 8.1.1 A pair $(\mathcal{M}, \mathbf{g})$, where $\mathcal{M}$ is a connected four-dimensional Hausdorff C^∞ manifold and $\mathbf{g}$ is a Lorentz metric, is a *Pitowsky spacetime* if there are future-directed timelike half-curves $\gamma_1, \gamma_2 \in \mathcal{M}$ such that $\int_{\gamma_1} d\tau = \infty$, $\int_{\gamma_2} d\tau < \infty$, and $\gamma_1 \subset I^-(\gamma_2)$, where $I^-(\gamma_2)$ denotes the past set (i.e., the collection of all past events of γ_2) [54].

Here γ_2 corresponds to Angelene and γ_1 to her colleagues and students. Pitowsky believes that his story is impossible simply because the operations described, demand an infinite computational space. Strictly speaking, this is not true, since it has been shown that it is possible to compute just the nth digit of many transcendentals in almost linear time and logarithmic space [5]. Also, there are spacetimes with infinite mass and space. In addition, Earman has spotted two flaws in Pitowsky's story. First of all, the magnitude of the acceleration that Angelene undergoes is $e^t / \sqrt{1 - e^{-2t}}$, which "blows up rapidly." Practically, this means that Angelene will be quickly crushed by enormous g-forces. Consequently, it is possible that she will never know whether there are three consecutive 7's in the decimal expansion of the number π even if such a sequence exists. The second problem is related to the "fact" that somehow Angelene in the end will know whether the answer to her question is affirmative or negative. In case it is affirmative, she will receive a message announcing that three consecutive 7's have been found in the decimal expansion of π. Otherwise, she will never receive any message. However, for Angelene it is not clear what the absence of a message means. It is reasonable for her to believe that the message she is eagerly awaiting may not yet have arrived. Nevertheless, it is equally reasonable for Angelene to believe that her colleagues have not found three consecutive 7's in the decimal expansion of π. Thus, at no definite moment in her life does Angelene know the answer to Wittgenstein's problem.

David Malament and Mark Hogarth, in order to solve the problems in Pitowsky's setup, have proposed an alternative spacetime structure.

Definition 8.1.2 A pair $(\mathcal{M}, g)$, where $\mathcal{M}$ is a connected four-dimensional Hausdorff C^∞ manifold and g is a Lorentz metric, is a Malament–Hogarth spacetime if there are a timelike half-curve $\gamma_1 \subset \mathcal{M}$ and a point $p \in \mathcal{M}$ such that $\int_{\gamma_1} d\tau = \infty$ and $\gamma_1 \subset I^-(p)$.

It is clear that in this case, our fictitious mathematician plays no direct role, since there is no reference to γ_2. In this spacetime, there is a future-directed timelike curve γ_2 stretching from a point q of the chronological past of p (i.e., $q \in I^-(p)$) to p. In other words, $\int_{\gamma_s(q,p)} d\tau < \infty$. This means that if Angelene's colleagues and students proceed as before to check out her favorite problem, then she will know for sure that if at event p she has received no message from her colleagues and students, then there are no three consecutive 7's in the decimal expansion of π. As Earman notes in [54], this setting can be used to "effectively decide" membership in a recursively enumerable but nonrecursive set of integers. Naturally, one may wonder why supertasks can be performed in a Malament–Hogarth spacetime. The answer lies in the following result.

Lemma 8.1.1 *A Malament–Hogarth spacetime is not globally hyperbolic.*

This simply means that in a Malament–Hogarth spacetime, events are not related to each other by cause and effect (i.e., Laplace's demon does not live there). Let us now see how we can construct a hypermachine $\mathcal{H}$ that can solve the halting problem in a Malament–Hogarth spacetime.

The construction is due to Oron Shagrir and Itamar Pitowsky [178]. Machine $\mathcal{H}$ consists of a pair of communicating standard computers, which we will denote by C_A and C_B. Machine C_B moves along γ_1, and C_A along a future-directed timelike curve joining the initial point q of γ_1 with p. Machine C_A travels from q to p in finite time, say one minute, while machine C_B moves along γ_1 in infinite time. Machine $\mathscr{H}$ operates as follows: initially, C_A takes as input a number $n \in \mathbb{N}$, which is emitted to C_B with a signal. Machine C_B is a universal machine that computes the Turing-computable function $f(n)$ that returns what the nth Turing machine computes with input the number n provided that this machine halts; otherwise, it returns no value. Suppose that C_B halts. Then it will send a message back to C_A, or else it never sends a message. If C_A receives no message, after, say, one minute, while it is traveling it will print out "yes;" otherwise it will print out "no." Thus, $\mathscr{H}$ computes the following function:

$$h(n) = \begin{cases} 0, & \text{if } f(n) \text{ is undefined,} \\ 1, & \text{otherwise.} \end{cases}$$

Function h is clearly noncomputable, but it is hypercomputable. In other words, $\mathscr{H}$ is a hypermachine. In spite of this, there are objections to the feasibility of this construction.

First of all, one should note that C_B demands infinite memory, which renders $\mathscr{H}$ a nonphysical device. There are two responses to this objection: first one should note that even a Turing machine demands infinite memory, and second, Reissner–Nordström spacetimes, which are specialized Malament–Hogarth spacetimes [54], are spatially infinite and allow the construction of $\mathscr{H}$. A second objection concerns the computational nature of $\mathscr{H}$: one may argue that this is not a computer at all, since it only delivers the values of h, but it does not compute them. However, this objection is based on the fact the C_B may never halt, and thus it cannot be classified as a machine performing a computational task, at least in the classical sense of the word. Clearly, in an expanded theory of computation this is not correct. After all, one may consider that C_B is an infinite-time Turing machine. According to the third objection, $\mathscr{H}$ is indeed a computer, but it is incapable of computing the function h. For instance, when the machine prints 0, then C_B ceases to exist, and so $\mathscr{H}$ cannot proceed with another computation. In view of this, $\mathscr{H}$ may not be able to compute h, but it does something that no Turing machine is able to do: it prints out the halting status of an arbitrary but fixed machine.

8.2 SAD Machines

Mark Hogarth [85, 86] has presented his SAD machines and their computational power. His construction is based on the notion of a *past temporal string*, or just *string*. A string is formed from a collection of nonintersecting open regions O_i that belong to a spacetime $(\mathcal{M}, \mathbf{g})$. The open regions O_i have the following properties:

(i) for all i, $O_i \subset I^-(O_{i+1})$, and

(ii) there is a point $q \in \mathscr{M}$ such that for all i, $O_i \subset I^-(q)$.

The upper left part of Figure 8.1 shows a schematic representation of a string.

Strings make it possible to construct complex spacetimes. In particular, the *arithmetic-sentence-deciding spacetimes of order n*, or SAD_n for short, form a hierarchy of spacetimes that is inductively defined as follows.

Definition 8.2.1 If a spacetime $(\mathscr{M}, g)$ is a Malament–Hogarth spacetime, then it is a SAD_1 spacetime. If a spacetime $(\mathscr{M}, g)$ admits strings of SAD_{n-1} spacetimes, then it is a SAD_n spacetime.

In general, a SAD_n spacetime is a spacetime that contains a string of SAD_{n-1} spacetimes. In this hierarchy of spacetimes, it is feasible to construct a corresponding hierarchy of *arithmetic-sentence-deciding computers of order n*, or just SAD_n. On the bottom of the hierarchy lies the finite Turing machine (FTM), which is an ordinary Turing machine that exists for only a finite time. Next in the hierarchy lies the ordinary Turing machine (OTM). Then we have the sequence of SAD_i machines. And on the top of the hierarchy lies the *arithmetic-deciding computer*, or just AD. Figure 8.1 shows a schematic representation of these computers. Notice that in these figures a lower-filled dot represents an initial event, an upper-filled dot represents a solution event (i.e., the latest point where the machine has to deliver the result or no-result of its computation, and it this point where the machine user, i.e., the distant observer, stays), a line represents a "hardware" world line, an empty dot represents "the edge of spacetime at infinity" (e.g., a point at infinity in the sense of compactification), and three dots represent an infinite sequence of hardware boxes. Thus, in the FTM diagram a simple Turing machine exists for a finite amount of time, but it never reaches a specified solution event. The situation is considerably different for the OTM diagram where the Turing machine surpasses the solution event. In the case of SAD_1 the whole world line of the Turing machine lies below the solution event, while the machine never stops, thus allowing it to decide "simple" relations, as we will see later on. A SAD_2 machine is a string of SAD_1 machines, while the AD machine is a string of increasingly more powerful SAD machines.

Let us now state a few results that indicate the power of SAD machines.

Lemma 8.2.1 *Some SAD_1 machine can decide any relation of the form either $S(z) = \exists x R(x, z)$ or $S(z) = \forall x R(x, z)$, where R is recursive.*

The previous result can be extended as follows. Assume that $R(x_1, x_2, x_3)$ is a recursive relation. Then either

$$S_2(x_3) = \forall x_1 \exists x_2 R(x_1, x_2, x_3) \quad \text{or} \quad S_2'(x_3) = \exists x_1 \forall x_2 R(x_1, x_2, x_3)$$

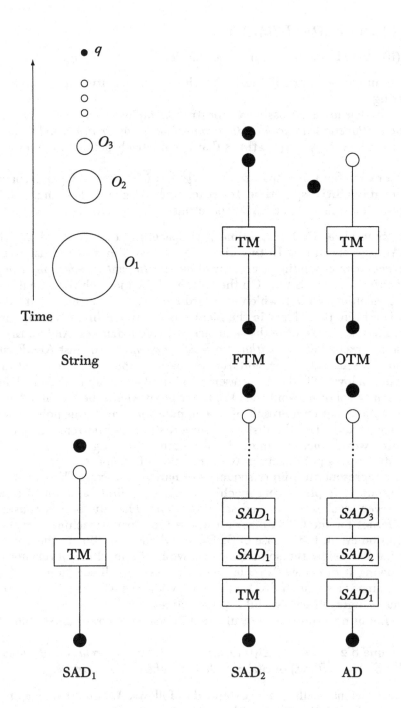

Figure 8.1: A string and Hogarth schemas of some Turing machine based computers.

is decidable by some SAD_2 machine. More generally, if $R(x_1, \ldots, x_{n+1})$ is a recursive relation, then either

$$S_{n+1}(x_{n+1}) = \forall x_1 \exists x_2 \cdots \forall x_{n-1} \exists x_n R(x_1, \ldots, x_{n+1})$$

or

$$S'_{n+1}(x_{n+1}) = \exists x_1 \forall x_2 \cdots \exists x_{n-1} \forall x_n R(x_1, \ldots, x_{n+1})$$

is decidable by some SAD_n machine. Even more generally, one can prove the following.

Proposition 8.2.1 *Arithmetic is decidable by the* AD *machine.*

Since AD can compute exactly $\aleph_0$ functions, there are functions that this machine cannot compute. The following fully characterizes the computational power of SAD_n machines.

Proposition 8.2.2 SAD_n *can decide* $\Pi_n^0 \cup \Sigma_n^0$ *but not* $\Pi_{n+1}^0 \cup \Sigma_{n+1}^0$.

Thus far, I have presented spacetimes and machines that operate in these particular spacetimes. Clearly, the important question is whether these spacetimes are physically possible and physically realistic. As has been noted above, a Reissner-Nordström spacetime is actually a Malament-Hogarth spacetime. This implies that at least some Malament-Hogarth spacetimes are physically possible. In addition, in Earman's own words "Malament-Hogarth spacetimes meet the (necessarily vaguer) criteria for physically realistic spacetime arenas." A serious problem with Malament-Hogarth spacetimes is that all of them violate Penrose's strong *cosmic censorship* hypothesis (i.e., the hypothesis that no singularity created by an imploding star is ever visible to any observer). In addition, there are Malament-Hogarth spacetimes that violate even the weak cosmic censorship hypothesis (i.e., the hypothesis that singularities are never "naked," that is, they do not occur unless surrounded by a shielding event horizon; this is an immaterial surface in spacetime that divides spacetime into two regions: that which can be observed, and that which cannot). There are many physicists who are convinced that the cosmic censorship conjecture is true, which makes the physical possibility of Malament-Hogarth spacetimes unlikely. However, in 1991, Stuart L. Shapiro and Saul A. Teukolsky performed computer simulations of a rotating plane of dust that indicated that general relativity allows for naked singularities (see [180] for details). Notwithstanding the validity of these computer simulations, it is possible to overcome the problem of cosmic censorship, and indeed, this is the subject of the next section.

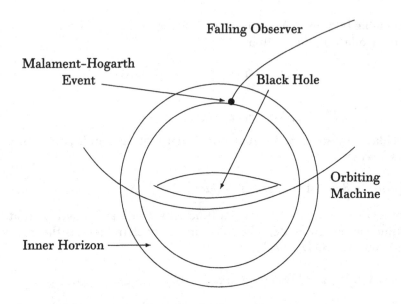

Figure 8.2: The three-dimensional setup of a relativistic computer.

8.3   Supertasks near Black Holes

In 1963, Roy Kerr published a paper giving a solution of Einstein's field equations that describes every rotating black hole that can possibly exist. In general, it is believed that there are many such objects in our universe. For example, astronomers are almost certain that a massive rotating black hole of several million times the mass of our sun resides at the core of the Milky Way. Rotating black holes with no electrical charge have been dubbed *Kerr* black holes. If a Kerr black hole is charged, then it is called a *Kerr-Newman* black hole. The exterior of such a black hole forms a Kerr-Newman space-time, which is actually a Malament-Hogarth spacetime. This observation has prompted Gábor Etesi and István Németi [58] to propose the construction of a *general* computing system (i.e., a computing system that is feasible, but may not exist yet due to current technological limitations only) that can perform supertasks.

The relativistic computer $G = (\gamma_P, \gamma_O)$ operates in a vacuum Kerr space-time $(\mathcal{M}, \mathbf{g})$, where γ_P and γ_O are timelike curves around a slowly rotating Kerr black hole. In particular, γ_P is a computer traveling around the Kerr black hole in a stable circular orbit in the equatorial plane, and γ_O is a freely falling observer that crosses the outer event horizon of the black hole and enters the inner horizon, which is not globally hyperbolic, but does not continue into the singularity (see Figure 8.2). The computer has as its sole task to check all theorems of ZFC[3] in order to see whether mathematics is consistent. Both the observer γ_O and the computing device γ_P start from the same point $q \in \mathscr{M}$. Also, the length of γ_P is infinite (i.e., $\|\gamma_P\| = \infty$), while the length of γ_O is finite (i.e., $\|\gamma_O\| < \infty$).

Assume that T is a Turing machine that enumerates all the theorems of ZFC, that is, T realizes a function

$$f_T : \mathbb{N} \to \{F \mid F \text{ is a ZFC formula}\}$$

such that the range of f_T is the set of all ZFC theorems. The computer has as a subsystem such a Turing machine. Also, the observer is accompanied by an identical Turing machine that will be used to verify the validity of any information received from γ_P. The observer departs on a journey toward the black hole, and the computer executes the following pseudocode while orbiting around the black hole:

```
i=0;
while (true) {
        Derive ith theorem from ZFC set theory;
        if (the ith theorem coincides with x ≠ x) {
                SendSignalTo(γ_O);
                break;
        }
        i++;
}
```

Suppose that at some moment the computer has found an $i \in \mathbb{N}$ such that the ith theorem of ZFC coincides with $x \neq x$. At this given moment, the computer has to send a message to the observer informing her that ZFC is inconsistent. The message has to be unique so that it cannot be confused with any other incoming signal. For example, this problem can be tackled by sending a Morse-like sequence of "short" and "long" light impulses. But let us see what is happening to the observer. She is traveling toward the black hole in order to reach the point p where the Malament-Hogarth event will take place. If the observer has reached p and she has received no message from the computer, she can be sure that ZFC is consistent. On the other hand, if she has received a message, then she is absolutely sure that ZFC is inconsistent. It is important to note that the observer never enters the black hole, so she can come back and inform her colleagues about the outcome of her experiment.

---

3. The axioms proposed by Ernst Friedrich Ferdinand Zermelo and Adolf Abraham Halevi Fraenkel as a foundation for set theory yield the Zermelo-Fraenkel set theory (ZF). When the axiom of choice (i.e., the postulate that given a set A having as elements nonempty sets, there exists a set B that contains exactly one element from each of the sets belonging to A) is included in the list of axioms, the resulting system is called ZFC (for example, see [88] for more information).

It is well known that there are infinitely many relations $R \in \Sigma_1^0 \setminus \Pi_1^0$ (i.e., relations that are recursively enumerable, but not decidable). Nonetheless, one can prove the following.

Proposition 8.3.1 *Assume that $R \in \Sigma_1^0 \setminus \Pi_1^0$. Then there is a relativistic computer $G = (\gamma_O, \gamma_P)$ that decides R.*

In addition, the following statement can be proved.

Proposition 8.3.2 *Suppose that $n > 0$; then there are infinitely many relations $R \in \Sigma_2^0 \setminus (\Sigma_1^0 \cup \Pi_1^0)$, $R \subset \mathbb{N}^n$, such that R is decidable by a relativistic computer.*

Relativistic computers can also solve the halting problem for Turing machines.

Proposition 8.3.3 *There is a relativistic computer that has as input the program of a Turing machine together with its input and is able to determine whether this Turing machine will halt on this input.*

In the description so far we have not explained why we need a Kerr black hole and not a Schwarzschild black hole (named for the German astronomer Karl Schwarzschild), that is, a nonrotating chargeless black hole. The answer is that in the case of a Kerr black hole there is a second inner event horizon. The spacetime between the outer event horizon and the inner event horizon has the properties of a Malament-Hogarth spacetime.

There are two objections related to the physical possibility of the relativistic computer described in this section. The first is related to black hole evaporation and the second is related to time granularity. In 1974, Stephen William Hawking [80] proposed that black holes emit thermal radiation, now known as Hawking radiation, due to quantum effects. Thus, any black hole will vanish sometime in the future. If Hawking radiation is indeed a real phenomenon, then it is possible that a relativistic computer G will not be able to finish a particular supertask it was assigned to finish. The reason is that the black hole that the computer orbits around might evaporate years before the computer completes its task. Moreover, Hawking radiation should play a role in cases in which the black hole has very small mass. For instance, a black hole of one solar mass will evaporate in 10^{67} years, while a black hole of 10^{16} kg will evaporate in 3 billion years. Let us now discuss the second issue.

It is a common belief among quantum-gravity theoreticians that spacetime becomes "foamy" at the Planck scale, that is, time intervals $\Delta t \leq t_P = \sqrt{\hbar G / c^5} \approx 10^{-44}$ sec, and consequently, with lengths that are less than or equal to $l_P = ct_P \approx 10^{-33}$ cm. More specifically, at the Planck scale, the topology of spacetime may take various forms with different probabilities. In other words, space and time cannot be accurately measured at the Planck

Figure 8.3: The white rings around the stars (white disks) are called Airy rings.

scale. This observation is crucial for the thought experiment presented, since observer γ_O is required to be able to measure time with any imaginable accuracy. Although it is widely believed that both time and space are discrete, still there is no experimental evidence to justify this belief. On the contrary, recently Richard Lieu and Lloyd Hillman [112] proposed (but see also [163]) a technique to detect spacetime foam[4] by observing images of distant galaxies. In particular, the detection of diffraction rings (also known as Airy rings; see Figure 8.3) in images of distant galaxies can be used to refute models of quantum gravity. Indeed, Lieu and Hillman applied their technique to images of the galaxy PSK1413+135 and used their findings to rule out the majority of modern models of quantum gravity, including the "standard" one. However, these incredible results have been challenged by Jack Ng [142], who argues that Lieu and Hillman arrived at their conclusion by wrongly calculating the *cumulative statistical phase dispersion* as

$$\Delta\varphi = 2\pi \frac{v_p}{v_g} \frac{L}{\lambda},$$

where v_p is the phase velocity of a light wave and v_g is the group velocity of propagation. Ng argues that the correct result is

$$\Delta\varphi = 2\pi a \frac{l_p^a L^{1-a}}{\lambda}.$$

Quite unexpectedly, Ng uses the Lieu–Hillman technique to rule out two of the three major models of quantum gravitation. However, it is clear that for the time being, nobody really knows the truth regarding spacetime granularity. So until we have undeniable experimental proof in favor of either view of the world, we can safely assume that γ_O can measure time with any accuracy she wishes.

For reasons of completeness, it is important to say that Németi and Gyula Dávid [140] have concluded that since γ_O need not observe an infinite sequence of events happening in its causal past, the time measurement

---

4. The expression spacetime foam should not be taken literally to mean that there is such a substance. On the contrary, it just refers to the hypothetical probabilistic structure of space and time at Planck scale.

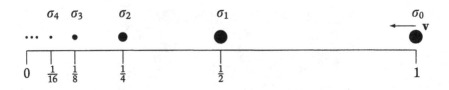

Figure 8.4: A classical supertask.

objection becomes void. Actually, the authors support the new idea that the general computing system involves a *pseudosupertask* and not a "proper" supertask. The term pseudosupertask has been coined by John David Barrow in [7] to characterize cases in which an observer sees a moving machine carrying out an infinite sequence of actions in what seems to be a finite amount of time.

8.4 Quantum Supertasks

The supertasks discussed in this section are not directly related to hyper-computation. Thus, readers not interested in supertasks in general can safely skip this section. On the other hand, this section is almost essential reading for those with an interest in supertasks.

Jon Pérez Laraudogoitia [106] (but see also [107]) has described one of the simplest classical supertasks; it illustrates the spontaneous acquisition of energy and momentum while sustaining indeterministic time developments. In particular, Laraudogoitia's system consists of an infinite set of elastic spheres, having the same mass m, that are placed along the open interval $(0, \frac{1}{2})$ using the following rule: sphere σ_i is placed at point $x_i = \frac{1}{2^i}$, where $i = 1, 2, 3, \ldots$ (see Figure 8.4). Notice that the size of the spheres must decrease, while their density must increase. At point $x_0 = 1$ there is another sphere, σ_0, with equal mass, that moves toward σ_1 with constant speed v. After some finite time, the two spheres collide and σ_0 stops at point $x_1 = \frac{1}{2}$ and will remain at this position, while sphere σ_1 moves with constant speed v toward sphere σ_2. The two spheres collide, exchange energy (i.e., σ_1 loses all its kinetic energy and stops at $x_2 = \frac{1}{4}$, and σ_2 starts moving), and a new collision takes place, and so on. In the end, all spheres σ_i will stop moving, while each of them will rest at point $\frac{1}{2^{i+1}}$.

In classical mechanics, time is reversible, and thus one may consider the reverse of this supertask. Initially, an infinite number of spheres σ_i, $i = 0, 1, 2, \ldots$, are at rest at positions $x_i = \frac{1}{2^i}$. Without any apparent external cause, a series of collisions begins at the end where an infinite number of spheres have accumulated and has as a final effect the ejection of the first

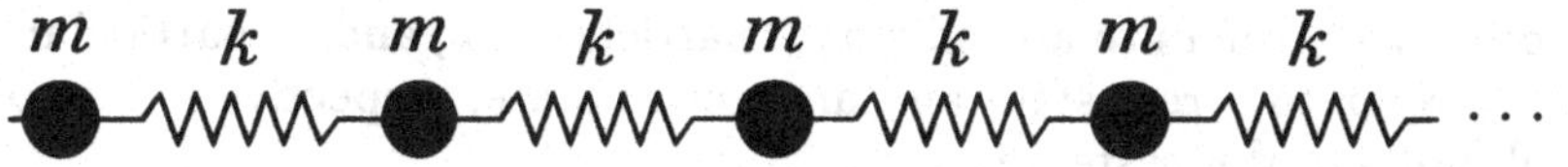

Figure 8.5: Masses and springs.

sphere. Clearly, this system is not deterministic and also violates the laws of energy and momentum conservation.

John Norton [143] argues that this supertask cannot be easily translated into a quantum setting. Therefore, he proposes another, quite similar, classical supertask that can be easily translated into a corresponding quantum-mechanical supertask [143]. In particular, this new supertask involves an infinite sequence of spheres that are connected by springs, all of them having spring constant k (see Figure 8.5). It is not hard to show that this system is indeterministic: while in an equilibrium state it can spontaneously set its masses in motion. Before proceeding, the reader should ponder the feasibility of a translation of this supertask into a quantum-mechanical setting.

To set up the quantum equivalent of the classical springs and masses supertask, Norton considers infinitely many particles, each having its own Hilbert space $\mathcal{H}_1$, $\mathcal{H}_2$, $\mathcal{H}_3$,.... The state vectors of particles in space $\mathcal{H}_i$, where $i = 1, 2, 3, \ldots$, will be written $|\Psi\rangle_i$. To make things simple, Norton assumes that each particle admits just two energy eigenstates $|0\rangle_i$ and $|1\rangle_i$ of the "particle Hamiltonian" H_i^{part} that acts in space H_i. Notice that $_i\langle 0|0\rangle_i = {}_i\langle 1|1\rangle_i = 1$, and thus

$$H_i^{\text{part}}|0\rangle_i = 0|0\rangle_i = 0, \quad H_i^{\text{part}}|1\rangle_i = 1|1\rangle_i = |1\rangle_i,$$

for $i = 1, 2, 3, \ldots$. The infinite particles of the supertask are represented by vectors of an infinite-dimensional product space

$$\mathcal{H}_1 \otimes \mathcal{H}_2 \otimes \mathcal{H}_3 \otimes \cdots.$$

The natural basis vectors of this infinite-dimensional space, which is not a Hilbert space since it admits vectors that cannot be normalized, are

$$|a_1\rangle_1 \otimes |a_2\rangle_2 \otimes |a_3\rangle_3 \otimes \cdots,$$

where $a_i \in \{0, 1\}$. These vectors are used to define other vectors (fundamental states) that describe interactions that mimic the classical supertask (only a few cases are shown):

$$|0\rangle = |0\rangle_1 \otimes |0\rangle_2 \otimes |0\rangle_3 \otimes |0\rangle_4 \otimes \cdots,$$
$$|1\rangle = |1\rangle_1 \otimes |0\rangle_2 \otimes |0\rangle_3 \otimes |0\rangle_4 \otimes \cdots,$$
$$|2\rangle = |0\rangle_1 \otimes |1\rangle_2 \otimes |0\rangle_3 \otimes |0\rangle_4 \otimes \cdots,$$
$$|3\rangle = |0\rangle_1 \otimes |0\rangle_2 \otimes |1\rangle_3 \otimes |0\rangle_4 \otimes \cdots.$$

Notice that $|j\rangle_i$ refers to an individual particle state, and in particular $|0\rangle_i$ and $|1\rangle_i$ refer to a rest state and an excited state, respectively. The total Hamiltonian of this system is

$$H = H^{\text{part}} + H^{\text{int}},$$

where

$$H^{\text{part}} = \sum_{n=1}^{\infty \text{ or } N} |n\rangle\langle n|, \tag{8.1}$$

$$H^{\text{int}} = \sum_{n=1}^{\infty \text{ or } N-1} ia|n+1\rangle\langle n| - ia|n\rangle\langle n+1|. \tag{8.2}$$

Observe that the Schrödinger equation requires that

$$i\frac{d}{dt}|\Psi(t)\rangle = H|\Psi(t)\rangle \tag{8.3}$$

for a state vector $|\Psi(t)\rangle = \sum_{n=0}^{\infty \text{ or } N} C_n(t)|n\rangle$. By substituting this expression into (8.3) and using expressions (8.1) and (8.2), we get the following set of equations:

$$i\frac{dC_0}{dt} = 0,$$

$$i\frac{dC_1}{dt} = C_1 - iaC_2,$$

$$i\frac{dC_2}{dt} = C_2 + ia(C_1 - C_3),$$

$$\vdots$$

$$i\frac{dC_n}{dt} = C_n + ia(C_{n-1} - C_{n+1}),$$

$$\vdots$$

An analysis of the time development of the state vector shows that if it is controlled only by (8.3), then it is indeterministic, which is the main result of Norton's work. For more details, the reader should consult Norton's paper [143].

Alisa Bokulich [17] addressed the question whether it is possible to perform an infinite number of quantum-mechanical measurements in a finite amount of time. Her starting point is *Zeno's paradox in quantum theory*, which was discovered by Baydyanath Misra and George Sudarshan. The first published account of this paradox appeared in [135]. It involves systems with unstable quantum states, such as a system that involves the radioactive disintegration of nuclei. Initially, the system is in some undecayed state. The system evolves, and we can always ask at any given moment for the probability that the system has decayed. The fundamental claim of Zeno's paradox in quantum theory is that the probability that the system has not decayed is proportional to the frequency of measurements made to determine whether the system has decayed. In other words, the more measurements we make, the higher the probability that the system will remain in its initial state. And if it is possible to perform an infinite number of measurements, the system will never change its initial state. But is it possible to perform such a measurement? Surprisingly, quantum nondemolition (QND) measurements, which do not necessarily lead to Zeno's paradox in quantum theory but also circumvent the limitations imposed by Heisenberg uncertainty principles, allow such measurements with respect to fundamentals. What exactly are these quantum nondemolition measurements?

It is a fundamental principle of quantum mechanics that a precise measurement at the microscopic scale is impossible without the introduction of "back action," which is inherent to the very fact of measurement. This principle can be directly related to Heisenberg's uncertainty principles. Suppose that A and B are some *observables* (i.e., linear operators representing "measurable" quantities of a quantum system). Then $AB \neq BA$, since A and B are noncommuting operators. The Heisenberg principles state that the product of the dispersions of A and B has a lower bound:

$$\Delta A \, \Delta B \geq \frac{1}{2} |\langle AB - BA \rangle|.$$

In other words, if A and B are represented by noncommuting operators, a very precise measurement of A resulting in a very small dispersion ΔA will cause a large dispersion ΔB. The real problem is that although this does not directly restrict the precision in the measurement of A, the large fluctuation induced in B most probably will couple back to A, which will result in "back action" in the measurement of A. To circumvent this problem, one has to resort to *quantum nondemolition measurements* [21], in which we pick a measurement strategy that avoids the undesirable effects of back action. This is accomplished by devising measurement schemes in which the "back action" noise is kept entirely within unwanted observables, so that the quantity of interest remains intact by a measurement thus allowing repeated measurements with arbitrarily high accuracy. Observables with such properties are called QND observables. Formally, a QND observable A is one that commutes with itself at all times of measurement:

$$A(t_i)A(t_j) - A(t_j)A(t_i) = 0.$$

For example, the momentum of a free particle is a continuous QND observable. In general, any observable that commutes with the Hamiltonian (i.e., $AH - HA = 0$ and $A(t) = A(t_0)$) is actually a QND observable. Also, no quantum mechanical principle imposes any limit to the frequency with which QND measurements can be made. In addition, if we identify the limit of an infinite number of discrete QND measurements with continuous measurements, then the latter are possible in principle. Ergo, a quantum measurement supertask is possible in principle.

8.5 Ultimate Computing Machines

At the end of Section 8.3 I discussed at some length efforts to resolve the issue of spacetime granularity. It was pointed out that the issue has not been resolved in spite of (controversial?) experimental findings. However, this does not seem to be an obstacle for researchers who are in favor of spacetime granularity to assume such granularity, in order to put forth "new" ideas. In particular, Seth Lloyd and Jack Ng [115] present a semipopular account of their search for the ultimate computing device (which, in my eyes, is quite similar to the quest for the Holy Grail). More specifically, Ng [141] claims that a black hole is actually a "simple" computer whose speed v (i.e., the number of operations per bit per unit of time) and the number I of bits of information in its memory space are both delimited by the following inequality:

$$Iv^2 \leq t_P^{-2} \approx 10^{86} \, \text{sec}^{-2}.$$

Notice that the number $\tilde{v}$ of operations per unit of time is given by $\tilde{v} = Iv$. In addition, Lloyd [114] argues that the "ultimate" laptop, which is a "computer" with a mass of 1 kg and a volume of 1 l, is able to perform $2mc^2 / \pi \hbar = 5.4248 \times 10^{50}$ logical operations per second on $\approx 10^{31}$ bits. The temperature inside the ultimate laptop is approximately 10^9 kelvins. To recapitulate: according to Lloyd and Ng there are limits imposed by nature on how fast we can compute, regardless of the meaning of the word "compute." In addition, a black hole is the ultimate computing device!

Lloyd and Ng went one step further and proposed that the whole universe (whatever that means) is a gigantic computer computing itself! Clearly, such a statement constitutes the apotheosis of computationalism. According to their view, the universe, "powered by Standard Model software," computes "quantum fields, chemicals, bacteria, human beings, stars and galaxies." But if one supposes that the universe is itself a computer and that John Archibald Wheeler's *it from bit*[5] hypothesis holds, it is reasonable

---

5. "It from bit symbolizes the idea every item of the physical world has at bottom–at a very bottom, in most instances–an immaterial source and explanation: that which we call reality arises in the last analysis from the posing of yes-no questions and the registering of equipment-evoked responses; in short, that all things physical are information-theoretic in origin and this is a *participatory universe*" [226].

to assume that all concrete objects (e.g., books, walls, etc.) are themselves computers. But what is the deeper meaning of this fatuous remark?

If everything is a computer, then the chair you are sitting on is a computer, the book you are reading now is a computer, the window you are looking through is a computer, the wall behind your back is a computer, and so on. But what can be said about the wall that is behind the back of Melany, who is making a presentation, and on which a standard projection system connected to her laptop computer is shining light? Searle [173] has explained how Melany, based on the standard textbook definition of computation and by assuming that there is no problem with universal realizability, can argue that the wall behind her back is *actually* implementing the presentation program that she is using! Now let us go one step further: if the universe computes itself, what does the chair you are sitting on compute? Also, does the book you are reading right now compute the same thing as the wall behind you? To answer these questions one must clearly define what is meant by "computation." In this book, we have presented various models of computation and all have as common denominator the ability to manipulate symbols. So, either we can very broadly define computation as a symbol manipulation procedure (recall that computing systems are Type V minds, see page 109) or we can adopt an elaborate definition like Stevan Harnad's.

Definition 8.5.1 Computation is an implementation-independent, systematically interpretable, symbol manipulation process [77].

Based on these remarks, what is the book you are reading right now computing? Searle argues [173] that "Computational states are not *discovered within* the physics, they are *assigned* to the physics." In other words, the book you are reading computes the sum of two numbers just because you have opted to *assign* this particular computational task to the book you are reading. Clearly, even digital computers compute things just because we interpret the outcome of a particular computational procedure the way we do. But on the other hand, we are not entirely free to assign to any object any computational task. For instance, Block [15] presents a good example that makes this point clear:

> [a]ny physical device that can be interpreted as an inclusive OR gate can also be interpreted as an AND gate (and conversely). To see this, note that an AND gate outputs a '1' just in case both inputs are '1'–and otherwise outputs a '0'. Any physical device that acts this way can have its states reinterpreted. Suppose the interpretation that made it an AND gate was: 4 volt potential is interpreted as '0', 7 volts as '1'. But we could reverse the interpretation, reading 4 volts as '1' and 7 volts as '0'. Then we would have a device that outputs a '0' just in case both inputs

are '0' (otherwise '1'), and that is an OR gate. So a mere change in interpretation can change an OR to an AND gate.

Although a physical device that can be interpreted as an AND gate can also be interpreted as an OR gate, it cannot nevertheless be interpreted as a NAND gate. And of course, the AND gate does execute a logical operation just because a conscious individual has constructed it to do exactly this and nothing else. In the light of these remarks, one can surely say that the book you are reading as well as a black hole compute absolutely nothing! On the other hand, a computer does actually compute something because it has been constructed for this particular purpose.

To be fair, it is important to note that Lloyd and Ng are not the first researchers to put forth the idea that the universe is a computer. In 1969, Konrad Zuse published a monograph entitled "Rechnender Raum" (Computing Universe) [236], in which he proclaimed the idea that the whole universe is a cellular automaton (i.e., a computing device). Furthermore, Stephen Wolfram developed ideas almost identical to Zuse's. His work, which has been summarized in his latest book [228], is an effort to show not that everything can be simulated by computers, but that everything is actually a computer! And of course Wolfram's ideas are based on the assumption that space and time are not continuous, or as Steven Weinberg puts it [220]:

> Only if Wolfram were right that neither space nor time nor anything else is truly continuous (which is a separate issue) would the Turing machine or the rule 110 cellular automata be computationally equivalent to an analog computer or a quantum computer or a brain or the universe.

8.6 Quantum Adiabatic Computation

The idea of using a computer that operates according to the laws of quantum mechanics was introduced to the public by Richard Feynman in 1982.[6] Generally speaking, the universal quantum Turing machine (i.e., the quantum computational counterpart of Turing's conceptual computing device) has the same computational power as its classical counterpart. This implies that the universal Turing machine can, in principle, simulate the operation of its quantum counterpart. However, its simulation is incredibly inefficient, so much so that the classical machine is incapable of feasibly performing many tasks that the quantum machine can easily perform. For

---

6. Strictly speaking, Paul Benioff was the first to propose the theoretical construction of a computer based solely on quantum-mechanical principles, which, however, had only the power of a classical computer.

completeness, let me describe in a nutshell the basic ingredients of quantum computing.

Generally speaking, quantum machines operate on quantum bits using quantum gates to manipulate them and thus perform a computation. A quantum bit, or qubit, is represented by a two-level quantum mechanical system, whose two basic states are conventionally labeled $|0\rangle$ and $|1\rangle$. For instance, the two polarization states of a photon would constitute a physical implementation of a qubit. Mathematically, a qubit is represented by a two-dimensional Hilbert space $\mathcal{H}_2$, and so a general state of a single qubit is a vector

$$c_0|0\rangle + c_1|1\rangle,$$

where $|c_0|^2 + |c_1|^2 = 1$. Roughly speaking, a quantum register is a 2^n-level, $n \in \mathbb{N}$, quantum system (e.g., for $n = 2$ the product space $\mathcal{H}_2 \otimes \mathcal{H}_2$ represents such a system). To put it simply, a quantum register is a sequence of qubits. Also, a quantum gate is just a mapping $\mathcal{H}_m \to \mathcal{H}_n$, for some $m = 2^k$ and $n = 2^l$.

As was pointed out above, a quantum system evolves according to the Schrödinger equation

$$i\hbar \frac{d}{dt}|\Psi(t)\rangle = H(t)|\Psi(t)\rangle.$$

If $H(t)$ is slowly varying, then we can use the *adiabatic theorem* of quantum mechanics to see how it will evolve. This capability was initially utilized by Edward Farhi, Jeffrey Goldstone, Sam Gutmann, and Michael Sipser to devise a quantum algorithm for solving instances of the satisfiability problem (see [60] for more details and Appendix A for a description of the satisfiability problem). The idea behind their solution is to find the ground state of a Hamiltonian H_P. Unfortunately, finding the ground state of the Hamiltonian of some problem may turn out to be a difficult task, although the specification of the Hamiltonian is straightforward. A solution to this problem is to consider another Hamiltonian H_B that is straightforward to construct and whose ground state is easy to find. The next step involves the deformation of H_B in time T into H_P through a time-dependent process:

$$H\left(\frac{t}{T}\right) = \left(1 - \frac{t}{T}\right) H_B + \frac{t}{T} H_P. \tag{A}$$

According to the adiabatic theorem, if the deformation is slow enough, the initial state will evolve into the desired ground state with high probability. The longer it takes for the deformation to take place, the higher the probability that it will evolve into the desired state. Note that another criterion for identifying the ground state is described in [95]. However, we will not describe it, and the reader is referred to Tien Kieu's paper for details.

The use of the adiabatic theorem in quantum computational processes to solve particularly hard problems inspired Kieu to construct a quantum algorithm that is supposed to solve Hilbert's tenth problem.[7] For the time being, there are no quantum computers to verify Kieu's algorithm, but then again, there are no quantum computers to verify the validity of any other quantum algorithm;[8] and of course no one has yet built any hypercomputer. Kieu's algorithm was originally published in [95], while an elaborated discussion of the algorithm and its properties is presented in [97, 96]. Before I present the algorithm itself, it would be useful to give a rough idea of the inner workings of the algorithm. For this purpose, we will consider a particular Diophantine equation

$$D(x, y, z) = (x + 2)^3 + y^2 - 4z^5 - 2xy = 0.$$

A quantum-mechanical method to check whether this particular equation has a nonnegative integer solution requires the realization of an infinite Fock space.[9] In general, the Hamiltonian corresponding to

$$D(x_1, x_2, \ldots, x_m)$$

has the following form:

$$H_P = \left(D(a_1^\dagger a_1, \ldots, a_m^\dagger a_m) \right)^2.$$

So, the Hamiltonian corresponding to the particular Diophantine equation above is

$$H_P = \left((a_x^\dagger a_x + 2)^3 + (a_y^\dagger a_y)^2 - 4(a_z^\dagger a_z)^5 + 2(a_x^\dagger a_x)(a_y^\dagger a_y) \right)^2.$$

Before proceeding, let me briefly explain the characteristics of the creation $a^\dagger$ and annihilation a operators. These operators arise in the case of the one-dimensional simple harmonic oscillator with Hamiltonian

$$H_{\text{SHO}} = P^2 + X^2 - 2,$$

which can be rewritten

$$H_{\text{SHO}} = a^\dagger a + \frac{1}{2}.$$

---

7. The use of the word *algorithm* in conjunction with Hilbert's tenth problem constitutes an oxymoron, but the word algorithm is used to denote a method or a procedure that is carried out to achieve a particular task.

8. Strictly speaking, there are no general-purpose quantum computers, although some researchers have already built some rudimentary quantum computers (see [92]). In addition, recently, D-Wave Systems, a private company based in Canada, announced the launch of the world's first "commercial" quantum computer. According to the company's founder and chief technology officer, their machine is a 16-qubit processor that employs the adiabatic theorem to deliver results. Although it is difficult to say when (commercial) general-purpose quantum computers will be widely available, Scott Aaronson was the first to impugn D-Wave Systems' project [27]. Interestingly, he has also criticized quantum adiabatic computing (see Appendix B).

9. A Fock or Fok space is a special Hilbert space introduced by Vladimir Alexandrovich Fok. It is used to analyze such quantum phenomena as the annihilation and creation of particles.

The relationship between the momentum and position operators and the creation and annihilation operators is defined by the following equations:

$$X = \frac{1}{\sqrt{2}}(a + a^\dagger),$$

$$P = \frac{i}{\sqrt{2}}(a - a^\dagger).$$

Observe that $[a, a^\dagger] = 1$ and $[a, a] = [a^\dagger, a^\dagger] = 0$, where in general, $[a, b] = ab - ba$. Also, a Fock space has as basis the states $|n\rangle$, $n \in \mathbb{N}$, with the following properties:

$$a^\dagger|n\rangle = \sqrt{n+1}|n+1\rangle,$$

$$a|n\rangle = \sqrt{n}|n-1\rangle,$$

$$(a^\dagger a)|n\rangle = n|n\rangle.$$

Here $|0\rangle$ is the vacuum state, which has the additional property that $a|0\rangle = 0$. Let us return to the Hamiltonian of the Diophantine equation.

The ground state $|g\rangle$ of H_P has the following properties:

$$N_j|g\rangle = n_j|g\rangle,$$

$$H_P|g\rangle = \left((a_x^\dagger a_x + 2)^3 + (a_y^\dagger a_y)^2 - 4(a_z^\dagger a_z)^5 + 2(a_x^\dagger a_x)(a_y^\dagger a_y)\right)^2|g\rangle$$

$$\equiv E_g|g\rangle,$$

where the n_i are the nonnegative integer eigenvalues of the number operators $N_i = a_i^\dagger a_i$ and $[N_i, H_P] = 0 = [N_i, N_j]$, for $i \neq j$. By projectively measuring the energy E_g of the ground state $|g\rangle$, we can determine whether the Diophantine equation we are studying has a solution. In particular, it has at least one integer solution if and only if $E_g = 0$ and none otherwise. Although it is possible to find out the values of various unknowns, this is not the main task of the algorithm, but rather a side effect. Let us recapitulate:

(i) Let $D(x_1, \ldots, x_m) = 0$ be a Diophantine equation; we have to simulate the quantum Hamiltonian

$$H_P = \left(D(a_1^\dagger a_1, \ldots, a_m^\dagger a_m)\right)^2$$

on some appropriate Fock space.

(ii) Assuming that the ground state can be found with high probability, while at the same time it can be verified that this particular ground state has the required properties, then a measurement of appropriate observables would lead to an answer to the decision problem.

So in order to solve this kind of decision problem we need to have at our disposal a countably infinite number of Fock states to be able to construct, or at least simulate, a suitable Hamiltonian and to determine and verify its ground state.

After this rather long but also quite condensed introduction, we can proceed with the presentation of the algorithm itself. As was remarked previously, it is rather easier to implement a Hamiltonian than to find its ground state. Instead, we define another Hamiltonian whose ground state is easily obtainable and then deform this Hamiltonian in time T into the Hamiltonian whose ground state we are looking for. The deformation goes through a time-dependent process that can be represented by an interpolating Hamiltonian $H(t \, / \, T)$. Let us assume that we start with the Hamiltonian

$$H_I = \sum_{i=1}^{m} (a_i^\dagger - \alpha_i^*)(a_i - \alpha_i),$$

which has as ground state the easily achievable coherent state

$$|g_I\rangle = |\alpha_1 \ldots \alpha_m\rangle.$$

Clearly, the next step involves the formation of the slowly changing Hamiltonian $H(t \, / \, T)$ (see equation (A) on page 155) that interpolates in the time interval $[0, T]$ between H_I and H_P:

(i) Set the evolution time T, a probability p, and an accuracy $0 < \varepsilon < 1$, which is arbitrarily small.

(ii) Perform the physical quantum process, which is time-dependent, is governed by $H(t \, / \, T)$, and terminates after time T.

(iii) Projectively measure either the observable H_P or the number operators $N_1, \ldots, N_m$ to obtain some state $|\ldots n_i \ldots\rangle$.

(iv) Repeat the physical process of the two previous steps in order to build a histogram of measurement frequencies. This loop will exit when we have obtained a probability distribution $P(T; \varepsilon)$ at time T with an accuracy ε for measured states. Note that the convergence of this repetitive process is guaranteed by the weak law of large numbers in probability theory.[10]

(v) On a classical machine, successively apply the displaced creation operators $b_i^\dagger \equiv (a_i^\dagger - \alpha_i^*)$ on the initial state and choose a truncated basis of M vectors made up of $|\alpha_1 \ldots \alpha_m\rangle$ and its excited states.[11]

---

10. Given a set of X_n, $n \geq 1$, of observations, the law of large numbers deals with the question, "when does $\overline{X_n} = \sum_{i=1}^{n} X_i \, / \, n$ converge to some parameter ξ?"
11. Kieu has claimed in a message posted to the FOM (Foundations Of Mathematics) mailing-list that "truncation is not essential to the algorithm at all."

(vi) On a classical machine, solve the Schrödinger equation in the basis for $\psi(T)$, with initial state $\psi(0) = |\alpha_1 \ldots \alpha_m\rangle$, to derive a probability distribution $P_{\text{est}}(T; M)$.

(vii) On a classical machine, enlarge the truncated basis by increasing the size of M when $|P_{\text{est}}(T; M) - P(T; \varepsilon)| \geq \varepsilon$. Repeat step (vi).

(viii) Since now the two probability distributions are uniformly within the desired accuracy (i.e., $|P_{\text{est}}(T; M) - P(T; \varepsilon)| < \varepsilon$), use this truncated basis on a classical machine to diagonalize H_P to get the appropriate ground state $|g'\rangle$ and its energy $E_{g'}$, with an accuracy that can be determined from ε.

(ix) On a classical machine, estimate in this truncated basis the gap between the ground state and the first excited state. Next, use the adiabatic theorem to choose a time T such that the system has a high probability of being mostly in the ground state:

$$\left| |\langle g'|\psi(T)\rangle|^2 - 1 \right| < \varepsilon.$$

(x) Go to step (ii) with this value of T to confirm that the candidate ground state is actually the real ground state.

Before proceeding with the presentation of some issues related to this algorithm, it is worth mentioning that Andrés Sicard, Mario Vélez, and Juan Ospina [182] have presented an alternative quantum algorithm that performs the same task. In particular, instead of using the simple harmonic oscillator, they use the infinite square well, that is, a particle under the influence of the following potential:

$$V(x) = \begin{cases} 0, & 0 \leq x \leq \pi l, \\ \infty, & (x < 0) \vee (x > \pi l). \end{cases}$$

In this case, the particle is free (i.e., no forces are applied to this particle) between $x = 0$ and $x = \pi l$, while it cannot escape this region since the forces at the edges are infinite. The Hamiltonian operator H^{ISW} and the energy levels E_n^{ISW} are

$$H^{\text{ISW}} = -\frac{\hbar^2}{2m}\frac{d^2}{dx^2} - \frac{\hbar^2}{2ml^2} \quad \text{and} \quad E_n^{\text{ISW}} = \frac{\hbar^2}{2ml^2}n(n+2),$$

respectively. In addition, $H^{\text{ISW}}|n\rangle = E_n^{\text{ISW}}|n\rangle$. The "constitutive elements" of this algorithm are drawn from the Lie algebra $\mathfrak{su}(1, 1)$ (see section D.2), which satisfies the following commutation relations:

$$[K_-, K_+] = K_3, \quad [K_-, K_3] = 2K_-, \quad [K_+, K_3] = -2K_+,$$

where K_+, K_-, and K_3 are called creation, annihilation, and Cartan operators, respectively. In addition, the following equalities hold:

$$K_+|n\rangle = \sqrt{(n+1)(n+3)}|n+1\rangle,$$
$$K_-|0\rangle = 0,$$
$$K_-|n\rangle = \sqrt{n(n+2)}|n-1\rangle,$$
$$K_3|n\rangle = (2n+3)|n\rangle.$$

From these, the Hamiltonian can be written as

$$H^{\text{ISW}} = \frac{\hbar^2}{2ml^2}K_+K_-,$$

while the new number operator N^{ISW} is defined as

$$N^{\text{ISW}} = \frac{1}{2}(K_3 - 3).$$

In this new solution, the Hamiltonian corresponding to a Diophantine equation has the following form:

$$H_B^{\text{ISW}} = \left(D(N_1^{\text{ISW}}, \ldots, N_k^{\text{ISW}})\right)^2.$$

The new initial Hamiltonian H_I^{ISW} is constructed from the creation and annihilation operators of $\mathfrak{su}(1,1)$:

$$H_I^{\text{ISW}} = \sum_{i=1}^{k}(K_{+i} - z_i^*)(K_{-i} - z_i),$$

where $|z\rangle$ are eigenstates of K_-. From these two equations, one can get the time-dependent Hamiltonian

$$H_A^{\text{ISW}}(t) = \left(1 - \frac{t}{T}\right)H_I^{\text{ISW}} + \left(\frac{t}{T}\right)H_B^{\text{ISW}}.$$

Let us now proceed with the presentation of some objections related to Kieu's algorithm.

A first remark concerning the algorithm just presented is that it terminates and solves Hilbert's tenth problem. However, in the introductory chapter it was stated that Matiyasevich proved that Hilbert's tenth problem is Turing undecidable, yet Kieu claims that his algorithm can decide Hilbert's tenth problem. Therefore, it seems that something is wrong here. However, one has to understand that Hilbert's tenth problem cannot be decided by a Turing machine, but in the light of hypercomputation, this does not imply that there is no way to solve this problem. Indeed, Kieu's algorithm is actually a hyperalgorithm.

Another objection to this algorithm is related to Cantor's diagonalization argument. In particular, since it has been shown using the diagonal construction that no Turing machine can solve its halting problem, the existence of any machine capable of solving any incomputable problem will lead to logical inconsistency. Thus, it is impossible to solve Hilbert's tenth problem. Before demonstrating why such a conclusion is at least misleading, let us briefly present the proof that no Turing machine can solve its halting problem.

The diagonalization argument was devised by Georg Ferdinand Ludwig Philip Cantor to show that the set of real numbers is not countably infinite. Is based on the diagonalization principle, a fundamental proof technique, which can be stated as follows:

Principle 8.6.1 (Diagonalization Principle) Assume that R is a binary relation on a set A. Also, assume that D, the diagonal set for R, is the set

$$\left\{ a \mid (a \in A) \wedge ((a,a) \notin R) \right\}.$$

For each $a \in A$, suppose that $R_a = \{b \mid (a,b) \in R\}$. Then D is distinct from each R_a.

Paulo Cotogno [39] has presented a simplified proof of the insolvability of the halting problem: Assume that ψ_1, ψ_2, ψ_3,... is an enumeration of the computable (partial) functions. In addition, let us define the halting function

$$f(x,y) = \begin{cases} 1, & \text{if } \psi_x(y) \text{ converges,} \\ 0, & \text{if } \psi_x(y) \text{ does not converge,} \end{cases}$$

and the diagonal monadic function

$$g(x) = \begin{cases} 1, & \text{if } f(x,x) = 0 \\ \text{undefined}, & \text{if } f(x,x) = 1. \end{cases}$$

Suppose that $g(x)$ is computable. Then there is an i such that $g(x) = \psi_i(x)$. This implies that $\psi_i(i) = 0$, that is, $g(i) = 0$. The last equation is equivalent to $f(i,i) = 0$ and this implies that $\psi_i(i)$ is undefined, which is obviously a contradiction.

The interesting thing about Turing's proof is that it holds for all definitions of computability. In other words, if we consider a class of hypermachines, then it is impossible for them to compute their own halting functions. However, this does not mean that some hypermachine cannot solve the halting problem for Turing machines—there is no logical inconsistency here. Indeed, most models of hypercomputation, including Kieu's algorithm, have been examined by Toby Ord and Tien Kieu [145], who found that none of them is able to solve its own halting problem. In particular, accelerating Turing machines cannot solve their own halting functions because the functions computed by these machines are closed under composition. Also, infinite-time Turing machines cannot compute their own halting functions because they cannot determine whether a coded machine diverges when applied to its own code. Moreover, Kieu's method cannot determine whether a given input encodes a machine in the class. And this simply means that there is nothing logically wrong with Kieu's method.

Even though there is nothing logically wrong with Kieu's algorithm, Warren Douglas Smith has spotted some "flaws" in it that are described in [186]. More specifically, Smith claims that Kieu was under the impression that he should consider only Diophantine equations with *unique* solutions. In this case, H_P has unique ("nondegenerate") ground states. Smith admits that this is not a serious error, since he has managed to find a way to repair t his flaw. However, Smith shows that a second error is serious. In particular, this error is due to the assumption that independently of the value $T > 0$, no nonground "decoy" state will ever achieve an occupation probability greater that $\frac{1}{2}$. Quite surprisingly, he claims that this is valid in a number of limiting cases. However, Smith's claims have prompted Kieu to investigate them thoroughly [99, 98]. Kieu's conclusion is that Smith's work is groundless and therefore poses no real threat to his research project.

8.7   Infinite Concurrent Turing Machines

It has been noted in the previous section that a quantum-mechanical method to check whether some Diophantine equation has a nonnegative integer solution requires the realization of an infinite Fock space. Very roughly, one may imagine that each dimension of an infinite Fock space corresponds to a Turing machine that solves a tiny part of the total problem. This idea prompted Ziegler [234] to investigate the computational power of an infinite number of classical Turing machines operating concurrently. Before presenting his key results, it is necessary to explain what it means for infinite concurrent Turing machines to solve a problem.

First of all, it is important to say that here the word "problem" is identified with a set $P \subseteq \mathbb{N}$. When we say that a countably infinite family $(\mathcal{M}_k)_{k \in \mathbb{N}}$ of Turing machines solves a problem P, then:

(i) each $\mathcal{M}_k$ eventually terminates when presented with some input $x \in \mathbb{N}$;

(ii) for any $x \in \mathbb{N}$, it holds that $x \in P$ if and only if there is at least one machine $\mathcal{M}_k$ that can "attest to" this fact;

(iii) when presented with some input $x \in \mathbb{N}$, all machines $\mathcal{M}_k$ terminate within some finite time that clearly depends on x;

(iv) a distinguished machine $\mathcal{M}_0$ is capable of computing the Gödel number of any machine $\mathcal{M}_k$, when it is fed with the number k.

Having made clear how infinite concurrent Turing machines operate, we proceed with the key results.

Theorem 8.7.1 *Infinite concurrent Turing machines can solve the halting problem.*

In other words, infinite concurrent Turing machines are a hypermachine.

Theorem 8.7.2 *A problem $P \subseteq \mathbb{N}$ is solvable by infinite concurrent Turing machines if and only if it is semidecidable.*

However, there are limits to what can be accomplished.

Theorem 8.7.3 *Infinite concurrent Turing machines cannot solve the totality problem, that is, they cannot decide whether an arbitrary Turing machine halts on all inputs.*

IX. Natural Computation and Hypercomputation

Hypercomputation is not only about the falsification of the Church-Turing thesis, but also about the broadening of the concept of *computation*. This implies that the Turing machine model of computation, which is based on a small number of assumptions, cannot and should not form the basis for proposing or studying new models of computation inspired by natural processes. Unfortunately, in many instances this is not the case and computational models inspired by nature are treated like some sort of exotic Turing machine. In this chapter we will discuss the general characteristics of natural computing. Next, there is a discussion of analog computation followed by a discussion of ideas that make evident that there are indeed formally incomputable natural phenomena. There is also a discussion of the relationship between neural networks and analog computation, a presentation of a new model of optical computation, and some ideas regarding cellular computing and hypercomputation. We conclude with a presentation of analog X-machines and their computational power.

9.1 Principles of Natural Computation

Natural computation is a broad term that encompasses disciplines that study computation inspired by nature. Such disciplines include DNA computing, analog computing, and cellular computing. In Section 8.5 it was stressed that in our own perspective, computation does not really occur in nature, but it is we that interpret certain sequences of events as computation. So when we speak about natural computing, we will mean exactly this: a natural system has been set up and its activity is perceived as a computation by a conscious agent. This assumption will not have a great impact on the discussion that follows, but it should be obvious that no cell or DNA strand or anything else performs computation ex nihilo.

Analog computation can be viewed as an important branch of natural computing. Indeed, Eriko Tokuda, Noboru Asahi, Takashi Yamada, and

Yoshihito Amemiya [203] define analog computation as

> a way of processing that solves a mathematical problem by apply-
> ing an analogy of a physical system to the problem. To solve the
> problem in this way, you prepare an appropriate physical system
> and represent each problem variable by a physical quantity in
> the system. If the mathematical relations between the physical
> quantities are analogous to those of the problem, then you can
> find the solution to the problem by observing the behavior of the
> system and measuring the corresponding physical quantities.

An important facility of analog computers is that they can perform operations in a truly parallel manner and operate in continuous time using
continuous variables. Obviously, these characteristics set them apart from
Turing machines and their accompanying theory of computability, which is
completely discrete.

In Section 8.5 we defined computation as a symbol-manipulation process. Certainly, the word *symbol* should not be taken literally to mean symbols that can be composed using some keyboard or a similar device. On
the contrary, it merely means something that represents an object by association, resemblance, or convention. Thus, we are in agreement with
MacLennan [119] who defines computation as follows.

Definition 9.1.1 Computation is a physical process [in the sense described
in the previous page] the purpose of which is the abstract manipulation of
abstract objects.

Obviously, there are differences between analog and digital computing that
are not captured by a simple definition of this kind. So apart from the
differences presented above, in an analog setting there is no notion of an
"algorithm" (but see Section 9.5), in the sense of a effective procedure that
can, for example, be carried out by a human using only paper and pencil. Of
course, one may come up with the analogue of an algorithm in the setting of
analog computing. In addition, there is no need to translate quantities into
some formal form, since variables are represented by physical quantities on
which operations are performed.

Continuity (and of course discontinuity) and discreteness may characterize the flow of time and/or the state space (i.e., the "collective state of all
the devices comprised by the computer's memory" [118]) of a computational
process. Thus, computational processes are classified into three important
categories:

C: Continuous-time process over continuous state space.

CD: Discrete-time process over continuous state space.

D: Discrete-time process over discrete state space.

Category DC, continuous-time processes over discrete state spaces, is excluded by the laws of physics we presently know. Any ordinary computer program belongs to class D; Newton's algorithm belongs to class CD; and systems of differential equations belong to class C.

MacLennan [119] presents a number of considerations that are relevant to natural computing in general. First of all, in natural computing the computational system/process must be able to respond in real time. This is an almost obvious requirement, since, for instance, organisms are, to a certain degree adaptable and so able to respond immediately to external stimuli. So any artificial system mimicking a biological system should be able to respond immediately to an external stimulus. Clearly, this is a requirement that even some digital systems must satisfy to be reliable (e.g., hard real-time operating systems in particular, and interactive systems in general). However, in a digital system the range of responses is usually somehow fixed, although it may be enlarged when a (remote) human operator intervenes in its operation and thus acts as an "oracle."

As was hinted in the previous paragraph, what matters is not only the speed with which a system responds but also whether its "arsenal" of responses is fixed or *flexible*, that is, whether the system can respond to a new, "never seen before," stimulus in a proper way. To get an idea of the importance of this property, think of how the immune system responds when a new unidentified microorganism enters the body. This property is closely related to the notion of *adaptability*. By definition, an immune system that can easily find a way to handle unknown microorganisms is one that is adaptable. Similarly, natural computational processes that can deal with new, unknown, external events are termed adaptable. It is possible to have natural computing systems that are not adaptable. However, these systems should easily accommodate adaptation in order to be characterized as natural.

Any animal, and of course any plant, may get hurt several times during its life. However, in most cases, the organism should be able to recover from the wound and so continue its life normally. Even when an organism is severely wounded, in many cases it can partially recover and continue living, albeit with problems. This implies that natural computing systems have to be able to recover from damage, faults, and errors and to be able to work under heavy noise.

Let us now see how these considerations may affect our efforts to specify a model of natural computation. Clearly, a natural computational system must be physically realizable. In particular, MacLennan assumes that physical realization implies that "all physically instantiated quantities must be finite."

Throughout this book it has been noted that most (if not all) discrete computing systems blindly manipulate symbols without paying any attention to the (possible) meaning of these symbols. Similarly, it is reasonable to suppose that for natural computational systems, the computation does not take into consideration any meaning that is possibly attached to the representations. In other words, natural computational systems ignore any semantic aspect of the ingredients of such a system and take into consideration only syntax (i.e., abstract relationships between symbols). Obviously, here we are talking about a formal system for which continuity is an essential aspect. Continuous formal systems have been called *simulacra* by MacLennan, who has studied them quite extensively in [117].

A simulacrum is continuous not only in syntax, but also in computation. Images are the notational vehicle for representing continuous formal systems. Images are not merely reproductions of form, but may be pictures, written language, maps, auditory signals (i.e., music, speech, etc.), gestures (which are classified as three-dimensional images), etc. In general, to each syntactic entity is attached some denotation, which assigns some meaning to it. This does not mean that the symbols themselves bear any meaning, but instead that a conscious being interprets the symbols in a certain way. Each syntactically correct expression has a denotation. For instance, the denotation of the expression 3 > 2 is *tt*, while the expression 3 ⊐ 2 has no denotation (i.e., it is *undefined*) if the relational operator ⊐ is not defined. In a continuous setting, one cannot merely assert that an image is syntactically correct or not. An image has a denotation to the degree that it is well formed (i.e., syntactically correct). Figuratively speaking, syntactic correctness of images is not a black-or-white matter, but rather a gray-scale matter. Let us demonstrate this idea with a simple example. Consider the following list of glyphs, which are images of the character "LATIN CAPITAL LETTER A":

Since the leftmost glyph has all the *known* characteristics of the LATIN CAPITAL LETTER A, it can be very easily identified as a faithful representation of this character. On the other hand, this does not hold true for the rightmost glyph, since is not clear whether this glyph represents this character. Situations like this are very common in everyday experiences, and the theory of fuzzy (sub)sets has been employed to model them mathematically. Fuzzy set theory is a theory that generalizes the concept of the set (for an overview, see, for example [101]; also, see [227] for a discussion of the power of classical fuzzy conceptual computing devices). In fuzzy set theory, an element of a fuzzy subset belongs to it to a degree, which is usually a number between 0 and 1. More specifically, given a set X, which we call a *universe*, a fuzzy subset of X is a function $A : X \rightarrow I$, where I is the unit interval (i.e., $I = [0, 1]$) or, more generally a frame (see Section D.1). Thus, when $A(x) = i$, we say that the degree to which $x \in X$ belongs to A is i. For example, one can construct a fuzzy subset having as elements the glyphs above in the following way:

$$G(\text{A}) = 1.00, \qquad G(\text{A}) = 0.98,$$
$$G(\text{A}) = 0.95, \qquad G(\textsf{A}) = 0.85,$$

$$\vdots \quad \vdots \quad \vdots \qquad \quad \vdots \quad \vdots \quad \vdots$$

The intermediate values are not the outcome of some "algorithm," which is how values are usually assigned, that is, nonalgorithmically. In this particular case, they have been chosen to make the whole point clear. Although MacLennan has developed a basic theory of interpretability, we will not go into the details, since we feel that the theory is not mature enough.

Any system of natural computation has to process continuous representations of information. This means that the system must process the information in a continuous way, which does not mean that it has to operate continuously. In addition, systems of natural computation should never terminate, and thus they violate one of the basic principles of Turing computability. This is a justified requirement, since a natural computing system should be able to interact continuously with its surrounding environment, and this interaction terminates only when the system ceases to exits.

9.2   Models of Analog Computation

This section is a short description of the two of the most important models of analog computation: the GPAC and the extended analog computer (EAC). Shannon defined the GPAC as a conceptual computing device that consists of a number of nodes that make up a finite directed graph probably with directed cycles. GPACs operate in continuous time. Functions are represented by connecting a number of five different types of nodes [157].

Integration: A two-input, one-output node with a setting for initial conditions. If $u(x)$ and $v(x)$ are inputs, the output will be the Riemann–Stieltjes integral $\int_{x_0}^{x} u(x)dv(x) + c$, where c is a constant that depends on the initial conditions. The Riemann-Stieltjes integral is a generalization of the definite integral normally encountered in calculus texts. Assume that $u(x)$ and $v(x)$ are real-valued bounded functions defined on a closed interval $[a,b]$. Also, consider a partition of the interval $a = x_0 < x_1 < x_2 \cdots < x_{n-1} < x_n = b$, and take the Riemann sum $\sum_{i=0}^{n-1} u(\xi_i)[v(x_{i+1}) - v(x_i)]$ with $\xi_i \in [x_i, x_{i+1}]$. If the sum tends to a fixed number k as $\max(x_{i+1} - x_i) \to 0$, then k is called the Riemann-Stieltjes integral of u with respect to v and is denoted by $\int u(x)dv(x)$.

Constant multiplier: For each real constant k, there is a node having as input a unary function $u(x)$ and as output the product $ku(x)$.

Adder: This node has as input the unary functions $u(x)$ and $v(x)$ and as output their sum $u(x) + v(x)$.

Variable multiplier: A node having as inputs two unary functions $u(x)$ and $v(x)$ and as output their product $u(x) \cdot v(x)$.

Constant function: This node has as input any unary function $u(x)$ and always as output the number 1.

Marian Boykan Pour-El [157] has given an alternative but equivalent definition of GPACs, which nevertheless is considered as the standard definition for GPACs nowadays.

Definition 9.2.1 The unary function $y(x)$ is generated by a general-purpose analog computer (GPAC) on the closed bounded interval I with nonempty interior if there exists a set of unary functions $y_2(x), \ldots, y_n(x)$ and a set of initial conditions $y_i(a) = y_i^*$, where $a \in I$, such that:

(i) $\{y_2, \ldots, y_n\}$ is the *unique* solution on I of a set of differential equations of the form

(E)
$$A(x, \vec{y}) \frac{d\vec{y}}{dx} = b(x, \vec{y})$$

satisfying the initial conditions and where the vector $\vec{y}$ has components $y_2, \ldots, y_n$; $A(X, \vec{y})$ is an $(n-1) \times (n-1)$ matrix; $b(x, \vec{y})$ is a $(n-1) \times 1$ matrix; and each entry of A and b must be linear in $1, x, y_2, \ldots, y_n$.

(ii) For some i such that $2 \le i \le n$, $y(x) \equiv y_i(x)$ on I.

(iii) $(a, y_2^*, \ldots, y_n^*)$ has a *domain of generation* with respect to (E), that is, there exist closed intervals $J_1, \ldots, J_n$ with nonempty interiors such that $(a, y_2^*, \ldots, y_n^*)$ is an interior point of $J_1 \times J_2 \times \cdots \times J_n$. In addition, whenever $(b, z_2^*, \ldots, z_n^*) \in J_1 \times J_2 \times \cdots \times J_n$ there exists a set of functions $\{z_2, \ldots, z_n\}$ such that

  (a) $z_i(b) = z_i^*$ for $i = 2, \ldots, n$;

  (b) $(z_2, \ldots, z_n)$ satisfies (E) on some interval I^* for which $b \in I^*$;

  (c) $(z_2, \ldots, z_n)$ is locally unique (i.e., unique on I^* and on any subinterval of I^* containing b).

It can be proved that if a function $y(x)$ is generable on I in the "graph-theoretic" sense, it is generable on I in the sense of the previous definition. More generally, if a function $y(x)$ is generable on I, then we say that it is *GPAC-computable*.

The major drawbacks of the GPAC is its inability to compute a number of important functions. For example, the function $\Gamma(x) = \int_0^\infty t^{x-1} e^{-t} dt$, known as Euler's gamma function, and Riemann's zeta function, which on the real line with $x > 1$ can be defined by $\zeta(x) = 1/\Gamma(x) \int_0^\infty \frac{u^{x-1}}{e^u - 1} du$, are not computable by a GPAC. This and some other inabilities of the GPAC provided the motivation for the design of new, more powerful conceptual analog computing devices. Such conceptual devices include the EAC and some extensions of the GPAC that were proposed by Daniel Silva Graça [71]. All these devices compute the Γ and ζ functions.

There is a relationship between computable analysis and GPAC-computability.

Theorem 9.2.1 *A function $f : [a, b] \to \mathbb{R}$ is computable if and only if it is GPAC-computable* [20].

As Lee Albert Rubel [168] has admitted, one of the main motivations for introducing the EAC was his conviction that the brain is an analog computer. Just like the GPAC, the EAC is a conceptual computing device that consists of a number of nodes that make up a finite directed graph, probably with directed cycles. It has a number of initial settings, $s_1, \ldots, s_m$, which can be arbitrary real numbers. In addition, an EAC has any finite number of independent variables, $x_1, \ldots, x_k$, and the output is a set of real-analytic functions of these variables (i.e., the output is a set of functions such that each of them has a Taylor series about each point x belonging to the domain of each corresponding function that converges to the function itself in an open neighborhood of x). Internally, there is a hierarchy of levels in which output generated at level i is fed as input to level $i+1$. At level zero, polynomials are manipulated algebraically. At level one, work is done with differentially algebraic functions that have real numbers as input, which are generated at level zero. The inputs and outputs are functions of a finite number of independent variables x_i. Computation is carried out by nodes, which are of the following types:

Constant: These nodes produce *arbitrary* real constants, which are not necessarily computable by a Turing machine.

Independent variable: Nodes with no input that produce any of the variables x_i.

Adders: These nodes have as input any two functions $u_1(x_1, \ldots, x_k)$ and $u_2(x_1, \ldots, x_k)$ and yield their sum $u_1(x_1, \ldots, x_k) + u_2(x_1, \ldots, x_k)$ as output.

Multipliers: These nodes have as input any two functions $u_1(x_1, \ldots, x_k)$ and $u_2(x_1, \ldots, x_k)$ and yield their product $u_1(x_1, \ldots, x_k) \cdot u_2(x_1, \ldots, x_k)$ as output.

Substituters: When the functions

$$u_1(x_1, \ldots, x_k), \ldots, u_l(x_1, \ldots, x_k)$$

and $v(x_1, \ldots, x_l)$ are inputs, this node produces as output the function

$$v(u_1(x_1, \ldots, x_k), \ldots, u_l(x_1, \ldots, x_k)).$$

Inverters: Assume that at level $n - 1$ the machine has produced the functions

$$f_1(x_1, \ldots, x_n, x_{n+1}, \ldots, x_{n+l}), \ldots, f_l(x_1, \ldots, x_n, x_{n+1}, \ldots, x_{n+l}).$$

Given the variables $x_1, \ldots, x_n, x_{n+1}, \ldots, x_{n+l}$ as input, the inverters solve the following equations:

$$f_1(x_1, \ldots, x_n, x_{n+1}, \ldots, x_{n+l}) = 0,$$

$$\vdots$$

$$f_l(x_1, \ldots, x_n, x_{n+1}, \ldots, x_{n+l}) = 0,$$

for $x_{n+1}, \ldots, x_{n+l}$ as well-defined real-analytic functions of $x_1, \ldots, x_n$.

Differentiators: For each function $f(x_1, \ldots, x_n)$, these nodes produce at level n any (mixed) partial derivative

$$\frac{\partial^{a_1 + \cdots + a_n} f}{\partial x_1^{a_1} \ldots \partial x_n^{a_n}}.$$

Analytic continuation: The nodes start with a function f such that $A = \mathrm{dom}(f)$, produced at level n, and a set A^* produced by that time, with $A \cap A^* \neq \emptyset$. It may be that f has a unique analytic continuation f^* (i.e., a way of extending the domain over which f is defined as an analytic function) from $A \cap A^*$ to all of A^*. This node produces, at level n, the function that is f on A and f^* on A^* if it is well-defined.

Quintessential: This is a "boundary-value-problem" node that solves a finite system of partial differential equations (PDE), which may include some ordinary differential equations (ODE), on a set A. The system of PDEs is subject to certain prescribed boundary values and bounds. Each PDE is of the form

$$F(x_1, \ldots, x_k : u, u_1, \ldots, u_l) = 0,$$

where F is a function computed at a previous level and the u_i are partial derivatives of u. An example of a typical boundary-value requirement is $u = u_0$ on a piece γ_0 of the boundary of A, where we use only functions u_0 that have been defined by level $n - 1$. The set A has to be defined by level $n - 1 + \frac{1}{2}$. Note that the machine is capable of producing certain sets in Euclidean space at "half-levels" such as $2\frac{1}{2}$.

If at level n, the machine has produced the function $f(x_1, \ldots, x_k)$, with $\Lambda = \mathrm{dom}(f)$, at level $n + \frac{1}{2}$ it can produce both

$$\Lambda_1 = \{(x_1, \ldots, x_k) \in \Lambda \mid f(x_1, \ldots, x_k) > 0\}$$

and

$$\Lambda_1' = \{(x_1, \ldots, x_k) \in \Lambda \mid f(x_1, \ldots, x_k) \geq 0\}.$$

If the sets $\Lambda_1, \ldots, \Lambda_l$ are produced at level $n + \frac{1}{2}$, then the machine can produce at the same level both their union and intersection. After this parenthesis, let us finish the presentation of quintessential nodes. The bounds, for example on a function u occurring in the boundary-value problem, should be defined by level n.

As it stands, the EAC can produce any real-analytic function. However, Rubel was not comfortable with this idea. He believed that any real or conceptual device can be called a computer only if there are some numbers or functions that it cannot compute. So he decided to restrict the capabilities of the EAC to make it a *real* computing device. More specifically, assume that a function g is produced at level $n - 1$ and a set A is produced by level $n - 1 + \frac{1}{2}$; also suppose that $B \subset A$ is also produced by level $n - 1 + \frac{1}{2}$. Then we allow the function φ, with $B = \mathrm{dom}(\varphi)$, if for every $x_0 \in B$,

$$\lim_{\substack{x \in A \\ x \to x_0}} g(x) = \varphi(x_0).$$

Similar requirements are put on the derivatives of φ. This process is "implemented" by *restricted limit* nodes.

In general, the nodes can be freely interconnected. However, no two outputs should be connected to the same input, and each input has to be hooked up to at least one output. Also, outputs of level n are connected only to inputs of level $n + \frac{1}{2}$, $n + 1$, $n + \frac{3}{2}$, $n + 2, \ldots$. We run the machine by successively running it at levels $0, 1, \ldots, n$, where n has been preselected. The outputs generated at any of these levels are the outputs of the machine.

The EAC is more powerful that the GPAC.

Theorem 9.2.2 *There are functions computable by EACs that no GPAC can compute.*

Also, one can prove the following.

Theorem 9.2.3 *The Γ function, the ζ function, and Barnes's G function, where G is defined by*

$$G(z + 1) = (2\pi)^{z/2} e^{-z(z+1)/2 - \gamma z^2/2} \prod_{n=1}^{\infty} \left\{ \left(1 + \frac{z}{n}\right)^n e^{-z + z^2/(2n)} \right\},$$

can be computed by EACs.

9.3   On Undecidable Problems of Analysis

In the years 1960-1961, Bruno Scarpellini constructed a set of functions representing predicates. Then he examined whether there is a function among these that represents a nonrecursive predicate. He managed to find such a function and thus to establish that certain natural phenomena are actually noncomputable. Originally, he published his work in German, but later it was published in English [170] along with a note [169] that presents his original results with a fresh look. In what follows we will briefly describe Scarpellini's work.

Assume that $P(n_1, \ldots, n_s)$ is a predicate of s arguments over the natural numbers including zero. Also, assume that $\varphi(\alpha_1, \ldots, \alpha_s)$ is a 2π-periodic analytic (possibly complex valued) function of real variables.

Definition 9.3.1 The function φ *represents* the predicate P if

(i) $\varphi(\alpha_1, \ldots, \alpha_s) = \sum\limits_{n_i \geq 0} A_{n_1 n_2 \ldots n_s} e^{in_1 \alpha_1} e^{in_2 \alpha_2} \cdots e^{in_s \alpha_s},$

(ii) $P(n_1, \ldots, n_s) \Leftrightarrow A_{n_1 n_2 \ldots n_s} > 0.$

The Fourier series appearing in the previous definition converges absolutely. In what follows we will use the notation $[\varphi]_{n_1 n_2 \ldots n_s}$ to stand for $A_{n_1 n_2 \ldots n_s}$.

Two functions $\varphi(\alpha_1, \ldots, \alpha_s)$ and $\psi(\alpha_1, \ldots, \alpha_s)$ are *similar* if

$$[\varphi]_{n_1 n_2 \ldots n_s} > 0 \Leftrightarrow [\psi]_{n_1 n_2 \ldots n_s} > 0.$$

In what follows, we will consider only functions whose Fourier coefficients $[\varphi]$ are nonnegative.

For any two functions $\varphi(\alpha_1, \ldots, \alpha_s)$ and $\psi(\alpha_1, \ldots, \alpha_s)$ we define the convolution operation as follows:

$$\varphi * [\alpha_1, \ldots, \alpha_s] \psi = \frac{1}{(2\pi)^s} \int_{-\pi}^{+\pi} \cdots \int_{-\pi}^{+\pi} \varphi(\alpha_1 - \beta_1, \ldots, \alpha_s - \beta_s) \psi(\beta_1, \ldots, \beta_s) d\beta^s.$$

The following result shows how one can represent the conjunction of two predicates.

Lemma 9.3.1 *Suppose that* $P(x_1, \ldots, x_s, z_1, \ldots, z_n)$ *is represented by*

$$\varphi(\alpha_1, \ldots, \alpha_s, \beta_1, \ldots, \beta_n)$$

and that $Q(x_1, \ldots, x_s, y_1, \ldots, y_m)$ *is represented by*

$$\psi(\alpha_1, \ldots, \alpha_s, \gamma_1, \ldots, \gamma_m).$$

Then the conjunction $P \wedge Q$ *is represented by* $\varphi * [\alpha_1, \ldots, \alpha_s] \psi$. *In particular, if* $s = 0$, *then* $P \wedge Q$ *is represented by* $\varphi \cdot \psi$.

It should be clear that if $P(x_1, x_2, \ldots, x_s)$ is represented by $\varphi(\alpha_1, \alpha_2, \ldots, \alpha_s)$, then the predicate $P(x_2, x_1, \ldots, x_s)$ is represented by $\varphi(\alpha_2, \alpha_1, \ldots, \alpha_s)$. In addition, given two s-ary predicates P and Q that are represented by the functions φ and ψ, respectively, then the disjunction $P \vee Q$ can be represented by $\varphi + \psi$, provided that both functions have nonnegative Fourier coefficients, which is always the case here. However, Scarpellini chose not to use this fact. Instead, he used the identity $a \vee b = \neg(\neg a \wedge \neg b)$ to express the conjunction of two predicates. Indeed, if P is an s-ary predicate that is represented by the function φ, then $f - \varphi$ is a representation of $\neg P$, where f is a function representing the predicate $(x_1 = x_1) \wedge \cdots \wedge (x_s = x_s)$, and $[f]_{n_1 n_2 \ldots n_s} = [\varphi]_{n_1 n_2 \ldots n_s}$ holds if P holds true. The function f is called a *unit* of φ. Now, if P and Q are two s-ary predicates represented by φ and ψ, respectively, and f and g are the units of φ and ψ, respectively, then $f * g - (f - \varphi) * (g - \psi)$ is a representation of $P \vee Q$ and $f * g$ is a unit of $\varphi * \psi$.

Lemma 9.3.2 *If $\varphi(\alpha_1, \ldots, \alpha_s, \zeta)$ is a representation of $P(x_1, \ldots, x_s, y)$, then $\varphi(\alpha_1, \ldots, \alpha_s, 0)$ is a representation of $(\exists y)P(x_1, \ldots, x_s, y)$.*

In what follows, Greek letters will denote variables that assume real values. In addition, F_n is the set of n-ary complex-valued functions $\varphi(\zeta_1, \ldots, \zeta_n)$ that are analytic in $\mathbb{R}^n$ and 2π-periodic with regard to each variable ζ_i. We put $F = \bigcup_n F_n$.

If $\mathcal{M} \subset F$, then the closure $\overline{\mathcal{M}}$ is the smallest set $\mathcal{M}_1$ with the following properties:

(i) $\mathcal{M} \subseteq \mathcal{M}_1$.

(ii) If $\varphi(\alpha, \beta) \in \mathcal{M}_1$, then $\varphi(\beta, \alpha), \varphi(\alpha, \alpha) \in \mathcal{M}_1$.

(iii) Suppose that $\varphi(\alpha) \in \mathcal{M}_1$. Then if ξ is a real number then $\varphi(\xi) \in \mathcal{M}_1$, and if β is another variable then $\varphi(\alpha \pm \beta) \in \mathcal{M}_1$.

(iv) If $\varphi, \psi \in \mathcal{M}_1$, then $\varphi \cdot \psi, \varphi \pm \psi \in \mathcal{M}_1$.

(v) If $\varphi, \psi \in \mathcal{M}_1$, then $\varphi * [\alpha_1, \ldots, \alpha_s]\psi \in \mathcal{M}_1$.

(vi) Assume that $g(\xi, \alpha_1, \ldots, \alpha_s), K(\xi, \eta, \alpha_1, \ldots, \alpha_s) \in \mathcal{M}_1$ and in addition assume that for no values of $\alpha_1, \ldots, \alpha_s$ does the integral equation

$$f(\xi) = \frac{1}{2\pi} \int_{-\pi}^{+\pi} K(\xi, \eta, \alpha_1, \ldots, \alpha_s) f(\eta) d\eta$$

have a solution other than zero in $L^2(-\pi, \pi)$ (i.e., a solution square integrable[1] over the interval $(-\pi, \pi)$). Then the (existing and unique)

---
1. A function $f(x)$ is said to be square integrable over the interval (a, b) if the integral $\int_a^b f(x)f^*(x)dx$ is finite, where $f^*(x)$ is the complex conjugate of $f(x)$.

continuous solution $f(\xi, \alpha_1, \ldots, \alpha_s)$ of the integral equation

$$f(\xi, \alpha_1, \ldots, \alpha_s) = g(\xi, \alpha_1, \ldots, \alpha_s)$$
$$+ \frac{1}{2\pi} \int_{-\pi}^{+\pi} K(\xi, \eta, \alpha_1, \ldots, \alpha_s) f(\eta) d\eta \qquad (9.1)$$

is in $\mathcal{M}_1$.

Equipped with these definitions, we can choose as set $\mathcal{M}$ a set $\mathcal{M}_0$ as follows.

Definition 9.3.2 A function $f(\alpha_1, \ldots, \alpha_s)$ is in $\mathcal{M}_0$ exactly if there are two polynomials $p(y_1, \ldots, y_s)$ and $q(y_1, \ldots, y_s)$ with real coefficients such that

$$f = p(e^{i\alpha_1}, \ldots, e^{i\alpha_s}) q(e^{i\alpha_1}, \ldots, e^{i\alpha_s})^{-1}$$

with $q \neq 0$ for all α_i, $i \leq s$.

One can prove the following theorem.

Theorem 9.3.1 *For every recursively enumerable set S there is a function f in $\overline{\mathcal{M}_0}$ that represents S.*

So far, we have considered functions that are generated by admitting solutions of *Fredholm integral equations* of the second kind (i.e., integral equations such as equation 9.1). If instead we consider solutions of Fredholm equations of the first kind (i.e., $f(x) = \int_a^b K(x,t)\varphi(t)dt$), we can easily construct a representation of

$$P(n) = \int_0^{2\pi} f(\alpha)\cos(n\alpha)d\alpha > 0$$

for every predicate $P \in \Sigma_k^0$ and every $k > 0$.

Assume that we opt to use the solutions of Volterra integral equations[2] instead of solutions of Fredholm equations. Then interesting problems arise. For example, one may ask whether it is possible to construct an analog computer that can generate functions $f(x)$ for which the predicate

$$\int f(x)\cos(nx)dx > 0$$

---

2. A Volterra integral equation of the first kind has the form

$$f(x) = \int_a^x K(x,t)\varphi(t)dt,$$

while a Volterra integral equation of the second kind is an integral equation of the form

$$\varphi(x) = f(x) + \int_a^x K(x,t)\varphi(t)dt.$$

They differ from the corresponding Fredholm equations by having a variable in one of the integration limits.

is not decidable while the machine itself decides by direct measurement whether $\int f(x)\cos(nx)dx$ is greater that zero. Clearly, the construction of such a machine, which is no easy task, would possibly illustrate the existence of noncomputable natural processes. Indeed, this is interesting by itself, since the established view is that classical mechanics is computable!

Jürg Peter Buser and Bruno Scarpellini [30] have described another method to obtain undecidable problems of analysis. This approach was first investigated by Buser [29]. This alternative method as well as the final result are described briefly in the rest of this section.

Assume that $\mathcal{F}$ is the set of functions

$$f(\alpha_1, \ldots, \alpha_s) = g(\alpha_1, \ldots, \alpha_s) + ih(\alpha_1, \ldots, \alpha_s),$$

where g and h are analytic functions in $\alpha_j \in [a_j, b_j]$, $j \leq s$, and a_j, b_j are computable reals in the following sense.

Definition 9.3.3 Suppose that $f, g : \mathbb{N} \to \mathbb{N}$ are recursive functions such that $g(n) \neq 0$. Then $a(n) = f(n)/g(n)$ is a recursive sequence of rationals. This sequence converges recursively if there is a recursive function $k : \mathbb{N} \to \mathbb{N}$ that has the following property: given any $m \in \mathbb{N}$, if $p \geq k(m)$ and $q \geq k(m)$, then $|a(p) - a(q)| \leq \frac{1}{m}$. A real number c is called computable if there is a recursive sequence $a(n)$ that converges recursively to c (i.e., $\lim a(n) = c$). A complex number $a + bi$ is computable if both a and b are computable.

Note that c is necessarily nonnegative. However, it is trivial to extend the definitions to negative real numbers.

If $\mathcal{M} \subseteq \mathcal{F}$, its *elementary hull* $\overline{\mathcal{M}}$ is the smallest set $\mathcal{M}_1$ with the following properties:

(i) $\mathcal{M} \subseteq \mathcal{M}_1$.

(ii) If g is defined on $D = \prod_{j=1}^{s}[a_j, b_j]$, is in $\mathcal{M}_1$, and is nonzero on D, then $g^{-1} \in \mathcal{M}_1$.

(iii) If f and g are defined on D and are in $\mathcal{M}_1$, then $f + g, f - g$, and fg are in $\mathcal{M}_1$.

(iv) If $f \in \mathcal{M}_1$, then $f^* \in \mathcal{M}_1$.

(v) Assume that $f(\alpha_1, \ldots, \alpha_s) \in \mathcal{M}_1$, where $\alpha_j \in [a_j, b_j]$, and that $A_j, B_j, C_j, a_j', b_j', a_j'', b_j''$ satisfy

$$A_j + B_j\beta_j + C_j\gamma_j \in [a_j, b_j] \text{ for } \beta_j \in [a_j', b_j'], \gamma_j \in [a_j'', b_j''],$$

$j \leq s$. Then the function

$$f(A_1 + B_1\beta_1 + C_1\gamma_1, \ldots, A_s + B_s\beta_s + C_s\gamma_s),$$

where $\beta_j \in [a_j', b_j']$ and $\gamma_j \in [a_j'', b_j'']$ for $j \leq s$, is in $\mathcal{M}_1$.

(vi) Suppose that $f(\alpha_1, \ldots, \alpha_s, \beta) \in \mathcal{M}_1$, where $\alpha_j \in [a_j, b_j]$, $\beta \in [c, d]$. Then

$$\int_c^d f(\alpha_1, \ldots, \alpha_s, \beta) d\beta$$

is in $\mathcal{M}_1$.

Assume that $D(\zeta)$, $L(\varepsilon)$ are polynomial $n \times n$ matrices, $H(\zeta)$ is a polynomial $m \times m$ matrix, $P(\zeta, \xi)$, $R(\varepsilon)$ are polynomial n-vectors, and $Q(\xi)$ is a polynomial m-vector, where $\zeta = (\zeta_1, \ldots, \zeta_n)$, $\xi = (\xi_1, \ldots, \xi_m)$, and $\varepsilon = (\varepsilon_1, \ldots, \varepsilon_n)$.

Definition 9.3.4 A vector function $y \in C^1([0, T] \times [a, b]; \mathbb{C}^n)$ is called *admissible* if there are D, L, H, P, Q, and R that are polynomial matrices and vectors of the kind above, and $z \in C^1([a, b]; \mathbb{C}^m)$, $g \in C^1([a, b]; \mathbb{C}^n)$ such that

(i) $D(y(t, \lambda))\frac{dy}{dt} = P(y(t, \lambda), z(\lambda))$, $H(z(\lambda))\frac{dy}{d\lambda} = Q(z(\lambda))$, and $L(g(\lambda))\frac{dg}{d\lambda} = R(g(\lambda))$, where $t \in [0, T]$ and $\lambda \in [a, b]$;

(ii) $\det(D(y(t, \lambda))) \neq 0$, $\det(H(z(\lambda))) \neq 0$, and $\det(L(g(\lambda))) \neq 0$, where $t \in [0, T]$ and $\lambda \in [a, b]$;

(iii) $y(0, \lambda) = g(\lambda)$, where $\lambda \in [a, b]$, and $z(a)$, $g(a)$ are computable.

A function $f \in C^1([0, T] \times [a, b]; \mathbb{C})$ is admissible if there is an admissible $y = (y_1, \ldots, y_n)$ such that $f = y_i$ for some $i \leq n$.

Assume that $\mathcal{M}_0$ is the set of functions $\lambda e_{js}(\alpha_1, \ldots, \alpha_s)$, where $\lambda \in \mathbb{C}$ is computable, and $e_{js}(\alpha_1, \ldots, \alpha_s) = e^{i\alpha_j}$ for $j \leq s$. Also, assume that $\mathcal{M}_2 \supseteq \mathcal{M}_0$.

Definition 9.3.5 A function g is in $\mathcal{M}_2$ if either $g \in \mathcal{M}_0$ or if g is admissible in the sense of definition 9.3.4.

Now, we are ready to state the main result of [30].

Theorem 9.3.2 *Assume that $P(x)$ is a recursively enumerable predicate. Then there is a $\varphi \in \mathcal{M}_2$ that represents $P(x)$, where $\mathcal{M}_2$ is the class of functions generated by a GPAC.*

The remarks presented above apply also to this particular method. So nothing more will be said.

9.4 Noncomputability in Computable Analysis

As was pointed out in Section 7.1, Weihrauch's theory of computable analysis is not the only approach. For example, Pour-El and Jonathan Ian Richards [158] have presented their own approach to computable analysis, which is based on a definition of computable real numbers that is identical to the fifth case of Lemma 7.1.2 on page 120. The work of Pour-El and Richards is interesting because they have managed to discover noncomputability in ordinary physical systems, such as wave-propagation.

In general, the following PDE describes the wave propagation phenomenon in three dimensions:

$$\nabla^2 \psi = \frac{1}{v^2} \frac{\partial^2 \psi}{\partial t^2}, \tag{9.2}$$

where v is the velocity of the wave. Assume that v is equal to 1 and let us consider the equation with initial conditions

$$\nabla^2 \psi - \frac{\partial^2 \psi}{\partial t^2} = 0,$$
$$\psi(x,y,z,0) = f(x,y,z), \tag{9.3}$$
$$\frac{\partial \psi}{\partial t}(x,y,z,0) = 0.$$

Pour-El and Richards considered the wave equation on compact domains. These domains must be large enough so that "light rays" from the outside cannot reach any point in the domain in any time considered. This leads to the definition of D_1 and D_2 as follows:

$$D_1 = \left\{ (x,y,z) \;\middle|\; |x| \le 1, |y| \le 1, |z| \le 1 \right\},$$
$$D_2 = \left\{ (x,y,z) \;\middle|\; |x| \le 3, |y| \le 3, |z| \le 3 \right\}.$$

Notice that if $0 < t < 2$, the solution of the wave equation on D_1 does not depend on the initial values $\psi(x,y,z,0)$ outside D_2. And this leads us to assume that f has domain D_2. With this assumption and using the "First Main Theorem" of [158], one can show the following.

Theorem 9.4.1 *Consider the wave equation (9.2). Moreover, let D_1 and D_2 be the two cubes defined above. Then there exists a computable continuous function $f(x,y,z)$ in D_2 such that the solution $u(x,y,z,t)$ of (9.3) at time $t = 1$ is continuous on D_1 but is not a computable function there.*

Results that deal with the computability/noncomputability of eigenvalues and spectra of linear operators $T : H \to H$, where H is a Banach space that is effectively a separable Hilbert space (i.e., a Hilbert space that contains a countable dense subset), are particularly important. Recall that Hilbert spaces are used to model physical phenomena. The main results of Pour-El and Richards concerning noncomputability and operators on Hilbert spaces follow.

Theorem 9.4.2 *There exists an effectively determined bounded self-adjoint operator $T : H \to H$ whose sequence of eigenvalues is not computable.*

Theorem 9.4.3 *There exists an effectively determined bounded self-adjoint operator $T : H \to H$ whose norm is not a computable real number.*

Theorem 9.4.4 *There exists an effectively determined bounded operator $T : H \to H$ (not self-adjoint or normal) that has a noncomputable real number as an eigenvalue.*

The results presented in this section prove that our universe has properties that are noncomputable. Whether noncomputability is a general property of this universe is an open problem.

9.5   The Halting Function Revisited

Newton Carneiro Affonso da Costa and Francisco Antonio Doria have shown that the halting function can be expressed in the language of calculus. As explained to the author by Doria in a personal communication, da Costa and Doria originally were looking for a Rice-like theorem in the language of classical analysis in order to derive from it the undecidability (and Gödel incompleteness) of chaos theory. Only after they had reached their goal did they notice that their main tool was an expression for the halting function in that language. Their work has appeared in various journals, but the current exposition is based on their presentation in [45], which appeared in a special issue of the *Applied Mathematics and Computation* journal devoted to hypercomputation.

In order to proceed, we need to know what a universal Diophantine polynomial is:

Definition 9.5.1 Assume that $U(a_1, \ldots, a_k, x_0, x_1, \ldots, x_m)$ is a polynomial with integer coefficients. Then U is a universal Diophantine polynomial if for any Diophantine equation

$$D(a_1, \ldots, a_k, z_1, \ldots, z_n) = 0,$$

we can find a code $c \in \mathbb{N}$ such that

$$\left(\exists z_1, \ldots, z_n \text{ with } D(a_1, \ldots, a_k, z_1, \ldots, z_n) = 0 \right)$$

$$\Longleftrightarrow \left(\exists x_1, \ldots, x_m \text{ with } U(a_1, \ldots, a_k, c, x_1, \ldots, x_m) = 0 \right).$$

Assume that $\varphi_e : \mathbb{N} \to \mathbb{N}$ is the partial recursive function with Gödel number e. Then the following result (essentially equivalent to the Matiyasevich–Davis–Robinson resolution of Hilbert's tenth problem, named after Matiyasevich, Martin Davis and Julia Bowman Robinson) provides a link between polynomials and partial recursive functions (see [48] for the proof).

Proposition 9.5.1 *We can algorithmically construct a polynomial p_e over the natural numbers such that*

$$[\varphi_e(m) = n] \Leftrightarrow [\exists x_1, \ldots, x_k \in \mathbb{N} : p_e(m, n, x_1, \ldots, x_k) = 0].$$

The following result is a steppingstone to our goal of defining the halting function in the language of the calculus:

Proposition 9.5.2 *There is a proper injective function $\varkappa_P : P \to \mathscr{A}$, where P is the algebra of $\mathbb{N}$-defined and $\mathbb{N}$-valued polynomials having a finite number of variables, and $\mathscr{A}$ is the real-valued and real-defined algebra of polynomials, trigonometric functions, including the number π, absolute value, and exponentials, closed under sum, product, function composition, derivatives, and integrals such that:*

(i) *$\varkappa_P$ is constructive, which means that if we are provided with the arithmetic expression of p, there is an effective procedure by means of which we can obtain the expression for $F = \varkappa_P(p)$ in $\mathscr{A}$.*

(ii) *Let $\mathbf{x} = (x_1, \ldots, x_n)$. Then there is $\mathbf{x} \in \mathbb{N}^n$ such that $p(m, \mathbf{x}) = 0$ if and only if there exists $\mathbf{x} \in \mathbb{R}^n$ such that $F(m, \mathbf{x}) = 0$ if and only if there is $\mathbf{x} \in \mathbb{R}^n$ such that $F(m, \mathbf{x}) \leq 1$, for $p \in P$ and $F = \varkappa_P(p) \in \mathscr{A}$.*

Let us define $h(x) = x \sin x$ and $g(x) = x \sin x^3$. Given $F(m, \mathbf{x})$, if we substitute each x_i according to the scheme

$$x_1 = h,$$
$$x_2 = h \circ g,$$
$$x_3 = h \circ g \circ g,$$

$$\vdots \quad \vdots \quad \vdots$$

$$x_{n-1} = \underbrace{h \circ g \circ \cdots \circ g,}_{n - 2 \text{ times}}$$

$$x_n = \underbrace{g \circ \cdots \circ g,}_{n \text{ times}}$$

we get the new function $G(m, x)$. Let $L(m, x) = G(m, x) - \frac{1}{2}$.

Proposition 9.5.3 *Assume that $\mathscr{A}_1$ is the subalgebra $\mathscr{A}$ of functions with only one variable. Then there exists a function $\varkappa' : P \to \mathscr{A}_1$ that is constructive and injective and such that the inclusion $\varkappa'(P) \subset \mathscr{A}_1$ is proper. In addition, there is $\mathbf{x} \in \mathbb{N}^n$ such that $p(m, \mathbf{x}) = 0$ if and only if there exists $x \in \mathbb{R}$ such that $L(m, x) = 0$ if and only if there is $x \in \mathbb{R}$ such that $G(m, x) \leq 1$.*

Suppose that $\sigma : \mathbb{R} \to \mathbb{R}$ is the sign function (i.e., $\sigma(\pm x) = \pm 1$ and $\sigma(0) = 0$).

Theorem 9.5.1 *The halting function $h(m, i)$ can be explicitly defined by*

$$h(m, i) = \sigma\left(G_{m,i}\right),$$

$$G_{m,i} = \int_{-\infty}^{+\infty} C_{m,i}(x)e^{-x^2}dx,$$

$$C_{m,i}(x) = |F_{m,i}(x) - 1| - (F_{m,i}(x) - 1),$$

$$F_{m,i}(x) = xp_{m,i},$$

where $p_{m,i}$ is a one-parameter universal Diophantine polynomial

$$p(\langle m, i \rangle, x_1, \ldots, x_n)$$

and $\langle .,. \rangle$ is the pairing function.

The solvability of the halting function in the language of calculus formed the basis for proposing *H-computation theory* (where the "H" stands for Hilbert), which was proposed by da Costa and Doria [41]. In particular, these researchers defined the notion of an H-algorithm in this extended theory of computation as follows.

Definition 9.5.2 An H-algorithm is a set of instructions described by a finite string of discrete symbols that operates on finite strings of discrete symbols such that:

(i) the computation consists of a finite number of discrete steps that can be coded as a finite string of discrete symbols;

(ii) if and when the computation terminates, the output is expressed by finite strings of discrete symbols;

(iii) it is always possible to decide whether two smooth lines within a plane rectangle intersect.

The last condition, which is called the *Geometric principle*, is enough to extend the theory of computation. For example, it can be proved that there is an H-algorithm that can solve Hilbert's tenth problem. The idea to include the geometric principle in an extended theory of computation was the result of a discussion between Doria and Morris Hirsch. Note that the discovery that Euclid's parallel postulate is independent of the remaining axioms of plane geometry was crucial, since

> it emphasizes the formal nature of an axiomatic system through the separation between syntax and semantics, and shows that a naive-looking, intuitively "true" geometric assertion can be unprovable from "natural" first principles [40].

9.6 Neural Networks and Hypercomputation

An artificial neural network, or ANN, is a computational system composed of many simple processing units operating in parallel whose function is determined by network structure, connection strengths, and the processing performed at nodes, or neurons. The connection strength is expressed by a number that is referred to as *weight*. ANNs have their roots in a paper written by Warren Sturgis McCulloch and Walter Pitts in 1943 [125]. In this paper, McCulloch and Pitts had developed a mathematical model for certain aspects of brain function. Generally speaking, in an ANN, information flows in only one direction. In the early 1980s, John Joseph Hopfield discovered "recurrent networks," in which information flows from a connection node back to itself via other nodes. Such an artificial network has complete connectivity, greater resemblance to a real neural network, and a memory of past events. More specifically, recurrent neural networks have a sort of long-term memory, but both feed-forward and recurrent neural networks can have long-term memory in their weights.

An ANN has input channels that mimic dendrites (i.e., fibers that carry input into the neuron), and output channels that represent the axons (i.e., fibers that deliver output from a neuron to other neurons). A synapse, which is a chemical gate between dendrites and axons, is modeled by an adjustable weight. ANNs have been very popular because of their capability to learn patterns from examples. In particular, a learning algorithm may adjust the weights of given interconnections to allow an ANN to learn. In addition, ANNs can create their own organization or representation of the information they receive during learning time. Finally we should stress that ANNs are inherently parallel in nature.

In general, it should be clear from this brief presentation why ANNs are considered a form of natural computation. However, ANNs are not explicitly continuous by their construction. Indeed, ANNs are discrete computational structures, and so they should not be classified as natural computing devices. However, if we insist that a network update itself continuously and utilize a continuous configuration space, then the resulting computational structure is indeed, analog and hence it can be classified as a natural computation device. Along these lines, Hava Siegelmann and her collaborator Eduardo Sontag proposed an *analog recurrent* neural network, or ARNN. The theory of ARNNs has been detailed in Siegelmann's book [183].

An ARNN is composed of a finite number of elementary processors called neurons. Each neuron is associated with a local state that depends on time. More specifically, neuron i is associated with the local state $x_i(t)$. At every time step, a vector u of binary inputs with m components, denoted by $u_j, j = 1, \ldots, m$, is fed to the network. The dynamics of the network are defined by a map

$$\mathcal{F} : \mathbb{R}^n \times \{0, 1\}^m \to \mathbb{R}^n,$$

where n is the number of neurons that make up the network, and which reads componentwise as

$$x_i(t+1) = \sigma\Big(\sum_{j=1}^{n} a_{ij}x_j(t) + \sum_{j=1}^{m} b_{ij}u_j(t) + c_i\Big), \quad i = 1,\ldots,n.$$

The letter σ represents the response function, which is usually either the logistic function $\frac{1}{1+e^{-x}}$ or the piecewise linear function

$$\sigma(x) = \begin{cases} 0, & \text{if } x < 0, \\ x, & \text{if } 0 \leq x \leq 1, \\ 1, & \text{if } x > 1. \end{cases}$$

Coefficients a_{ij}, b_{ij}, and c_i are real numbers and are called *weights* of the neural network. These coefficients play the same role as the coefficients c^2 and $\hbar$ in the equations $E = mc^2$ and $E = \hbar\nu$. However, these coefficients are not some sort of universal constants: they are just numbers that affect the behavior of an ARNN. Although a neural network with irrational coefficients may seem highly infeasible, many equations describing physical phenomena involve irrational coefficients. Thus, it is not unreasonable to consider ARNNs with irrational coefficients. Each neuron updates its response value continuously, and these values are not restricted. Thus, one may characterize ARNNs as analog computational devices. But how powerful are the ARNNs? In other words, what is it that these devices can compute?

A model of computation is called *nonuniform* when given a problem P, a different algorithm is allowed for each input size. Contrast this with Turing machines, which are uniform models of computation, since a particular machine solves the same problem for inputs of all sizes. In Section 5.4 we briefly described Turing machines with advice. These conceptual computing devices constitute a nonuniform model of computation, because the different advice strings cannot be generated from finite rules. They clearly surpass the computational power of (ordinary) Turing machines. In particular, the P/poly class of functions contains functions that are not Turing-computable. It has been proved that ARNNs can compute in polynomial time exactly the functions in P/poly. In other words, ARNNs are hypermachines with an extrinsically defined computational class.

9.7 An Optical Model of Computation

It is surprising how some everyday operations performed by scientists, engineers, and ordinary people have led to the development of new models of computation (e.g., the Turing machine is a conceptual computing device most probably inspired by production lines of factories at Turing's time). Indeed, a new model of computation, dubbed the optical model of computation, introduced by Damien Woods and Thomas J. Naughton in [229], arises as a realization (possibly physical) of their *continuous space machine* (CSM), which was inspired by common optical-information-processing operations. A CSM operates in discrete time steps over a finite number of two-dimensional complex-valued images of finite size and infinite spatial resolution. Various optical operations are performed by a finite control.

A CSM consists of a memory that contains a program and an input. In this respect, CSMs are similar to von Neumann machines. Generally, the memory has the form of a two-dimensional grid of rectangular elements as shown in Figure 9.1. This grid has finite size, while each rectangular element is associated with a unique address. In addition, there is a specific start address labeled **sta** and two well-known addresses labeled **a** and **b**. The instruction set contains commands that effect optical image-processing-tasks.

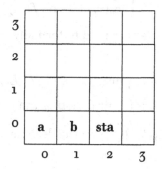

Figure 9.1: The memory of a CSM.

A CSM manipulates images, which are complex-valued functions f : $[0, 1) \times [0, 1) \to \mathbb{C}$. The set of all such images is denoted by $\mathcal{I}$. The function $f \in \mathcal{I}$ gives the one-dimensional Fourier transformation of its two-dimensional argument and is defined as

$$h(f(x,y)) = h'(F(\alpha,y)),$$

where $F(\alpha,y)$ is the Fourier transformation in the x-direction of $f(x,y)$ defined as

$$F(\alpha,y) = \int_{-\infty}^{+\infty} f(x,y)e^{i2\pi\alpha x}\,dx,$$

where $h'(F(\alpha,y)) = F(\vartheta\alpha,y)$, and where ϑ is a constant that is used to linearly rescale F so that F is defined over $[0, 1) \times [0, 1)$. Similarly, the function $v : \mathcal{I} \to \mathcal{I}$ gives the Fourier transformation in the y-direction of its two-dimensional argument and is defined as

$$F(x, \beta) = \int_{-\infty}^{+\infty} f(x, y) e^{i2\pi\beta y} \, dy,$$

where $v'(F(x, \beta)) = F(x, \vartheta\beta)$. The function $* : \mathcal{I} \to \mathcal{I}$ returns the complex conjugate of its argument:

$$*(f(x, y)) = f^*(x, y).$$

The functions $\cdot : \mathcal{I} \times \mathcal{I} \to \mathcal{I}$ and $+ : \mathcal{I} \times \mathcal{I} \to \mathcal{I}$ return the pointwise complex product and sum of their arguments, respectively. The function $\varrho : \mathcal{I} \times \mathcal{I} \times \mathcal{I} \to \mathcal{I}$ performs amplitude thresholding[3] of its first argument using the other two arguments, which are real-valued (i.e., $z_l, z_u : [0, 1) \times [0, 1) \to \mathbb{R}$), as lower and upper amplitude thresholds, respectively:

$$\varrho(f(x, y), z_l(x, y), z_u(x, y)) = \begin{cases} z_l(x, y), & \text{if } |f(x, y)| < z_l(x, y), \\ |f(x, y)|, & \text{if } z_l(x, y) \leq |f(x, y)| \leq z_u(x, y), \\ z_u(x, y), & \text{if } |f(x, y)| > z_u(x, y). \end{cases}$$

The operations defined so far are used to formally define CMSs in [229] as follows.

Definition 9.7.1 A CSM is a quintuple $\mathcal{M} = (D, L, I, P, O)$, where

- $D = (m, n)$, $m, n \in \mathbb{N}$, is a pair denoting the grid dimensions;

- $L = \left((s_\xi, s_\eta), (a_\xi, a_\eta), (b_\xi, b_\eta) \right)$ are the designated addresses **sta**, **a**, and **b**;

- $I = \left\{ (i_1, j_1), \ldots, (i_k, j_k) \right\}$ are the addresses of the k input images;

- $P = \left\{ (\xi_1, p_1, q_1), \ldots, (\xi_r, p_r, q_r) \right\}$, $\xi_i \in (\{h, v, *, \cdot, +, \varrho, \text{st}, \text{ld}, \text{br}, \text{hlt}\} \cup \mathcal{N}) \subset \mathcal{I}$ are the programming symbols and their addresses, and $\mathcal{N}$ is a finite set of images that encode the CSM's addresses;

- $O = \left\{ (\varphi_1, \psi_1), \ldots, (\varphi_l, \psi_l) \right\}$ are the addresses of the l output images.

The programming symbols and their informal semantics are presented in Table 9.1.

A configuration of a CSM $\mathcal{M}$ is a pair $\langle c, e \rangle$, where $c \in \{0, \ldots, m - 1\} \times \{0, \ldots, n - 1\}$ is an address called the control. Also,

$$e = \left((i_{00}, 0, 0), \ldots, (i_{(m-1)(n-1)}, m - 1, n - 1) \right),$$

---

3. Amplitude thresholding is a generalized clipping filter. An example is the clipping of a 3D surface to a view frustum by setting z_u and z_l to constants corresponding to the depth of the hin and yon planes. Because z_u and z_l are themselves images, this operation can also achieve, for example, a nonuniform cross-dissolve to a higher-value image by increasing $|f|$ over time.

Symbol	Arguments	Description
h	0	Perform a horizontal one-dimensional Fourier transformation on the two-dimensional image that is stored in **a** and store the result in **a**.
v	0	Perform a vertical one-dimensional Fourier transformation on the two-dimensional image that is stored in **a** and store the result in **a**.
*	0	Replace the image stored in **a** with its complex conjugate.
·	0	Multiply (point by point) the two images stored in **a** and **b** and store the resulting image in **a**.
+	0	Perform a complex addition of the images stored in **a** and **b** and store the resulting image in **a**.
ϱ	2	Filter the image stored in **a** by amplitude using the first and second arguments as lower and upper amplitude threshold images and store the resulting image in **a**.
st	4	Copy the image in **a** (automatically rescalling) into the rectangle of images designated by the four arguments of this command; more specifically, the address of its lower left corner is specified by the first and the third arguments and the address of its upper right corner is specified by the second and the fourth arguments.
ld	4	Copy into **a** (automatically rescaling) the rectangle of images designated by the four arguments of this command, which specify the rectangle of images, just as the four arguments of the st command specify the corresponding rectangle.
br	2	Unconditionally branch to the address specified by the two arguments of the command.
hlt	0	Halt program execution.

Table 9.1: The CSM programming symbols; when a command has arguments it is assumed that they are stored in consecutive squares.

where $i_{kl} \in \mathcal{I}$ is an image stored at address (k, l). Initially, the configuration of a CSM is $\langle c_{sta}, e_{sta} \rangle$, where $c_{sta} = (s_\xi, s_\eta)$ is the address of **sta**, and e_{sta} contains all the commands and the images stored in the memory. At the end of a computation, the configuration of a machine has the form

$$\langle (\gamma, \delta), (u, (\text{hlt}, \gamma, \delta), w) \rangle.$$

It is fairly straightforward to define a binary relation $\vdash_{\mathcal{M}}$ on configurations in order to formally define the semantics of the commands presented in Table 9.1 (see [229] for details).

CSMs are interesting analog computing devices, but are they feasible or are they just another conceptual computing device? The answer is that there is indeed a realistic optical model of computation. For instance, a complex-valued image could be represented physically by a spatial coherent optical wavefront, which can be produced by a laser. The functions h and v could be physically implemented by two convex cylindrical lenses, oriented horizontally and vertically, respectively, while the constant ϑ, which is used in the definition of h and v, could be implemented using Fourier-spectrum size reduction techniques. The function $*$ could be effected using a phase-conjugate mirror. The function $\cdot$ could be realized by placing a spatial light modulator encoding an image g in the path of a wave front encoding another image h. The wave front immediately behind the modulator would be the product of the two images. The function $+$ could be implemented using a $50 : 50$ beam splitter. And the function ϱ could be realized using an electronic camera or a liquid-crystal light valve.

The optical model of computation presented so far can be characterized as a model of computation once we have at our disposal a concrete way to encode data as images and decode the result of a computation. Indeed, it is not difficult to provide such an encoding/decoding scheme. Assume that $B = \{0, 1\}$. Then if $\psi \in B$, the following image encodes ψ:

$$f_\psi(x, y) = \begin{cases} 1, & \text{if } (x = 0.5) \wedge (y = 0.5) \wedge (\psi = 1), \\ 0, & \text{otherwise.} \end{cases}$$

There are two ways to represent bit strings: Assume that $w \in B^+$. Then w can be encoded as

$$f_w(x, y) = \begin{cases} 1, & \text{if } \left(x = 1 - \dfrac{3}{2^{k-i+2}} \right) \wedge (y = 0.5) \wedge (w_i = 1), \\ 0, & \text{otherwise,} \end{cases}$$

where $i = 1, \ldots, k = |w|$. We see that (f_w, k) uniquely encodes w. Alternatively, the bit string w can be encoded as follows:

$$f_w(x, y) = \begin{cases} 1, & \text{if } \left(x = \dfrac{2i - 1}{2k} \right) \wedge (y = 0.5) \wedge (w_i = 1), \\ 0, & \text{otherwise.} \end{cases}$$

Similarly, we see that (f_w, k) uniquely encodes w. A real number r can be encoded as an image as follows:

$$f_r(x,y) = \begin{cases} r, & \text{if } (x = 0.5) \wedge (y = 0.5), \\ 0, & \text{otherwise.} \end{cases}$$

Here, the real number r is represented by an image with a single peak of value r.

It also possible to encode an $m \times n$ matrix A of real values as follows:

$$f_A(x,y) = \begin{cases} a_{ij}, & \text{if } \left(x = 1 - \dfrac{1 + 2k}{2^{j+k}}\right) \wedge \left(y = \dfrac{1 + 2l}{2^{i+l}}\right), \\ 0, & \text{otherwise,} \end{cases}$$

where

$$k = \begin{cases} 1, & \text{if } j < n, \\ 0, & \text{if } j = n, \end{cases} \qquad l = \begin{cases} 1, & \text{if } i < m, \\ 0, & \text{if } i = m. \end{cases}$$

The core of this optical model of computation having been presented, what is left is to discuss the computational power of the CSMs. The main result concerning the computational power of CSMs can be stated as follows.

Theorem 9.7.1 *There exists a CSM $\mathcal{M}$ such that for each ARNN $\mathcal{A}$, $\mathcal{M}$ computes $\mathcal{A}$'s input/output map, using the Wood-Naughton ARNN input-output representation.*

This result implies that CSMs have at least the computational power of ARNNs.

9.8   Fuzzy Membrane Computing

Membrane computing is a model of computation inspired by the way cells live and function. P systems are conceptual membrane-computing devices built of nested compartments surrounded by porous membranes that define and confine these compartments. The nested compartments form a tree structure, called a *membrane structure*. Figure 9.2 depicts a characteristic membrane structure.Before proceeding, let us give a formal definition of membrane structure.

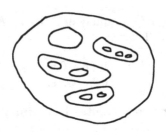

Figure 9.2: A typical membrane structure.

Definition 9.8.1 Let $V = \{[,]\}$ be an alphabet. The set MS is the least set inductively defined as follows:

(i) $[] \in$ MS;

(ii) if $\mu_1, \mu_2, \ldots \mu_n \in$ MS, then $[\mu_1 \ldots \mu_n] \in$ MS.

Initially, each compartment contains a number of possibly repeated objects (i.e., multisets of objects). When "computation" commences, the compartments exchange objects according to a number of multiset processing rules that are associated with each compartment; in the simplest case, these processing rules are just multiset rewriting rules. The activity stops when no rule can be applied. The result of the computation is equal to the number of objects that reside in a designated compartment called the *output membrane*. The general theory of P systems has been developed by Gheorghe Păun and his colleagues, and the major results concerning P systems are presented in [147].

From the previous short presentation it should be obvious that membrane computing is not really a form of natural computing, since continuity is used nowhere. In addition, although there is provision for some sort of interaction between a membrane structure and its surrounding environment, still it is assumed that the membrane structure lives in a quiet and calm environment, which definitely does not correspond to what happens in the real world. However, since P systems evolved from an abstraction of a biological structure, one can view them as a marginal type of natural computing.

As they stand, P systems provide no real insight into either computability theory or complexity theory. For instance, P systems have at most the computational power of Turing machines (see [147]). However, by properly extending the definition of P systems, we may get new systems with interesting properties. For instance, by fuzzifying the data manipulated by a P system, we get a new structure capable of computing any positive real number. Also, by replacing the calm and quiet environment that surrounds ordinary P systems with an active environment that continuously and reciprocally affects membrane structures, we get truly interactive systems.

P systems with fuzzy data were first defined in [196], leading to the fuzzification of P systems. When presented with an element x, this either belongs or does not belong to a set A. As was explained above (see page 168), in the case of a fuzzy subset, an element belongs to it to a degree i, which is a real number in the unit interval I. Assume that we have a multiset that draws elements from some universe (i.e., a fixed set X); then the multiset contains a number of copies of each element of the universe. A "fuzzy multiset" should be a structure that contains the elements of a given multiset to a degree. These structures have been dubbed *multi-fuzzy sets* and are defined as follows [196].

Definition 9.8.2 Assume that $M : X \to \mathbb{N}$ characterizes a multiset M. Then a multi-fuzzy subset of M is a structure $\mathscr{A}$ that is characterized by a function $\mathscr{A} : X \to \mathbb{N} \times I$ such that if $M(x) = n$, then $\mathscr{A}(x) = (n, i)$. In addition, the expression $\mathscr{A}(x) = (n, i)$ denotes that the degree to which each of the n copies of x belong to $\mathscr{A}$ is i.

Given a multi-fuzzy set $\mathscr{A}$, we can define the following two functions: the *multiplicity* function $\mathscr{A}_\pi : X \to \mathbb{N}$ and the *membership* function $\mathscr{A}_\sigma : X \to I$. If $\mathscr{A}(x) = (n, i)$, then $\mathscr{A}_\pi(x) = n$ and $\mathscr{A}_\sigma(x) = i$. The cardinality of a multi-fuzzy set is defined as follows.

Definition 9.8.3 Suppose that $\mathscr{A}$ is a multi-fuzzy set having the set X as its universe. Then its cardinality, denoted by card $\mathscr{A}$, is defined as

$$\text{card } \mathscr{A} = \sum_{a \in X} \mathscr{A}_\pi(a) \mathscr{A}_\sigma(a).$$

With these preliminary definitions, we can formally define P systems with fuzzy data.

Definition 9.8.4 A P system with fuzzy data is a construction

$$\Pi_{\text{FD}} = (O, \mu, w^{(1)}, \ldots, w^{(m)}, R_1, \ldots, R_m, i_0),$$

where:

(i) O is an alphabet (i.e., a set of distinct entities) whose elements are called *objects*;

(ii) μ is the membrane structure of degree $m \geq 1$, which is the depth of the corresponding tree structure; membranes are injectively labeled with successive natural numbers starting with one;

(iii) $w^{(i)} : O \to \mathbb{N} \times I$, $1 \leq i \leq m$, are functions that represent multi-fuzzy sets over O associated with the region surrounded by membrane i;

(iv) R_i, $1 \leq i \leq m$, are finite sets of multiset rewriting rules (called *evolution rules*) over O. An evolution rule is of the form $u \to v$, $u \in O^*$ and $v \in O_{TAR}^*$, where $O_{TAR} = O \times TAR$,

$$TAR = \{here, out\} \cup \{in_j | 1 \leq j \leq m\}.$$

The keywords "here," "out," and "in$_j$" are used to specify the current compartment (i.e., the compartment the rule is associated with), the compartments that surrounds the current compartment, and the compartment with label j, respectively. The effect of each rule is the removal of the elements of the left-hand side of the rule from the current compartment (i.e., elements that match the left-hand side of a rule are removed from the current compartment) and the introduction of the elements of the right-hand side to the designated compartments. Also, the rules implicitly transfer the fuzzy degrees to membership in their new "home set";

(v) $i_0 \in \{1, 2, \ldots, m\}$ is the label of an elementary membrane (i.e., a membrane that does not contain any other membrane), called the *output membrane*.

Before stating the main result concerning the computational power of these systems let us consider a simple P system with fuzzy data, as depicted in Figure 9.3.

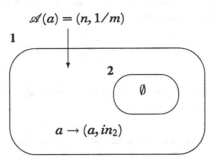

Figure 9.3: A simple P system with fuzzy data.

This P system contains n objects to the degree $1/m$ in compartment 1, which will be transferred into compartment 2, which is initially empty. The result of the computation (i.e., the cardinality of the multi-fuzzy set contained in compartment 2) is equal to n/m. Thus, the result of this particular computation is a positive rational number. However, there is nothing that prevents one from computing any real number. This can be summarized in the following statement.

Theorem 9.8.1 *P systems with fuzzy data can compute any positive real number.*

Skeptical readers may doubt whether P systems with fuzzy data can actually compute any real number at all. In particular, one may argue that by associating a number (i.e., a membership degree) with a group of identical objects, one does not get a concrete way to represent a number. First of all, I believe that it is important to recall that a Turing machine or a P system performs a computation because we have set up them up in such a way that the outcome of their operations corresponds to a "computable" number. Also, since we have agreed on the form of the input data, it follows that the output data will have the same form. In other words, if we feed a system with strokes or multi-fuzzy sets, we will get strokes or multi-fuzzy sets, respectively. In our case, we have opted to represent the input data with multi-fuzzy sets. Thus the output data will be multi-fuzzy sets. Naturally, the result of a computation is a multi-fuzzy set, which represents a number, just as the symbol 2.77 is a representation of a number. Whether we can "translate" this number into a familiar notation is an entirely different issue, which will not concern us here.

A P system that continuously interacts with its environment (e.g., by consuming or by dumping objects) is a first step toward a truly natural computing device that is based on cells and their properties. For this reason, these systems have been dubbed *C systems*, where the C stands for cell. The theory of C systems is being developed by the present author and his colleague Efstratios Doumanis, and the first results have been reported in [197]. Roughly, speaking, a C system never ceases to operate, and its operation is history-sensitive. Since the theory is not mature enough, we will not go into any other details.

9.9   Analog X-Machines

X-machines were introduced in 1974 by Samuel Eilenberg, who together with Saunders Mac Lane introduced category theory back in the 1940s. Roughly speaking, an X-machine is a labeled transition system, or LTS, whose states are objects of type X and whose transition labels are functions that operate on states (i.e., objects of type X). For completeness, let us recall the definition of an LTS.

Definition 9.9.1 A labeled transition system (LTS) is a triple

$$\left(S, T, \{ \xrightarrow{t} : t \in T \} \right),$$

where S is a set of *states*, T is a set of *transition labels*, and $\xrightarrow{t} \subseteq S \times S$ is a *transition relation* for each $t \in T$.

Intuitively, an LTS can be depicted as a labeled directed graph, where the labels attached to each node form the set of states, the labels that are attached to each arc form the set of transition labels, and the triples (s_1, t, s_2), where t is the label of an arc that directly connects the nodes with labels s_1 and s_2, form the transition relation.

One may think of a text-formatter as a stream machine, where a stream is a finite sequence of ASCII or Unicode characters. Indeed, any text-formatter supports a number of operations that can be used to insert, delete, etc., portions of text and thus alter a stream. Thus, one may view the text-editing commands as the arcs of an X-machine and the text before and after the application of these commands as the nodes that these arcs connect. Similarly, a (simple) pocket calculator can be viewed as a number machine, and so on. In general, X-machines cannot compute beyond the Turing barrier. In other words, they have at most the computational power of Turing machines. However, an analog version of the X-machine model of computation, which was introduced by Stannett [189], seems to be more powerful than Turing machines. But what is the main idea behind analog X-machines?

Suppose that we want to construct an integer-machine that computes the function $f(n) = 2n$. Obviously, such a machine can be represented by the diagram in Figure 9.4.

Figure 9.4: A diagram representing a simple integer-machine.

In this representation, the computation is informally equivalent to the traversal of the arc. Thus, when we are in the middle of the arc, the result is half-computed; when we in the first third of the arc, the result is one-third computed, and so on. Clearly, this implies that if we replace an endpoint with another that is closer to the first endpoint, we define a new function. And this is exactly the idea behind analog X-machines. Since we are going to work in a continuous setting, it makes sense to work with topological paths[4] and not with arrows. Let us now define analog X-machines [189].

Definition 9.9.2 An analog X-machine is a 10-tuple

$$\mathcal{M} = (X, \Phi, Q, P, Y, Z, \alpha, \beta, \text{delay}, \text{comp}),$$

---

4. A topological space X is said to be path-connected if for any two points $x, y \in X$ there exists a continuous function $f : [0, 1] \to X$ with $f(0) = x$ and $f(1) = y$. This function is called a path from x to y.

where X is a nonempty set called the *fundamental datatype*; Φ is a set of relations on X; Q is a topological space called the *state space*; P is a set of piecewise continuous paths in Q, that is, piecewise continuous functions $p : [0, 1] \rightarrow Q$; Y and Z are the input and output types, respectively; $\alpha : Y \rightarrow X$ and $\beta : X \rightarrow Z$ are encoding and decoding functions, respectively; delay : $P \times [0, 1] \rightarrow \mathbb{R}$ is a function that is both continuous and monotonically increasing with respect to its second argument; and comp : $P \times [0, 1] \rightarrow \Phi$ is a function that assigns to each point $p(r)$ along a path p a relation comp$(p, r) \in \Phi$.

Now let us briefly describe how an analog X-machine operates. The machine can handle only data of type X, but it is assumed that it consumes data of type Y and produces data of type Z. Consequently, we first need to encode the input data by applying the encoding function α to the input data. Similarly, the results of the computation will be decoded using the decoding function β. For convenience, we may imagine that the paths of the machine are slightly oblique. At the top of each path we place an imaginary ball bearing and all of them are released simultaneously when the machine begins its operation. The ball bearings move down the paths as time passes. A ball that moves on path $p \in P$ gets to point $p(r)$, $r \in [0, 1]$, in time delay(p, r). During this time, the ball has carried out some computation that is represented by comp(p, r).

Suppose that this machine has been running for some time t. In order to find the current output, we first need to determine the current position of each ball bearing (i.e., for each $p \in P$ we need to find an r such that delay$(p, r) = t$). Next, we find the associated relations comp(p, r) and apply each of them to the given (encoded) inputs. Then, we take these results and decode them using the function β so to get the current outputs. Let us now see how the analog X-machine can be used to decide the halting problem.

Assume that (P_n) and (I_n) are effective enumerations of Turing machine programs and their potential tape configurations, respectively. Also, assume that $P_m(I_n) \downarrow z$ denotes that the program P_m halts with output z when presented with the input tape I_n. Let us now formulate the halting problem in a form suitable for analog X-machines: is there a program P that when presented with some suitable coding *code* of the natural numbers m and n has the following property?

$$P(code) \downarrow tt \quad \text{if } P_m(I_n) \text{ halts,}$$
$$P(code) \downarrow ff \quad \text{if } P_m(I_n) \text{ does not halt.}$$

If P is an analog X-machine, then the answer to this problem is affirmative. But let us see how we can construct such an analog X-machine.

Assume that $\zeta \in [0, 1]$ is an irrational number. Then we define a bijection $g_\zeta : (0, 1] \rightarrow (0, 1]$ as follows:

$$g_\zeta(r) = \begin{cases} r + \zeta & \text{if } 0 < r \leq (1 - \zeta), \\ r + \zeta - 1 & \text{if } (1 - \zeta) < r \leq 1. \end{cases}$$

Take $\xi = 0.101001000100001\ldots$ (notice that the first one is followed by one zero, the second one by two zeros, the third one by three zeros, the fourth one by four zeros, and so on). Also, the letter Q will denote the set

$$Q = \left\{ g_\xi^n(1) \mid n \in \mathbb{N} \right\},$$

and for each $a \in \mathbb{N}$, the symbol Q_a will denote the set

$$Q_a = \left\{ g_\xi^{na}(1) \mid n \in \mathbb{N} \right\}.$$

Now we are ready to state an important result.

Lemma 9.9.1 *Each Q_a is dense in $[0,1]$.*

For brevity, we will denote $g_\xi^n(1)$ by q_n.

Suppose that a Turing machine $P_i(I_j)$ has executed n statements. Then its tape configuration is denoted by $c(i,j;n)$ (or the terminal configuration if the machine halts after executing fewer than n statements). In general, a tape configuration is a pair (s,t), where s is a machine state and t is a finite string consisting of the symbols printed on the cells of tape so far. Now, for simplicity we can assume that a tape configuration is just the string t. Let $x \in \mathbb{N}$ and $r \in (0,1]$. Then we define a set of configurations as follows:

$$f(x,r) = \begin{cases} \emptyset, & \text{if } x \neq 2^i 3^j, \\ \bigcap_{\delta \to 0} \left\{ c(i,j;n) \mid q_n \in (r - \delta, r - \delta^2) \right\}, & \text{otherwise.} \end{cases}$$

Let $i,j \in \mathbb{N}$. Then define $p_{ij} : [0,1] \to 2^{\mathrm{CONF}}$, where

$$\mathrm{CONF} = \{I_n \mid n \in \mathbb{N}\},$$

that is, the set of all configurations, by

$$p_{ij}(0) = \{I_j\},$$
$$p_{ij}(r) = f(2^i 3^j, r), r \in (0,1].$$

The following result characterizes p_{ij}.

Theorem 9.9.1 *The function p_{ij} is constant on $(0,1]$ with image a singleton if and only if $P_i(I_j)$ halts.*

Now we are ready to define an analog X-machine $\mathscr{X}$ capable of solving the classical halting problem.

Definition 9.9.3 The specification of $\mathscr{X}$ is as follows.

- The machine will input two natural numbers and output a Boolean. Therefore $X = \mathbb{N} \times \mathbb{N} \times \mathbb{B}$, where $\mathbb{B} = \{t\!\!t, f\!\!f\}$, $Y = \mathbb{N} \times \mathbb{N}$, and $Z = \mathbb{B}$. The encoding and decoding functions are given by $\alpha(i,j) = (i,j,t\!\!t)$ and $\beta(x,y,z) = z$, respectively.

- The topological space Q and the set P of piecewise continuous paths in Q are the sets 2^{CONF} and $\{p_{ij} \mid i,j \in \mathbb{N}\}$, respectively.

- The function delay is defined by $\text{delay}(p_{ij}, r) = r$.

- The relation $\text{comp}(p_{ij}, r)$ is defined to be the relation φ_{ijr} on X, which, in turn, is defined as follows: Assume that $d : (0,1] \to (0,1] \times (0,1]$ is a bijection and that d_1, d_2 are the associated projections (i.e., $d(r) = (d_1(r), d_2(r))$). Next, we define the predicates $\mathcal{A}_{ij}$ on $[0,1]$ as $\mathcal{A}_{ij}(a) = (p_{ij}(d_1(a)) = p_{ij}(d_2(a)))$. And finally,

$$\varphi_{ijr}(x,y,z) = \left(x,y, \wedge \left\{ \mathcal{A}_{ij}(b) \mid b \in [0,r] \right\} \right).$$

This uncountable conjunction is well-defined.

- The set Φ of relations on X is the collection of all φ_{ijr}.

Stannett [191, page 136] notes that the proof of the following result has an error. More specifically, a certain conjunction that comes up in the proof is true if and only if p_{ij} is constant on $(0,1]$. The truth of this conjunction is used to establish the ability of this analog X-machine to decide the classical halting problem. However, as required by Theorem 9.9.1, in order to arrive at the desired result, one needs also to show that the image of p_{ij} is a singleton. But it is not clear to what extent this affects the validity of the following result.

Theorem 9.9.2 *The analog X-machine $\mathscr{X}$ can decide the classical halting problem.*

In order to overcome the problem mentioned above, Stannett [190] proposed a very general extension of the X-machine model of computation, dubbed "general-timed X-machines." Here is the definition of general-timed X-machines, which is slightly different from the one that appears in [190].

Definition 9.9.4 A general-timed X-machine is an octuple

$$\mathscr{T} = (X, A, I, T, \mathcal{I}, \mathcal{O}, \Sigma, \Xi),$$

where X is the fundamental datatype, A is a set of all function paths $a : [0,1) \to X^X$, while $I \subset A$ and $T \subset A$, $\mathcal{I}$ and $\mathcal{O}$ are spaces representing the input and output types, $\Sigma : \mathcal{I} \times A \to A$, and $\Xi : X \times X^X \to \mathcal{O}$ are the import and export functions, respectively.

The general-timed X-machine is general enough, since every X-machine is actually such a machine. In addition, the general-timed X-machine is a demonstrably hypercomputational model of computation.

A. The $P = NP$ Hypothesis

Roughly, there are two kinds of solvable problems that are not too difficult–those that can be solved easily and those that can be solved with difficulty. In particular, when we say that a problem is difficult, we mean that (i) if there is an algorithmic solution to this problem we can quickly check it and (ii) an algorithmic solution will require an impossibly long time to yield an output. Let us denote by E the class of problems that can be solved easily and by D the class of problems that can be solved with difficulty. Then it is interesting to see whether these two classes are equal (i.e., whether $E = D$). Although it seems obvious to state that $E \neq D$, this is a long-standing open problem of computer science and mathematics. The problem is not directly connected to hypercomputation, but an affirmative answer to the problem (i.e., a proof that $P = NP$, which is the "real" name of the problem) will have a great impact on computer science and consequently on hypercomputation.

Da Costa and Doria have obtained some interesting results concerning the $P = NP$ problem. However, one cannot fully appreciate their importance without understanding the $P = NP$ problem. Thus, in the next two paragraphs I will briefly present the relevant theory. As usual, readers familiar with this theory can safely skip the next two paragraphs.

A Turing machine that has more than one next state for some combinations of the symbol just read and the current state is called a nondeterministic Turing machine. A polynomial-time Turing machine is a Turing machine that produces output in polynomially bounded time t (i.e., a machine that always halts after at most $p(n)$ steps, where n is the length of the input and $p(n)$ is a polynomial; see footnote on page 80). The class of decision problems that can be solved by a polynomially bounded deterministic Turing machine is denoted by P. Also, the class of decision problems that can be solved by a polynomially bounded nondeterministic Turing machine is denoted by NP. The $P = NP$ hypothesis can be precisely specified in terms of the Boolean satisfiability problem, or SAT problem for short; therefore, we need to explain SAT.

Assume that $X = \{x_1, x_2, \dots, x_n\}$ is a finite set of Boolean variables and $\overline{X} = \{\overline{x_1}, \overline{x_2}, \dots, \overline{x_n}\}$, where $\overline{x_1}, \overline{x_2}, \dots, \overline{x_n}$ are new symbols standing for the negations of $x_1, x_2, \dots, x_n$. The set $X \cup \overline{X}$ is called the set of (positive and negative) literals. A clause C is a nonempty set of literals, that is, $C \subseteq X \cup \overline{X}$. A Boolean formula in conjunctive normal form is a set of clauses defined on X. A truth assignment for a formula F is a function from X to the set $\{tt, ff\}$. A truth assignment T satisfies F if for all $C \in F$ there is at least one variable x_i such that either $T(x_i) = tt$, where $x_i \in C$, or $T(x_i) = ff$, where $\overline{x_i} \in C$. A formula F is called *satisfiable* if there is a truth assignment that satisfies it. More generally, we denote by SAT the following problem: given a Boolean formula F in conjunctive normal form, is it satisfiable?

According to da Costa and Doria, the $P = NP$ hypothesis can be (informally) stated as follows: There is a polynomial-time Turing machine $\mathcal{M}_m$, where m is its Gödel number, such that it correctly "guesses" a satisfying line of truth values for every input $x \in$ SAT. The authors start from an exotic formulation of the $P = NP$ hypothesis, which is consistent with ZFC, and from it they derive a consistency result for $P = NP$. More specifically, if we assume that f is a strictly increasing total recursive function with one argument, then we make the following hypothesis.

Hypothesis A.1 There is a Turing machine $\mathcal{M}_m$, with Gödel number m, and natural numbers a, b such that for every $x \in$ SAT, the output $\Psi^1_{\mathcal{M}}(x)$ is a satisfying line for x, and the number $t_m(x)$ of steps performed by the machine with input x is at most $|x|^{f(a)} + f(b)$, where $|x|$ denotes the length of the input in bits.

This hypothesis will be written $[P = NP]^f$, while the standard formulation of the $P = NP$ hypothesis will be written $[P = NP]$. Using a special function F, da Costa and Doria have proved the following result (see [43] for more details and [42] for a discussion of earlier results).

Proposition A.1

(i) *If* ZFC *has a model with standard arithmetic, the equivalence*

$$[P = NP]^F \leftrightarrow [P = NP]$$

holds for that model.

(ii) *If* ZFC *is consistent, then* $[P = NP]^F$ *is consistent with* ZFC.

(iii) *If* ZFC $+ [P = NP]^F$ *is ω-consistent,*[1] *then* $[P = NP]$ *is consistent with* ZFC.

The last result can be rephrased as follows: if there is a model for a consistent theory ZFC $+ [P = NP]^F$, where formal polynomial Turing machines act as intuitively expected, then ZFC $+ [P = NP]$ is consistent. In addition, we note that these results are in the line of previous results

---

1. A system F is said to be ω-consistent if there is no formula $\varphi(x)$ such that F proves $\neg\varphi(n)$ for each natural number n, and yet F proves $\exists x\, \varphi(x)$.

by Richard DeMillo and Richard Lipton (consistency of $[P = NP]$ with fragments of arithmetic; see [49]) and more recently by Attila Máté (consistency of $[P = NP]$ with Peano arithmetic, given an involved technical model–theoretic condition; see [120]).

The point is that if $[P = NP]$ is proved by ZFC, then the da Costa-Doria condition holds trivially. Yet it is known that if $[P = NP]$ is independent of ZFC, then $[P = NP]$ will hold only for models for ZFC with nonstandard arithmetic, and it is not immediately apparent why there should be a nonstandard model with the nice, desirable behavior they are asking for. Their condition for the consistency of $[P = NP]$ with a strong theory is simple and intuitive: in plain words, there is a model for the theory where formal objects behave as expected by our intuition.

Although the results presented so far seem to be supportive of the equality of the two classes, still there are results that seem to be supportive of exactly the opposite. In particular, Ralf-Dieter Schindler [171] defined the classes classes P_{ω^ω} and NP_{ω^ω}, which are supposed to be the corresponding P and NP classes for infinite-time Turing machines. Then he showed that $P_{\omega^\omega} \neq NP_{\omega^\omega}$. Also, Vinay Deolalikar, Joel Hamkins, and Ralf Schindler [50] have shown by extending previous results and by defining new classes of problems, just as Schindler did, that $P_\alpha \neq NP_\alpha \cap \text{co-}NP_\alpha$. But all these contradicting results show that the $P = NP$ problem is far from being settled.

B. Intractability and Hypercomputation

In classical computation theory, first of all it is important to know whether a problem is solvable. And when a problem is solvable, it is equally important to see whether it can be solved efficiently. For example, if there is a problem that is solvable in principle, but whose solution can be computed only in millions of years, then this problem is *practically* not solvable. Generally speaking, complexity theory is the branch of the theory of computation that studies whether computable problems are practically computable, that is, whether the resources required during computation to solve a problem are reasonable.

In Appendix A we presented the class of problems that can be solved by a polynomially bounded nondeterministic Turing machine, that is, the class NP. When some problem can be solved by an algorithm that can be *reduced* to one that can solve any problem in NP, then it is called NP-hard. A problem that is both NP and NP-hard is called NP-complete.

Assume that we have a problem Π that is as difficult as the halting problem (formally, its degree of insolvability is at most $0'$). It follows that if a hypermachine can solve Π, it will be able to solve any NP-complete problem, since NP-complete problems can be solved by some algorithm. Clearly, when one finds a general solution to an noncomputable problem, then no one will care whether the solution is optimal, provided it is feasible. In other words, in cases like this, efficiency becomes an empty word. However, a number of researchers in complexity theory have questioned the ability of certain hypermachines to efficiently solve NP-complete problems, and thus question the feasibility of these machines. In particular, Aaronson [1] presented a summary of such objections. Aaronson examines a number of approaches to hypercomputation and by using a number of supposedly knockout arguments aimed at showing that hypercomputation proposals cannot solve NP-complete problems and thus cannot solve noncomputable problems.

First of all, one should not forget that it is one thing to efficiently solve NP-complete problems and another to solve noncomputable problems. Compare airplanes and cars: airplanes can cross oceans and continents, something no car can do, but airplanes cannot be used to go to work every morning. For the moment, I will ignore this objection in order to present the arguments against hypercomputation. There are two basic objections to the feasibility of hypermachines. These two objections can be summarized as follows: first, it is not known whether quantum mechanics remains valid in the regime tested by quantum computing (in other words, are quantum computers feasible?), and second, it is not known whether quantum gravity imposes limits that make infeasible various models of hypercomputation that are based on properties of spacetime.

The reader may recall that the second objection has been discussed in Chapter 8. Our response was that there is no experimental evidence that time and space are granular, but on the contrary, there are experimental indications that space and time are continuous. Quantum gravity is based on the hypothesis that space and time are granular, while relativity theory assumes that space and time are continuous. Also, at least one model of hypercomputation does not rely on the space and time granularity hypothesis. Thus, hypercomputation cannot by ruled out based on this hypothesis. And since there is no proof of the space and time granularity hypothesis, we can safely assume that space and time are indeed continuous. The first objection is more serious despite the vast literature on quantum computing. Nowadays, there are no general-purpose quantum computers available. Indeed, there are many obstacles that scientists and engineers have to overcome before the first general-purpose quantum computer is constructed. However, it seems that most problems are being successfully tackled one after the other (for example, see [14, 6, 165, 59, 32]). So it is not unreasonable to expect that general-purpose quantum computers will be constructed in a few years. After all, it took only a few years to go from the Turing machine to the first general-purpose digital computer.

C. Socioeconomic Implications

As mentioned on page 85, cognitive scientists were probably the first scholars to fully adopt the computational metaphor in their research programs. Later, the computational metaphor was adopted by economists, sociologists, and others. In particular, economists who bought into the metaphor were hoping, and still hope, to be able to convincingly *explain* fluctuations in oil and currency prices, *predict* upcoming stock market crashes, *forecast* economic growth, etc. Naturally, one may wonder whether such expectations are reasonable. Certainly, one should not expect to find a full-fledged answer to this question in an appendix of a book on hypercomputation. Nevertheless, this appendix serves as a brief exposition of our ideas concerning the use of the computational metaphor in economics and sociology in the light of hypercomputation and the view that the human mind has capabilities that transcend the Church–Turing barrier.

John Forbes Nash's noncooperative game theory has a central importance in modern economic theory. More specifically, this theory deals with how intelligent individuals interact with one another in an effort to achieve their own goals. Consequently, an economic system is a very complex system, which, nevertheless, can be modeled by computers, as Axel Stig Bengt Leijonhufvud has suggested [110]. In addition, Leijonhufvud went on to give a (new) formulation of what an economy is.

Conjecture C.1 *An economy is best conceived of as a network of interacting processors, each one with less capability to process information than would be required of a central processor set to solve the overall allocation problem for the entire system.*

Consequently, by assuming this conjecture, Leijonhufvud's further claim that "[T]he economy should be looked at as a machine that has to 'compute' the equilibrium" is not an exaggeration at all. Needless to say, these ideas had a profound impact on the development of the field of *computational economics* (i.e., a new field of economics that utilizes the computational metaphor to analyze economic phenomena).

Agent-based computational economics (ACE) "is the computational study of economic processes modeled as dynamic systems of interacting agents."[1] Observe that ACE is based on Leijonhufvud's conjecture regarding the "true" nature of an economy. More specifically, ACE is based on the assumption that agents (i.e., individuals, social groups, institutions, biological entities, and physical entities) are computable entities, which is a hypothesis we contest in this book. On the other hand, it is possible that in certain cases the interaction of noncomputable agents may result in a computable behavior, but this is something no one can really guarantee. Also, if we assume that economic behavior is hypercomputational, then we may use the theory presented in this book as a starting point for a hypercomputational economics. Indeed, the economist Wolfram Latsch proposed something similar in [108], but he argues for a noncomputable economic theory using Penrose's ideas as a starting point.

Latsch examines evolutionary economics and its relationship to complexity. More specifically, he notes that "evolutionary economics is interested in the emergence of order out of complex processes" and then shows how evolutionary economics is related to Wolfram's view of the cosmos. In particular, Wolfram is convinced that cellular automata, which are self-reproducing finite-state machines that may show very complex behavior from very simple rules, are computing devices that can simulate, if not *implement*, everything in this world. Thus, one would expect that the use of cellular automata would be a panacea for economics. However, da Costa and Doria have shown that if there is a mathematical model for some market economy, it is not possible to algorithmically decide whether the economy has reached some equilibrium set of prices (see [44] for a recent, but not so formal, discussion of these results). A direct consequence of this result is that one cannot practically "compute the future."

Kumaraswamy Vela Velupillai discussed in [211] why, in his opinion, mathematical economics is unreasonably ineffective. This has prompted him to look for an alternative formalization of economics. So he has concluded that a "reasonable and effective mathematisation of economics entails Diophantine formalisms." This implies that economics should suffer from all the limits and constraints imposed by the Church-Turing thesis. A broad-minded view should seriously take into consideration hypercomputation as presented in this book, at least as a basis for a foundation of economics.

An economy is part of a society, and it is not an exaggeration to say that economic activities are actually social activities. So it was not surprising to see the computational metaphor find its way into the social sciences. Indeed, *computational sociology* is a recently developed branch of sociology that uses the computational metaphor to analyze social phenomena (see [65] for a thorough presentation of this new branch of sociology).[2]

---

1. See http://www.econ.iastate.edu/tesfatsi/ace.htm for more information.
2. In a way, computational sociologists try to analyze social phenomena by creating virtual worlds much like the virtual worlds presented in movies like "The Matrix" (written and

The techniques, the methodologies, and the ideas employed in computational sociology are similar, if not identical, to those employed in computational economics. Consequently, computational sociology should and, in our opinion does, suffer from the same problems computational economics does. Apart from this, *culture*³ is one aspect of any society that has to be taken into account in any serious analysis of social phenomena.

Roy F. Baumeister [10] has examined how culture has affected our mental capabilities. More specifically, he asserts that meaning and language actually prove that human thought cannot be reduced to brain activity. Baumeister argues that thought is more than just neuron firing. For him, "[H]uman thought generally uses language and meaning, which are social realities that are not contained in the brain." Obviously, this idea is akin to Searle's biological naturalism in particular, and hypercomputation in general. Note that this view is actually an attack against reductionism in neurobiology, which assumes that thinking can be reduced to neuron firing.

In order to defend his ideas, Baumeister argues that culture, with its meaning and language, is like the Internet. In particular, he asserts that maintaining that "human thought is contained in the brain, or is nothing more than brain cell activity, is like saying that the Internet is contained inside your computer, or that the Internet is nothing more than electrical activity inside your computer" [10, p. 185]. As was explained in Chapter 5, the Internet cannot be described by the operation of a single computer, while computers connected to the Internet can actually accomplish more than isolated machines. Similarly, brains connected to culture do more and better things than an isolated brain.

In conclusion, one may say that computer simulations in economics and sociology may provide some insight into certain aspects of economic or social phenomena, but they cannot give any definitive answers to crucial problems of computation.

---

directed by Andy Wachowski and Larry Wachowski; see http://whatisthematrix. warnerbros.com/ for more information) and "The Thirteenth Floor" (screenplay by Josef Rusnak and Ravel Centeno-Rodriguez, based on the book "Simulacron 3" by Daniel Francis Galouye, and directed by J. Rusnak; see http://www.imdb.com/title/tt0139809/ for more information).

3. For example, see http://www.isanet.org/portlandarchive/bada.html for a brief discussion of what culture actually is.

D. A Summary of Topology and Differential Geometry

D.1 Frames

The presentation of this section is based on [212].

Definition D.1.1 A poset (or partially ordered set) is a set P equipped with a binary relation $\leq$ called a partial order that satisfies the following laws:

reflexivity $a \leq a$, for all $a \in P$;

transitivity if $a \leq b$ and $b \leq c$, then $a \leq c$, for all $a, b, c \in P$;

antisymmetry if $a \leq b$ and $b \leq a$, then $a = b$ for all $a, b \in P$.

Definition D.1.2 A totally ordered set is a poset $(P, \leq)$ whose binary relation satisfies the following additional law, making it a total order.

comparability (trichotomy law) for any $a, b \in P$ either $a \leq b$ or $b \leq a$.

Two totally ordered sets $(A, \leq)$ and $(B, \leq')$ are order isomorphic if there is a bijection $f : A \to B$ such that for all $a_1, a_2 \in A$, if $a_1 \leq a_2$ then $f(a_1) \leq' f(a_2)$. The order type is the property of a totally ordered set that remains when the set is considered not with respect to the properties of its elements but with respect to their order. The order type of $(A, \leq)$ is denoted by $|A|$. For example, the order type of $(\mathbb{N}, \leq)$ is ω.

Definition D.1.3 Assume that $(P, \leq)$ is a poset, $X \subseteq P$ and $y \in P$. Then y is a *meet* (or *greatest lower bound*) for X if

- y is a *lower bound* for X, that is, if $x \in X$ then $y \leq x$, and

- if z is any other lower bound for X then $z \leq y$.

The meet for X is denoted by $\bigwedge X$. If $X = \{a, b\}$, then the meet for X is denoted by $a \wedge b$.

Definition D.1.4 Suppose that $(P, \leq)$ is a poset, $X \subseteq P$, and $y \in P$. Then y is a *join* (or *least upper bound*) for X if

- y is an *upper bound* for X, that is, if $x \in X$, then $x \leq y$, and

- if z is any other upper bound for X then $y \leq z$.

The join for X is denoted by $\bigvee X$. In addition, if $X = \{a, b\}$, then the join for X is denoted by $a \vee b$.

Definition D.1.5 A poset $(A, \leq)$ is a *frame* if

(i) every subset has a join,

(ii) every finite subset has a meet, and

(iii) binary meets distribute over joins:

$$x \wedge \bigvee Y = \bigvee \{x \wedge y : y \in Y\}.$$

A function between two frames is a frame homomorphism if it preserves all joins and finite meets.

D.2   Vector Spaces and Lie Algebras

In general, we can say that an algebraic structure (or algebra) consists of one or more sets closed under one or more operations satisfying some axioms. A subalgebra consists of subsets of the sets an algebra consists of, while the algebraic operations are now restricted to these subsets. Let us define some common algebraic structures.

Definition D.2.1 A quadruple $(G, \cdot, ^{-1}, 1)$, where G is a set, $\cdot : G \times G \to G$ a binary operation, $^{-1} : G \to G$ a unary operation, and $1 \in G$ a distinguished element called the *unit* element, is an *abelian* group if

(i) $\forall g_1, g_2, g_3 \in G : g_1 \cdot (g_2 \cdot g_3) = (g_1 \cdot g_2) \cdot g_3$,

(ii) $\forall g \in G : g \cdot 1 = 1 \cdot g = g$,

(iii) $\forall g \in G : g \cdot g^{-1} = g^{-1} \cdot g = 1$, and

(iv) $\forall g_1, g_2 \in G : g_1 \cdot g_2 = g_2 \cdot g_1$.

Definition D.2.2 A set S together with two binary operators + (the "addition" operator) and * (the "multiplication" operator) is called a ring if it satisfies the following properties:

(i) $(a + b) + c = a + (b + c)$,

(ii) $a + b = b + a$,

(iii) $0 + a = a + 0 = a$,

(iv) $a + (-a) = (-a) + a = 0$,

(v) $(a * b) * c = a * (b * c)$, and

(vi) $a * (b + c) = (a * b) + (a * c)$ and $(b + c) * a = (b * a) + (c * a)$.

Definition D.2.3 A commutative ring (i.e., $a * b = b * a$) with a "multiplication" unit 1 (i.e., $1 * a = a * 1 = a$) with the property that for all $a \neq 0$ there exists an element a^{-1} such that $a^{-1} * a = a * a^{-1} = 1$, is called a field.

The set $\mathbb{R}$ ($\mathbb{C}$) and the operations of real (complex) number addition and multiplication define a field.

Definition D.2.4 A *vector* or *linear* space over the field F is an abelian group V, whose group operation is usually written as +, that is equipped with *scalar multiplication*, which is a mapping $F \times V \to V$ that is usually denoted by $(c, \mathbf{x}) \mapsto c\mathbf{x}$. In addition, the following axioms must be fulfilled for all $c, c_1, c_2 \in F$ and $\mathbf{x}, \mathbf{x}_1, \mathbf{x}_2 \in V$:

(i) $c_1(c_2\mathbf{x}) = (c_1c_2)\mathbf{x}$,

(ii) $(c_1 + c_2)\mathbf{x} = c_1\mathbf{x} + c_2\mathbf{x}$,

(iii) $c(\mathbf{x}_1 + \mathbf{x}_2) = c\mathbf{x}_1 + c\mathbf{x}_2$, and

(iv) $1\mathbf{x} = \mathbf{x}$.

Note that the unit element of V is denoted by $\mathbf{0}$. Also, the elements of V are called vectors. A finite subset $\{\mathbf{x}_1, \cdots, \mathbf{x}_n\}$ of a linear space V is called *linearly independent* if

$$k_1\mathbf{x}_1 + k_2\mathbf{x}_2 + \cdots + k_n\mathbf{x}_n = \mathbf{0} \Rightarrow k_1 = k_2 = \cdots = k_n = 0.$$

Every expression of the form $k_1\mathbf{x}_1 + \cdots + k_n\mathbf{x}_n$ is called a *linear combination* of $\mathbf{x}_1, \ldots, \mathbf{x}_n$. A subset $B \subset V$ is a basis of the linear space V if it is linearly independent and every element of V is a linear combination of B. The dimension of a linear finite-dimensional space X is equal to the cardinality of a basis of X. A linear space that is not finite-dimensional is an infinite-dimensional space.

Lie algebras are special cases of vector spaces.

Definition D.2.5 A Lie algebra L is a vector space over some field together with a bilinear multiplication $[,] : L \times L \to L$, called the bracket, that satisfies two simple properties:

(i) $[a, b] = -[b, a]$ (anticommutativity) and

(ii) $[a[b, c]] = [[a, b], c] + [a, [b, c]]$ (Jacobi identity).

An associative algebra L, that is, an algebraic structure with a product ab that is associative (i.e., $a(bc) = (ab)c$), can be transformed into a Lie algebra $\bar{L}$ by the bilinear multiplication

$$[a, b] = ab - ba.$$

D.3   Topological Spaces: Definitions

The presentation that follows is based on [113].

Definition D.3.1 Let X be a nonempty set. A class $\mathcal{T}$ of subsets of X is a *topology* on X if $\mathcal{T}$ satisfies the following axioms:

(i) the (trivial) subsets X and the empty set $\emptyset$ are in $\mathcal{T}$;

(ii) the intersection of any *finite number* of members of $\mathcal{T}$ is a member of $\mathcal{T}$; and

(iii) the union of any (even infinite) number of members of $\mathcal{T}$ is a member of $\mathcal{T}$.

The members of $\mathcal{T}$ are called *open sets* and the pair $(X, \mathcal{T})$ is called a *topological space*. If $\mathcal{O}$ is an open set containing a point $x \in X$, then $\mathcal{O}$ is called an *open neighborhood* of x.

   Let Σ be an alphabet; we are going to define some of the standard topologies on Σ^* and Σ^ω. The class $\tau_* = 2^{\Sigma^*} = \{A \mid A \subseteq \Sigma^*\}$ is the discrete topology on Σ^*. The Cantor topology on Σ^ω is $\tau_C = \{A\Sigma^\omega \mid A \subseteq \Sigma^*\}$, and (Σ^ω, τ_C) is called the Cantor space over Σ. Note that if $A, B \subseteq \Sigma^*$, then $AB = \{ab \mid a \in A, b \in B\}$.

   Assume that $(P, \leq)$ is a poset; a nonempty subset $S \subseteq P$ is *directed* if for all $x, y \in S$ there is a $z \in S$ such that $x, y \leq z$.

Definition D.3.2 A poset $(P, \leq)$ is a *directed complete partial order* (or *dcpo*, for short) when every directed subset has a join.

A subset U of a dcpo D is *Scott open* if

(i) U is an upper set, that is if $x \in U$ and $x \leq y$ this implies that $y \in U$, and

(ii) U is inaccessible by directed joins, that is for every directed $S \subseteq D$,

$$\bigvee S \in U \Rightarrow S \cap U \neq \emptyset.$$

The collection of all Scott open sets on D is called the *Scott topology* and is denoted by σ_D.

Definition D.3.3 Let $(X, \mathcal{T})$ be a topological space. A point $p \in X$ is an *accumulation point* of a subset A of X if every open set $\mathcal{O}$ containing p also contains a point of A different from p, that is,

$$\mathcal{O} \text{ open}, p \in \mathcal{O} \Rightarrow (\mathcal{O} \setminus \{p\}) \cap A \neq \emptyset.$$

Definition D.3.4 Assume that $(X, \mathcal{T})$ is a topological space. Then a subset A of X is a *closed set* if its complement $A^{\complement}$ is an open set.

Definition D.3.5 Suppose that A is a subset of X, where $(X, \mathcal{T})$ is a topological space. Then the *closure* of A, denoted by $\mathrm{Cl}(A)$, is the intersection of all closed supersets of A.

Definition D.3.6 Assume that A is a subset of X, where $(X, \mathcal{T})$ is a topological space. Then a point $p \in A$ is called an *interior point* of A if p belongs to an open set $\mathcal{O}$ that is a subset of A. The set of interior points of A is denoted by $\mathrm{Int}(A)$.

Definition D.3.7 A subset A of X, where $(X, \mathcal{T})$ is a topological space, is *nowhere dense in X* if $\mathrm{Int}(\mathrm{Cl}(A)) = \emptyset$.

Definition D.3.8 A subset A of X, where $(X, \mathcal{T})$ is a topological space, is called *dense* if $\mathrm{Cl}(A) = X$.

Definition D.3.9 Suppose that p is a point in X, where $(X, \mathcal{T})$ is a topological. Then a subset N of X is a *neighborhood* of p if and only if N is a superset of an open set $\mathcal{O}$ containing p.

Definition D.3.10 Let $(X, \mathcal{T})$ be a topological space. A class $\mathcal{B}$ of open subsets of X is a *base* for the topology $\mathcal{T}$ if every open set $\mathcal{O} \in \mathcal{T}$ is the union of members of $\mathcal{B}$.

Definition D.3.11 Let $(X, \mathcal{T})$ be a topological space. A class $\mathcal{S}$ of open subsets of X is a *subbase* for the topology $\mathcal{T}$ if finite intersections of members of $\mathcal{S}$ form a base for $\mathcal{T}$.

Now we need to define the notion of a map between topological spaces.

Definition D.3.12 Assume that $(X, \mathcal{T}_1)$ and $(Y, \mathcal{T}_2)$ are topological spaces. Then a function $f : X \to Y$ is *continuous* if the inverse image $f^{-1}(\mathcal{O})$ of every open subset $\mathcal{O}$ of Y is an open subset of X.

Metric spaces are special cases of topological spaces. In addition, a metric space induces a topological space. Let us now define a metric space.

Definition D.3.13 Suppose that X is a nonempty set. Then a function $f :$ $X \times X \to \mathbb{R}$ is called a *metric* or *distance function* on X if it satisfies, for every $a, b, c \in X$, the following axioms:

(i) $d(a, a) = 0$;

(ii) $d(a, b) > 0$ if $a \neq b$;

(iii) $d(a, b) = d(b, a)$; and

(iv) $d(a, c) \leq d(a, b) + d(b, c)$.

The real number $d(a, b)$ is called the *distance* from a to b.

Given a metric space (X, d), the distance between a point $p \in X$ and a nonempty subset A of X is defined by

$$d(p, A) = \inf\left\{ d(p, a) | a \in A \right\}.$$

In addition, the distance between two nonempty subsets A and B of X is defined by

$$d(A, B) = \inf\left\{ d(a, b) | a \in A, b \in B \right\}.$$

The *diameter* of a nonempty subset A of X is defined by

$$d(A) = \sup\left\{ d(a, b) | a, b \in A \right\}.$$

The *open sphere* with center p and radius δ is defined by

$$S(p, \delta) = \left\{ x | d(p, x) < \delta \right\}.$$

Equally important is the notion of a *normed space*.

Definition D.3.14 Assume that V is a vector space over the field F. Then a function that assigns to each vector $\mathbf{v} \in V$ the quantity $\|\mathbf{v}\| \in F$ is a *norm* on V if it satisfies, for all $\mathbf{v}, \mathbf{u} \in V$ and $k \in F$, the following axions:

(i) $\|\mathbf{v}\| \geq 0$ and $\|\mathbf{v}\| = 0$ if $\mathbf{v} = \mathbf{0}$;

(ii) $\|\mathbf{v} + \mathbf{u}\| \leq \|\mathbf{v}\| + \|\mathbf{u}\|$;

(iii) $\|k\mathbf{v}\| = k\|\mathbf{v}\|$.

A vector space V together with a norm is called a *normed vector space*.

A *cover* of a subset A of a topological space is a collection $\{C_i\}$ of subsets of X such that $A \subset \cup_i C_i$. In addition, if each C_i is open, then it is called an *open cover*. Furthermore, if a finite subcollection of $\{C_i\}$ is also a cover of A, then $\{C_i\}$ includes a *finite subcover*.

Definition D.3.15 A subset A of a topological space X is *compact* if every open cover of A contains a finite subcover.

Two subsets A and B of a topological space X are said to be *separated* if

(i) A and B are disjoint and

(ii) neither contains an accumulation point of the other.

Definition D.3.16 A subset A of a topological space X is *disconnected* if there exist open subsets $\mathcal{O}$ and $\mathcal{O}'$ of X such that $A \cap \mathcal{O}$ and $A \cap \mathcal{O}'$ are disjoint nonempty sets whose union is A. In this case, $A \cup \mathcal{O}$ is called a *disconnection* of A. A set is *connected* if it is not disconnected.

An easy way to construct a new topological space from existing ones is by *multiplying* them.

Definition D.3.17 Assume that $\{(X_i, \mathscr{T}_i)\}$ is a collection of topological spaces and that $X = \prod_i X_i$ (i.e., X is the product of the sets X_i). The smallest topology $\mathscr{T}$ on X with respect to which all the projections $\pi_i : X \to X_i$ are continuous is called the *product topology*. The product set X with the product topology $\mathscr{T}$ (i.e., $(X, \mathscr{T})$) is called the *product (topological) space*.

Suppose that X is a metric space. A sequence $a_1, a_2, \ldots$ in X is a *Cauchy sequence* if for every $\varepsilon > 0$ there is an $n_0 \in \mathbb{N}$ such that for all $n, m > n_0$ it holds that $d(a_n, a_m) < \varepsilon$. Similarly, if X is a normed vector space, then $\mathbf{a}_1, \mathbf{a}_2, \ldots$ is a Cauchy sequence if for every $\varepsilon > 0$, there is an $n_o \in \mathbb{N}$ such that for all $n, m > n_0$ it holds that $\|\mathbf{a}_n - \mathbf{a}_m\| < \varepsilon$.

A metric space (X, d) is complete if every Cauchy sequence $a_1, a_2, \ldots$ in X converges to some point $p \in X$.

Definition D.3.18 A topological space X is a *Hausdorff space* if each pair of distinct points $a, b \in X$ belong to disjoint open sets.

D.4   Banach and Hilbert Spaces

Definition D.4.1 A Banach space is a normed vector space over $\mathbb{R}$ or $\mathbb{C}$ that is complete in the metric $\|\mathbf{x} - \mathbf{y}\|$.

We denote by $C([a, b])$ the Banach space of all continuous functions f on $[a, b]$, endowed with the uniform norm $\| f \|_\infty = \sup_x \{| f(x)|\}$. By obvious modifications the interval $[a, b]$ can be replaced by cubes (i.e., subsets of $\mathbb{R}^3$), squares (i.e., subsets of $\mathbb{R}^2$), etc.

Definition D.4.2 A Hilbert space H is a Banach space in which the norm is given by an inner product $H \times H \to F \mapsto \langle x|y \rangle$. The inner product of a Hilbert space induces a vector norm in a natural way:

$$\|x\|^2 = \langle x|x \rangle.$$

A function $T : X \to Y$, where X and Y are linear spaces over the same field F, is called an operator.

Definition D.4.3 An operator $T : X \to Y$ is called *linear* if

  (i) for all $x_1, x_2 \in X$, $T(x_1 + x_2) = T(x_2) + T(x_2)$, and

  (ii) for all $k \in F$ and all $x \in X$, $T(kx) = kT(x)$.

It customary to write Tx instead of $T(x)$. Let us now define some special linear operators.

Definition D.4.4 A linear operator $T : X \to Y$ is called bounded if there is a constant $m \geq 0$ such that

$$\|Tx\| \leq m \cdot \|x\|, \quad \forall x \in X.$$

The smallest m satisfying the inequality above is called the norm of the operator T. In addition, the domain of the operator $T : X \to Y$ is usually not X but a subspace $\mathscr{D}(T)$ that is dense in X.

Definition D.4.5 A linear operator $T : \mathscr{D}(T) \to Y$ is called closed if for $(x_n) \in \mathscr{D}(T)$,

$$\left(\|x_n - x\| \to 0 \right) \wedge \left(\|Tx_n - y\| \to 0 \right) \Rightarrow \left((x \in \mathscr{D}(T)) \wedge (Tx = y) \right).$$

Let $T : H \to H$ be a bounded linear operator. Then the adjoint operator T^* is defined by

$$\langle Tx \mid y \rangle = \langle x \mid T^* y \rangle, \quad \forall x, y \in H.$$

A closed operator $T : H \to H$ is called self-adjoint if $T = T^*$.

Suppose that T is a closed operator. Then a number λ belongs to the spectrum of T if the operator $(T - \lambda)$ does not have a bounded inverse. A number λ is called an eigenvalue of an operator T if there exists a nonzero vector x, which is the corresponding eigenvector, such that $T(x) = \lambda x$.

A closed operator $T : H \to H$ is *effectively determined* if there is a computable sequence $\{e_n\}$ in H such that the pairs $\{(e_n, Te_n)\}$ form an effective generating set for the graph of T. Note that *effective generating set* means that $\{(e_n, Te_n)\}$ is computable in $H \times H$ and that the linear span of $\{(e_n, Te_n)\}$ is dense in the graph of T.

D.5   Manifolds and Spacetime

The short exposition of manifolds that follows is based on the introduction to differential geometry provided in [79].

Let us denote by $\mathbb{R}^n$ the set of n-tuples $(x_1, \ldots, x_n)$, where $-\infty < x_i < +\infty$. This set forms an n-dimensional vector space over $\mathbb{R}$ called *Euclidean space of dimension n*. Since a Euclidean space is a metric space, it is also a topological space with the natural topology induced by the metric. The metric topology on $\mathbb{R}^n$ is called the Euclidean topology. We say that $(x_1, \ldots, x_n) \in \frac{1}{2}\mathbb{R}^n$ if $x_i \leq 0$, $i = 1, \ldots, n$. A map φ of an open set $\mathcal{O} \subset \mathbb{R}^n$ to an open set $\mathcal{O}' \subset \mathbb{R}^m$ is of class C^r if the coordinates $(x_1', \ldots, x_m') = \varphi(p)$ in $\mathcal{O}'$ are r-times continuously differentiable functions (i.e., the rth derivatives exist and are continuous) of the coordinates $(x_1, \ldots, x_n)$ of $p \in \mathcal{O}$. When a map is C^r for all $r \geq 0$, then it is called a C^∞ map.

A function $f : \mathcal{O} \to \mathcal{O}$, where $\mathcal{O}$ is an open subset of $\mathbb{R}^n$, is locally Lipschitz if for each open set $\mathcal{U} \subset \mathcal{O}$ with compact closure, there is a constant C such that for all $p, q \in \mathcal{U}$, $|f(p) - f(q)| \leq C|p - q|$, where $|p|$ means

$$\sqrt{\left(x_1(p)\right)^2 + \cdots + \left(x_n(p)\right)^2}.$$

A map φ is locally Lipschitz, denoted by C^{1-}, if the coordinates of $\varphi(p)$ are locally Lipschitz functions of the coordinates of p. In addition, a map φ is C^{r-} if it is C^{r-1} and if the $(r-1)$th derivatives of the coordinates of $\varphi(p)$ are locally Lipschitz functions of the coordinates of p.

Suppose that $P \subset \mathbb{R}^n$ and $P' \subset \mathbb{R}^m$. Then a map $\varphi : P \to P'$ is a C^r map if it is the restriction of a map $\psi : \mathcal{O} \to \mathcal{O}'$, where $\mathcal{O}$ and $\mathcal{O}'$ are open sets and include P and P', respectively. We are now ready to give a general definition of the notion of C^r manifold.

Definition D.5.1 A C^r n-dimensional manifold $\mathcal{M}$ is a set $\mathcal{M}$ together with a C^r *atlas* $\{\mathcal{U}_i, \varphi_i\}$, $i = 1, \ldots, n$, which is a collection of *charts* $(\mathcal{U}_i, \varphi_i)$, where each $\mathcal{U}_i$ is a subset of $\mathcal{M}$ and φ_i injectively maps $\mathcal{U}_i$ to open sets in $\mathbb{R}^n$ such that

(i) the sets $\mathcal{U}_i$ cover $\mathcal{M}$, that is,

$$\mathcal{M} = \bigcup_i \mathcal{U}_i,$$

(ii) if $\mathcal{U}_k \cap \mathcal{U}_l \neq \emptyset$, the map $\varphi_k \circ \varphi_l^{-1}$, which maps $\varphi_l(\mathcal{U}_k \cap \mathcal{U}_l)$ to $\varphi_k(\mathcal{U}_k \cap \mathcal{U}_l)$, is a C^r map of an open subset of $\mathbb{R}^n$ to an open subset of $\mathbb{R}^n$.

Each $\mathcal{U}_i$ is a *local coordinate neighborhood*, and the local coordinates x^i are defined by the map φ_i, that is, if $p \in \mathcal{U}_i$, then the coordinates of p are the coordinates of $\varphi_i(p)$ in $\mathbb{R}^n$.

An atlas $\{\mathcal{U}_i, \varphi_i\}$ is *locally finite* if every $p \in \mathcal{M}$ has an open neighborhood that intersects only a finite number of the sets $\mathcal{U}_i$. A manifold $\mathcal{M}$ is called *paracompact* if for every atlas $\{\mathcal{U}_i, \varphi_i\}$ there is a locally finite atlas $\{\mathcal{V}_j, \psi_j\}$ such that each $\mathcal{V}_j$ is contained in some $\mathcal{U}_i$. A connected Hausdorff manifold is paracompact if there is a countable collection of open sets such that any open set is the union of members of this collection.

A C^k *curve* $\lambda(t)$ in $\mathcal{M}$ is a C^k map of an interval of the real line $\mathbb{R}^1$ into $\mathcal{M}$. The *vector* (contravariant vector) $(\partial/\partial t)_\lambda|_{t_0}$ tangent to the C^1 curve $\lambda(t)$ at the point $\lambda(t_0)$ is the operator that maps each C^1 function f at $\lambda(t_0)$ into the number $(\partial/\partial t)_\lambda|_{t_0}$. This means that $\left(\frac{\partial f}{\partial t}\right)_\lambda$ is the derivative of f in the direction of $\lambda(t)$ with respect to the parameter t, or

$$\left(\frac{\partial f}{\partial t}\right)_\lambda \bigg|_t = \lim_{s \to 0} \frac{1}{s}\left\{ f(\lambda(t+s)) - f(\lambda(t)) \right\}.$$

The curve parameter t obeys the relation $\left(\frac{\partial}{\partial t}\right)_\lambda t = 1$.

If $(x^1, \ldots, x^n)$ are local coordinates in a neighborhood of p, then

$$\left(\frac{\partial f}{\partial t}\right)_\lambda \bigg|_{t_0} = \sum_{j=1}^n \frac{dx^j(\lambda(t))}{dt}\bigg|_{t=t_0} \cdot \frac{\partial f}{\partial x^j}\bigg|_{\lambda(t_0)} = \frac{dx^j}{dt}\frac{\partial f}{\partial x^j}\bigg|_{\lambda(t_0)}.$$

This means that every tangent vector at a point p can be expressed as a linear combination of the coordinate derivatives

$$\left(\frac{\partial}{\partial x^1}\right)\bigg|_p, \ldots, \left(\frac{\partial}{\partial x^n}\right)\bigg|_p.$$

The space of all tangent vectors to $\mathcal{M}$ at p, denoted by T_p, is an n-dimensional vector space. A *one-form* ω at p is a real-valued linear function on the space T_p of vectors at p. The space of all one-forms at p is denoted by T_p^*. From the spaces T_p and T_p^* we can form the Cartesian product

$$\Pi_r^s = \underbrace{T_p^* \times \cdots \times T_p^*}_{r \text{ factors}} \times \underbrace{T_p \times \cdots \times T_p}_{s \text{ factors}}.$$

Clearly, if $(\omega_1, \ldots, \omega_r, a_1, \ldots, a_s) \in \Pi_r^s$, then the a_i's are vectors and the ω_is are one-forms. A *tensor of type* (r, s) *at* p is a function on Π_r^s that is linear in each argument.

A *metric tensor* **g** at a point $p \in \mathcal{M}$ is a symmetric tensor of type $(0, 2)$ at p. A tensor **T** of type $(0, 2)$ is symmetric if $T_{ab} = \frac{1}{2}(T_{ab} + T_{ba})$. The *signature* of **g** at p is the number of positive eigenvalues of the matrix (g_{ab}) at p, minus the negative ones. A metric whose signature is $(n - 2)$ is called a *Lorentz metric*. We are now ready to give the definition of the mathematical model of a spacetime.

Definition D.5.2 A spacetime, that is, the collection of all events, is a pair $(\mathcal{M}, g)$, where $\mathcal{M}$ is a connected four-dimensional Hausdorff C^∞ manifold and g is a Lorentz metric.

References

[1] AARONSON, S. NP-complete Problems and Physical Reality. *ACM SIGACT News 36*, 1 (2005), 30-52.

[2] ABBOTT, E. A. *Flatland: A Romance of Many Dimensions.* Dover Publications, New York, 1992. Unabridged, corrected republication of Flatland (first publication: Seeley & Co. Ltd., London, 1884).

[3] ADOLPHS, R., TRANEL, D., AND DAMASIO, A. R. Dissociable neural systems for recognizing emotions. *Brain and Cognition 52*, 1 (2003), 61-69.

[4] AGHA, G. *Actors: A Model of Concurrent Computation in Distributed Systems.* The MIT Press, Cambridge, MA, USA, 1986.

[5] BAILEY, D., BORWEIN, P., AND PLOUFFE, S. On the Rapid Computation of Various Polylogarithmic Constants. *Mathematics in Computation 66*, 218 (1997), 903-913.

[6] BARRETT, M. D., CHIAVERINI, J., SCHAETZ, T., BRITTON, J., ITANO, W. M., JOST, J. D., KNILL, E., LANGER, C., LEIBFRIED, D., OZERI, R., AND WINELAND, D. J. Deterministic quantum teleportation of atomic qubits. *Nature 429* (2004), 737-739.

[7] BARROW, J. D. How to do an infinite number of things before breakfast. *New Scientist*, 29 January issue (2005), 28-32.

[8] BARWISE, J., AND MOSS, L. *Vicious Circles.* CSLI Publications, Stanford, CA, USA, 1996.

[9] BATES, J. L., AND CONSTABLE, R. L. Proofs as Programs. *ACM Transactions on Programming Languages and Systems 7*, 1 (1985), 113-136.

[10] BAUMEISTER, R. F. *The Cultural Animal: Human Nature, Meaning, and Social Life.* Oxford University Press, Oxford, UK, 2005.

[11] BELL, J. L. Infinitary logic. In *The Stanford Encyclopedia of Philosophy*, E. N. Zalta, ed. Spring 2006. http://plato.stanford.edu/archives/spr2006/entries/logic-infinitary/.

[12] BENACERRAF, P. Tasks, Super-Tasks, and the Modern Eleatics. *Journal of Philosophy 59* (1962), 765-784.

[13] BENACERRAF, P. God, the Devil, and Gödel. *The Monist 51*, 1 (1967), 9-32. Electronic version available from http://www.univ.trieste.it/~dipfilo/etica_e_politica/2003_1/3_monographica.htm.

[14] BENJAMIN, S. C., AND BOSE, S. Quantum Computing with an Always-On Heisenberg Interaction. *Physical Review Letters 90*, 24 (2003). Electronic version avalaible from http://xxx.lanl.gov/abs/quant-ph/0210157.

[15] BLOCK, N. Searle's Argument against Cognitive Science. In Preston and Bishop [159], pp. 70-79.

[16] BLUM, L., CUCKER, F., SHUB, M., AND SMALE, S. *Complexity and Real Computation*. Spinger-Verlag, New York, 1998.

[17] BOKULICH, A. Quantum measurements and supertasks. *International Studies in the Philosophy of Science 17*, 2 (2003), 127-136.

[18] BOOLOS, G. S., BURGESS, J. P., AND JEFFREY, R. C. *Computability and Logic*, fourth ed. Cambridge University Press, Cambridge, UK, 2002.

[19] BOUDOL, G., AND LANEVE, C. λ-Calculus, Multiplicities and the π-Calculus. In *Proof, Language, and Interaction: Essays in Honour of Robin Milner*, G. Plotkin, C. Stirling, and M. Tofte, eds. The MIT Press, Cambridge, MA, USA, 2000, pp. 659-689. Electronic version available at ftp://ftp.inria.fr/INRIA/publication/publi-pdf/RR/RR-2581.pdf.

[20] BOURNEZ, O., CAMPAGNOLO, M. L., GRAÇA, D. S., AND HAINRY, E. The General Purpose Analog Computer and Computable Analysis are Two Equivalent Paradigms of Analog Computation. In *TAMC2006: Theory and Applications of Models of Computation, Beijing, China, 15th-20th May, 2006*, J.-Y. Cai, S. B. Cooper, and A. Li, eds., no. 3959 in Lecture Notes in Computer Science. Springer-Verlag, Berlin, 2006, pp. 631-643.

[21] BRAGINSKY, V. B., VORONTSOV, Y. L., AND THORNE, K. S. Quantum nondemolition measurements. *Science 209* (1980), 547-557.

[22] BRATTKA, V., AND HERTLING, P. Feasible Real Random Access Machines. *Journal of Complexity 14* (1998), 490-526.

[23] BRINGSJORD, S., AND ARKOUDAS, K. The modal argument for hypercomputing minds. *Theoretical Computer Science 317*, 1-3 (2004), 167-190.

[24] BRINGSJORD, S., BELLO, P., AND FERRUCCI, D. Creativity, the Turing Test, and the (Better) Lovelace Test. *Minds and Machines 11* (2001), 3-27.

[25] BRINGSJORD, S., KELLETT, O., SHILLIDAY, A., TAYLOR, J., VAN HEUVELN, B., YANG, Y., BAUMES, J., AND ROSS, K. A new Gödelian argument for hypercomputing minds based on the busy beaver problem. *Applied Mathematics and Computation 176*, 2 (2006), 516-530.

[26] BRINGSJORD, S., AND ZENZEN, M. *Superminds: People Harness Hypercomputation, and More*. Kluwer Academic Publishers, Dordrecht, the Netherlands, 2003.

[27] BRUMFIEL, G. Quantum leap of faith. *Nature 446* (15 March 2007), 245.

[28] BURGIN, M. *Super-Recursive Algorithms*. Springer-Verlag, New York, 2005.

[29] BUSER, J. P. Darstellung von Prädikaten durch analytische Funktionen. Diplomarbeit, Universität Basel, 1972.

[30] BUSER, P., AND SCARPELLINI, B. Undecidable Propositions by ODE's. *Annales Academiæ Scientiarum Fennicæ, Mathematica 32* (2007), 317-340.

[31] CASTI, J. L. *Five Golden Rules: Great Theories of 20th-Century Mathematics-and Why They Matter*. John Wiley & Sons, New York, 1997.

[32] CHOI, K., DENG, H., LAURAT, J., AND KIMBLE, H. Mapping photonic entanglement into and out of a quantum memory. *Nature 452* (2008), 67-71.

[33] CLELAND, C. E. On Effective Procedures. *Minds and Machines 12* (2002), 159-179.

[34] COPELAND, B. J. Accelerating Turing Machines. *Minds and Machines 12* (2002), 281-301.

[35] COPELAND, B. J. Hypercomputation in the Chinese Room. In *Unconventional Models of Computation*, C. Calude, M. Dinneen, and F. Peper, eds., vol. 2509 of *Lecture Notes in Computer Science*. Springer-Verlag, Berlin, 2002, pp. 15-26.

[36] COPELAND, B. J. The Church-Turing Thesis. In *The Stanford Encyclopedia of Philosophy*, Edward N. Zalta, ed. Fall 2002. http://plato.stanford.edu/archives/fall2002/entries/church-turing/.

[37] COPELAND, B. J., AND PROUDFOOT, D. Alan Turing's forgotten ideas in computer science. *Scientific American 280* (1999), 76-81.

[38] COPELAND, B. J., AND SYLVAN, R. Beyond the universal Turing machine. *Australasian Journal of Philosophy 77*, 1 (1999), 44-66.

[39] COTOGNO, P. Hypercomputation and the Physical Church-Turing Thesis. *The British Journal for the Philosophy of Science 54*, 2 (2003), 181-223.

[40] DA COSTA, N. C. A., AND DORIA, F. A. Undecidability and Incompleteness in Classical Mechanics. *International Journal of Theoretical Physics 30*, 8 (1991), 1041-1073.

[41] DA COSTA, N. C. A., AND DORIA, F. A. Variations on an Original Theme. In *Boundaries and Barriers: On the Limits to Scientific Knowledge*, J. L. Casti and A. Karlqvist, eds. Diane Publishing Co., Collingdale, PA, USA, 1996, pp. 37-56.

[42] DA COSTA, N. C. A., AND DORIA, F. A. On a total function which overtakes all total recursive functions. Electronic document available from http://arxiv.org/math/0106099, 2001.

[43] DA COSTA, N. C. A., AND DORIA, F. A. Consequences of an exotic definition for $P = NP$. *Applied Mathematics and Computation 145* (2003), 655-665.

[44] DA COSTA, N. C. A., AND DORIA, F. A. Computing the Future. In *Computability, Complexity and Constructivity in Economic Analysis*, K. V. Velupillai, ed. Blackwell Publishing, Malden, MA, USA, 2005, pp. 15-50.

[45] DA COSTA, N. C. A., AND DORIA, F. A. Some thoughts on hypercomputation. *Applied Mathematics and Computation 176*, 1 (2006), 83-92.

[46] DAVIDSON, R. J., AND HUGDAHL, K., eds. *Brain Asymmetry* (Cambridge, MA, USA, 1996), The MIT Press.

[47] DAVIES, E. B. Building Infinite Machines. *The British Journal for the Philosophy of Science 52*, 4 (2001), 671-682.

[48] DAVIS, M. *Computability and Unsolvability*. Dover Publications, Inc., New York, 1982.

[49] DEMILLO, R. A., AND LIPTON, R. J. The Consistency of "$P = NP$" and Related Problems with Fragments of Number Theory. In *STOC* (1980), ACM, pp. 45-57.

[50] DEOLALIKAR, V., HAMKINS, J. D., AND SCHINDLER, R.-D. $P \neq NP \cap$ co-NP for infinite time turing machines. *Journal of Logic and Computation 15*, 5 (2005), 577-592.

[51] DEUTSCH, D. Quantum theory, the Church-Turing principle and the universal quantum computer. *Proceedings of the Royal Society of London A 400* (1985), 97-115.

[52] DUBOSE, D. A. The Equivalence of Determinacy and Iterated Sharps. *The Journal of Symbolic Logic 55* (1990), 502-525.

[53] DUFFY, D. A. *Principles of Automated Theorem Proving.* John Wiley & Sons, Chichester, England, 1991.

[54] EARMAN, J. *Bangs, Crunches, Whimpers, and Shrieks.* Oxford University Press, New York, 1995.

[55] EBERBACH, E. Is Entscheidungsproblem Solvable? Beyond Undecidability of Turing Machines and Its Consequences for Computer Science and Mathematics. In *Computational Mathematics, Modelling and Algorithms*, J. C. Misra, ed. Narosa Publishing House, New Delhi, 2003, pp. 1-32.

[56] EKDAHL, B. Interactive computing does not supersede Church's thesis. In *The Association of Management and the International Association of Management, 17th Annual International Conference, San Diego, California USA, Proceedings Computer Science*, R. Y. Lee, ed., vol. 17. Maximilian Press Publishers, Virginia Beach, VA, USA, 1999, pp. 261-265.

[57] ELIASMITH, C. The myth of the Turing machine: the failings of functionalism and related theses. *Journal of Experimental & Theoretical Artificial Intelligence 14* (2002), 1-8.

[58] ETESI, G., AND NÉMETI, I. Non-Turing Computations Via Malament-Hogart Space-Times. *International Journal of Theoretical Physics 41*, 2 (2002), 341-370.

[59] F. DE MELO, F., WALBORN, S., BERGOU, J. A., AND DAVIDOVICH, L. Quantum Nondemolition Circuit for Testing Bipartite Complementarity. *Physical Review Letters 98* (2007), 250501.

[60] FARHI, E., GOLDSTONE, J., GUTMANN, S., AND SIPSER, M. Quantum Computation by Adiabatic Evolution. Electronic document available from http://arxiv.org/quant-ph/0001106, 2000.

[61] FEFERMAN, S. Penrose's Gödelian Argument. *PSYCHE 2*, 7 (May 1995). Article in electronic form available from http://psyche.cs.monash.edu.au/v2/psyche-2-07-feferman.html.

[62] FETZER, J. H. People are not computers: (most) thought processes are not computational procedures. *Journal of Experimental & Theoretical Artificial Intelligence 10* (1998), 371-391.

[63] GAVRILOV, G. P., AND SAPOZHENKO, A. A. *Problems and Exercises in Discrete Mathematics.* Kluwer Academic Publishers, Dordrecht, the Netherlands, 1996.

[64] GIERE, R. N. The role of computation in scientific cognition. *Journal of Experimental & Theoretical Artificial Intelligence 15* (2003), 195-202.

[65] GILBERT, N., AND TROITZSCH, K. G. *Simulation for the Social Scientist*, 2nd ed. Open University Press, Berkshire, UK, 2005.

[66] GIRARD, J.-Y. Locus Solum: From the rules of logic to the logic of rules. *Mathematical Structures in Computer Science 11* (2001), 301-506.

[67] GIRARD, J.-Y., LAFONT, Y., AND TAYLOR, P. *Proofs and Types.* Cambridge University Press, Cambridge, UK, 1989. Available from http://www.cs.man.ac. uk/~pt/stable/Proofs+Types.html.

[68] GOLD, E. M. Limiting Recursion. *The Journal of Symbolic Logic 30*, 1 (1965), 28-48.

[69] GOLDIN, D. Q. Persistent Turing Machines as a Model of Interactive Computation. In *Foundations of information and knowledge systems*, K.-D. Schewe and B. Thalheim, eds., vol. 1762 of *Lecture Notes in Computer Science*. Springer-Verlag, Berlin, 2000, pp. 116-135.

[70] GOLDIN, D. Q., SMOLKA, S. A., ATTIE, P. C., AND SONDEREGGER, E. L. Turing Machines, Transitions Systems, and Interaction. *Information and Computation 194* (2004), 101-128.

[71] GRAÇA, D. S. Some recent developments on Shannon's General Purpose Analog Computer. *Mathematical Logic Quarterly 50*, 4/5 (2004), 473-485.

[72] GUREVICH, Y. Platonism, Constructivism, and Computer Proofs vs. Proofs by Hand. In *Current Trends in Theoretical Computer Science: Entering the 21st Century*, G. Păun, G. Rozenberg, and A. Salomaa, eds. World Scientific, Singapore, 2001, pp. 281-302.

[73] HAMKINS, J. D. Infinite Time Turing Machines. *Minds and Machines 12* (2002), 521-539.

[74] HAMKINS, J. D., AND LEWIS, A. Infinite time Turing machines. *The Journal of Symbolic Logic 65*, 2 (2000), 567-604.

[75] HAMKINS, J. D., AND LEWIS, A. Post's problem for supertasks has both positive and negative solutions. *Archive for Mathematical Logic 41* (2002), 507-523.

[76] HAMKINS, J. D., AND SEABOLD, D. E. Infinite Time Turing Machines with Only One Tape. *Mathematical Logic Quarterly 47*, 2 (2001), 271-287.

[77] HARNAD, S. Computation Is Just Interpetable Symbol Manipulation; Congnition Isn't. *Minds and Machines 4*, 4 (1995), 379-390.

[78] HAUSER, M. D., AND AKRE, K. Asymmetries in the timing of facial and vocal expressions by rhesus monkeys: implications for hemispheric specialization. *Animal Behaviour 61* (2001), 391-400.

[79] HAWKING, S., AND ELLIS, G. *The Large Scale Structure of Space-Time.* Oxford University Press, Oxford, UK, 1973.

[80] HAWKING, S. W. Particle Creation by Black Holes. *Communications in Mathematical Physics 43* (1975), 199-220. Article in electronic form available from http://projecteuclid.org/Dienst/UI/1.0/Summarize/euclid. cmp/1103899181.

[81] HERTLING, P. Is the Mandelbrot set computable? *Mathematical Logic Quarterly 51*, 1 (2005), 5-18.

[82] HEYTING, A. *Intuitionism: An Introduction*. North-Holland, Amsterdam, 1976.

[83] HINTIKKA, J. *Language, Truth and Logic in Mathematics*. Kluwer Academic Publishers, Dordrecht, the Netherlands, 1997.

[84] HIRVENSALO, M. *Quantum Computing*, 2nd ed. Springer-Verlag, Berlin, 2004.

[85] HOGARTH, M. Non-Turing Computers and Non-Turing Computability. In *Proceedings of the 1994 Biennial Meeting of the Philosophy of Science Association*, D. Hull, M. Forbes, and R. M. Burian, eds. Michigan State University, East Lansing, MI, USA, 1994, pp. 126-138.

[86] HOGARTH, M. Deciding Arithmetic Using SAD Computers. *The British Journal for the Philosophy of Science 55*, 4 (2004), 681-691.

[87] HOROWITZ, E., AND SAHNI, S. *Fundamentals of Data Structures in Pascal*. Computer Science Press, 1984.

[88] HRBACEK, K., AND JECH, T. *Introduction to Set Theory*, 3rd ed. CRC Press, Boca Raton, FL, USA, 1999.

[89] JACKSON, F. What Mary Didn't Know. *Journal of Philosophy 83*, 3 (1986), 291-295.

[90] JACQUETTE, D. Metamathematical Criteria for Minds and Machines. *Erkenntnis 27* (1987), 1-16.

[91] JESSIMER, M., AND MARKHAM, R. Alexithymia: A Right Hemisphere Dysfunction Specific to Recognition of Certain Facial Expressions? *Brain and Cognition 34*, 2 (1997), 246-258.

[92] JONES, J. A., AND MOSCA, M. Implementation of a quantum algorithm on a nuclear magnetic resonance quantum computer. *Journal of Chemical Physics 109* (1998), 1648-1654.

[93] KALMÁR, L. An Argument against the Plausibility of Church's Thesis. In *Constructivity in Mathematics*, A. Heyting, ed. Noth-Holland, Amsterdam, 1959, pp. 72-80.

[94] KARP, R. M., AND LIPTON, R. J. Some connections between nonuniform and uniform complexity classes. In *Proceedings of the twelfth annual ACM symposium on Theory of computing* (1980), pp. 302-309.

[95] KIEU, T. D. Computing the non-computable. *Contemporary Physics 44*, 1 (2003), 51-71.

[96] KIEU, T. D. Hypercomputability of quantum adiabatic processes: Fact versus Prejudices. Electronic document available from http://arxiv.org/quant-ph/0504101, 2005.

[97] KIEU, T. D. Quantum Adiabatic Algorithm for Hilbert's Tenth Problem: I. The Algorithm. Electronic document available from http://arxiv.org/quant-ph/0310052, 2005.

[98] KIEU, T. D. A Mathematical Proof for a Ground-State Identification Criterion. Electronic document available from http://arxiv.org/quant-ph/0602146, 2006.

[99] KIEU, T. D. On the Identification of the Ground State Based on Occupation Probabilities: An Investigation of Smith's Apparent Counterexamples. Electronic document available from http://arxiv.org/quant-ph/0602145, 2006.

[100] KLEENE, S. C. General recursive functions of natural numbers. *Mathematische Annalen 112* (1936), 727-742.

[101] KLIR, G. J., AND YUAN, B. *Fuzzy Sets and Fuzzy Logic : Theory and Applications.* Prentice Hall (Sd), 1995.

[102] KUGEL, P. Thinking may be more than computing. *Cognition 22* (1986), 137-198.

[103] KUGEL, P. Toward a theory of intelligence. *Theoretical Computer Science 317,* 1-3 (2004), 13-30.

[104] KUGEL, P. It's Time To Think Outside the Computational Box. *Communications of the ACM 48,* 11 (2005), 33-37.

[105] LAFITTE, G. How Powerful Are Infinite Time Machines? In *Fundamentals of Computation Theory: 13th International Symposium, FCT 2001, Riga, Latvia,* R. Freivalds, ed., no. 2138 in Lecture Notes in Computer Science. Springer-Verlag, Berlin, 2001, pp. 252-263.

[106] LARAUDOGOITIA, J. P. A Beautiful Supertask. *Mind 105* (1996), 81-83. Electronic version available from http://www.findarticles.com.

[107] LARAUDOGOITIA, J. P. Infinity Machines and Creation Ex Nihilo. *Synthese 115* (1998), 259-265.

[108] LATSCH, W. Androids and agents: do we need a non-computable economics? *Journal of Economic Methodology 10,* 3 (2003), 375-396.

[109] LEA, D. *Concurrent Programming in Java.* Addison-Wesley, Reading, MA, USA, 1997.

[110] LEIJONHUFVUD, A. S. B. Towards a Not-Too-Rational Macroeconomics. *Southern Economic Journal 60,* 1 (1993), 1-13. Electronic version available from http://www.allbusiness.com/periodicals/article/391968-3.html.

[111] LEWIS, H. R., AND PAPADIMITRIOU, C. H. *Elements of the Theory of Computation,* 2nd ed. Peasron Education, Harlow, UK, 1998.

[112] LIEU, R., AND HILLMAN, L. W. The Phase Coherence of Light from Extragalactic Sources: Direct Evidence against First-Order Planck-Scale Fluctuations in Time and Space. *The Astrophysical Journal Letters 585,* 2 (2003), 77-80. Electronic version available from http://arxiv.org/astro-ph/0301184.

[113] LIPSCHITZ, S. *General Topology.* Schaum Publishing Co., New York, 1965.

[114] LLOYD, S. Ultimate Physical Limits to Computation. *Nature 406* (2000), 1047-1054.

[115] LLOYD, S., AND NG, Y. J. Black Hole Computers. *Scientific American 291,* 5 (2004), 53-61.

[116] LUCAS, J. R. Minds, Machines and Gödel. *Philosophy 36* (1961), 112-127.

[117] MACLENNAN, B. J. Continuous Formal Systems: A Unifying Model in Language and Cognition. In *Proceedings IEEE Workshop on Architectures for Semiotic Modeling and Situation Analysis in Large Complex Systems* (1995), pp. 161-172. Electronic version available from http://cogprints.org/541/.

[118] MacLennan, B. J. "Words Lie in Our Way." *Minds and Machines 4* (1995), 421-437.

[119] MacLennan, B. J. Natural computation and non-Turing models of computation. *Theoretical Computer Science 317*, 1-3 (2004), 115-145.

[120] Máté, A. Nondeterministic polynomial-time computations and models of arithmetic. *Journal of the ACM 37*, 1 (1990), 175-193.

[121] McCall, S. Can a Turing Machine Know that the Gödel Sentence is True? *The Journal of Philosophy 96* (1999), 525-532.

[122] McCall, S. On "Seeing" the Truth of the Gödel Sentence. *Facta Philosophica 3*, 1 (2001), 25-29.

[123] McCarthy, J. Notes on Self-Awareness. Electronic document available at http://www-formal.stanford.edu/jmc/selfaware.pdf, 2004.

[124] McCarthy, J. Awareness and Understanding in Computer Programs. *PSYCHE 2*, 11 (July 1995). Article in electronic form available from http://psyche.cs.monash.edu.au/v2/psyche-2-11-mccarthy.html.

[125] McCulloch, W. S., and Pitts, W. A logical calculus of the ideas immanent in nervous activity. *Bulletin of Mathematical Biophysics 5* (1943), 115-133.

[126] Mendelson, E. On Some Recent Criticism of Church's Thesis. *Notre Dame Journal of Formal Logic IV*, 3 (1963), 201-205.

[127] Michalewicz, Z. *Genetic Algorithms + Data Structures = Evolution Programs*, second ed. Springer-Verlag, Berlin, 1994.

[128] Miller, J. F., and Thomson, P. Cartesian Genetic Programming. In *EuroGP 2000*, R. Poli, W. Banzhaf, W. B. Langdon, J. Miller, P. Nordin, and T. C. Fogarty, eds., no. 1802 in Lecture Notes in Computer Science. Springer-Verlag, Berlin, 2000, pp. 121-132.

[129] Milner, R. *Communication and Concurrency*. Prentice Hall, New York, 1989.

[130] Milner, R. Functions as Processes. *Mathematical Structures in Computer Science 2* (1992), 119-141.

[131] Milner, R. Elements of Interaction. *Communications of the ACM 36*, 1 (1993), 78-89.

[132] Milner, R. *Communicating and Mobile Systems: The π-Calculus*. Cambridge University Press, Cambridge, UK, 1999.

[133] Milner, R., Parrow, J., and Walker, D. A calculus of mobile processes. *Information and Computation 100*, 1 (1992), 1-77. Parts I and II.

[134] Minsky, M. *Computation: Finite and Infinite Machines*. Prentice-Hall, Englewood Cliffs, NJ, USA, 1967.

[135] Misra, B., and Sudarshan, G. The Zeno's paradox in quantum theory. *Journal of Mathematical Physics 18*, 4 (1977), 756-763.

[136] Moore, C. Recursion theory on the reals and continuous-time computation. *Theoretical Computer Science 163*, 1 (1996), 23-44.

[137] Nagasawa, Y. Thomas vs. Thomas: A New Approach to Nagel's Bat Argument. *Inquiry 46* (2003), 377-394.

[138] NAGEL, E., AND NEWMAN, J. R. *Gödel's proof*. New York University Press, New York, 2001. Edited and with a new forward by Douglas R. Hofstadter.

[139] NAGEL, T. What Is It Like To Be a Bat? *The Philosophical Review 83* (1974), 435-450. Available on-line at http://members.aol.com/NeoNoetics/Nagel_Bat.html.

[140] NÉMETI, I., AND DÁVID, G. Relativistic computers and the Turing barrier. *Applied Mathematics and Computation 176*, 1 (2006), 118-142.

[141] NG, Y. J. From Computation to Black Holes and Space-Time Foam. *Physical Review Letters 86*, 14 (2001), 2946-2949.

[142] NG, Y. J., CHRISTIANSEN, W., AND VAN DAM, H. Probing Plank-scale physics with Extragalactic Sources? *The Astrophysical Journal Letters 591*, 2 (2003), 83-86. Electronic version available from http://arxiv.org/astro-ph/0302372.

[143] NORTON, J. D. A Quantum Mechanical Supertask. *Foundations of Physics 29*, 8 (1999), 1265-1302.

[144] OPPY, G., AND DOWE, D. The Turing Test. In *The Stanford Encyclopedia of Philosophy*, E. N. Zalta, ed. Winter 2005.

[145] ORD, T., AND KIEU, T. D. The Diagonal Method and Hypercomputation. *The British Journal for the Philosophy of Science 56*, 1 (2005), 147-156.

[146] PANKSEPP, J. At the interface of the affective, behavioral, and cognitive neurosciences: Decoding the emotional feelings of the brain. *Brain and Cognition 52* (2003), 4-14.

[147] PĂUN, G. *Membrane Computing: An Introduction*. Springer-Verlag, Berlin, 2002.

[148] PĂUN, G., ROZENBERG, G., AND SALOMAA, A. *DNA Computing*. Springer-Verlag, Berlin, 1998.

[149] PEITGEN, H.-O., JÜRGENS, H., AND SAUPE, D. *Chaos and Fractals: New Frontiers of Science*. Springer-Verlag, New York, 1992.

[150] PENROSE, R. *The Emperor's New Mind: Concerning Computers, Minds, and the Laws of Physics*. Oxford University Press, Oxford, UK, 1989.

[151] PENROSE, R. *Shadows of the Mind: A Search for the Missing Science of Consciousness*. Oxford University Press, New York, 1994.

[152] PENROSE, R. *The Road to Reality*. Alfred A. Knopf, New York, 2005.

[153] PENROSE, R. Beyond the Doubting of a Shadow. *PSYCHE 2*, 23 (January 1996). Article in electronic form available from http://psyche.cs.monash.edu.au/v2/psyche-2-23-penrose.html.

[154] PÉTER, R. Rekursivität und Konstruktivität. In *Constructivity in Mathematics*, A. Heyting, ed. Noth-Holland, Amsterdam, 1959, pp. 226-233.

[155] PITOWSKY, I. The Physical Church Thesis and Physical Computational Complexity. *Iyyun: A Jerusalem Philosophical Quarterly 39* (1990), 81-99. Available on-line from http://edelstein.huji.ac.il/staff/pitowsky/.

[156] PORTE, J. Quelques Pseudo-Paradoxes de la "Calculabilitè Effective". In *Actes du 2me Congrès International de Cybernetique, Namur, [Belgium] 26-29 June 1956*. Gauthier-Villars, Paris, 1958, pp. 332-334.

[157] POUR-EL, M. B. Abstract Computability and its Relation to the General Purpose Analog Computer (Some Connections between Logic, Differential Equations and Analog Computers). *Transactions of the American Mathematical Society 199*, 1 (1974), 1-28.

[158] POUR-EL, M. B., AND RICHARDS, J. I. *Computability in Analysis and Physics.* Springer-Verlag, Berlin, 1989.

[159] PRESTON, J., AND BISHOP, M., eds. *Views into the Chinese Room* (Oxford, UK, 2002), Oxford University Press.

[160] PUTNAM, H. Trial and Error Predicates and the Solution to a Problem of Mostowski. *The Journal of Symbolic Logic 30*, 1 (1965), 49-57.

[161] PUTNAM, H. Philosophy and Our Mental Life. In *Mind, Language, and Reality*, H. Putnam, ed. Cambridge University Press, New York, 1975, pp. 291-303.

[162] RAATIKAINEN, P. McCall's Gödelian Argument Is Invalid. *Facta Philosophica 4*, 1 (2002), 167-169.

[163] RAGAZZONI, R., TURATTO, M., AND GAESSLER, W. The Lack of Observational Evidence for the Quantum Structure of Spacetime at Planck Scales. *The Astrophysical Journal Letters 587*, 1 (2003), L1-L4. Electronic version available from http://arxiv.org/astro-ph/0303043.

[164] REDHEAD, M. Mathematics and the Mind. *The British Journal for the Philosophy of Science 55* (2004), 731-737.

[165] RIEBE, M., HÄFFNER, H., ROOS, C. F., HÄNSEL, W., BENHELM, J., LANCASTER, G. P. T., KÖRBER, T. W., BECHER, C., SCHMIDT-KALER, F., JAMES, D. F. V., AND BLATT, R. Deterministic quantum teleportation with atoms. *Nature 429* (2004), 734-737.

[166] ROGERS, JR., H. *Theory of Recursive Functions and Effective Computability.* The MIT Press, Cambridge, MA, USA, 1987.

[167] ROITMAN, J. *Introduction to Modern Set Theory.* John Wiley & Sons, New York, 1990.

[168] RUBEL, L. A. The Extended Analog Computer. *Advances in Applied Mathematics 14*, 1 (1993), 39-50.

[169] SCARPELLINI, B. Comments on "Two Undecidable Problems of Analysis." *Minds and Machines 13*, 1 (2003), 79-85.

[170] SCARPELLINI, B. Two Undecidable Problems of Analysis. *Minds and Machines 13*, 1 (2003), 49-77.

[171] SCHINDLER, R.-D. $P \neq NP$ for Infinite Time Turing Machines. *Monatshefte für Mathematik 139*, 4 (2003), 335-340.

[172] SEARLE, J. R. Minds, Brains and Programs. *Behavioral and Brain Sciences 3* (1980), 417-424.

[173] SEARLE, J. R. Is the Brain a Digital Computer? *Proceedings and Addresses of the American Philosophical Association 64* (1990), 21-37.

[174] SEARLE, J. R. Is the Brain's Mind a Computer Program? *Scientific American 262*, 1 (1990), 26-31.

[175] SEARLE, J. R. *The Mystery of Consciousness.* New York Review Books, New York, 1997.

[176] SEARLE, J. R. *Mind: A Brief Introduction.* Oxford University Press, Oxford, UK, 2004.

[177] SERGEYEV, Y. D. *Arithmetic of Infinity.* Edizioni Orizzonti Meridionali, Cosenza, Italy, 2003.

[178] SHAGRIR, O., AND PITOWKSY, I. Physical Hypercomputation and the Church-Turing Thesis. *Minds and Machines 13* (2003), 87-101.

[179] SHAPIRO, S. Incompleteness, Mechanism, and Optimism. *The Bulletin of Symbolic Logic 4*, 3 (1998), 273-302.

[180] SHAPIRO, S. L., AND TEUKOLSKY, S. A. Formation of naked singularities: The violation of cosmic censorship. *Physical Review Letters 66*, 8 (1991), 994-997.

[181] SHATZ, C. J. The Developing Brain. In *The Scientific American Book of the Brain*, The Editors of Scientific American, ed. The Lyons Press, 2001, pp. 3-16.

[182] SICARD, A., VÉLEZ, M., AND OSPINA, J. A possible hypercomputational quantum algorithm. In *Quantum Information and Computation III*, E. J. Donkor, A. R. Pirich, and H. E. Brandt, eds., vol. 5815 of Proc. of SPIE. SPIE, Bellingham, WA, USA, 2005, pp. 219-226. Electronic version available from http://arxiv.org/quant-ph/0406137.

[183] SIEGELMANN, H. T. *Neural Networks and Analog Computation: Beyond the Turing Limit.* Birkhäuser, Boston, 1999.

[184] SIMON, H. A., AND EISENSTADT, S. A. A Chinese Room that Understands. In Preston and Bishop [159], pp. 95-108.

[185] SMITH, S. D., AND BULMAN-FLEMING, M. B. An examination of the right-hemisphere term hypothesis of the lateralization of previous termemotion. *Brain and Cognition 57*, 2 (2005), 210-213.

[186] SMITH, W. D. Three counterexamples refuting Kieu's plan for "quantum adiabatic hypercomputation"; and some uncomputable quantum mechanical tasks. *Applied Mathematics and Computation 178*, 1 (2006), 184-193.

[187] SØRENSEN, M. H. B., AND URZYCZYN, P. Lectures on the Curry-Howard Isomorphism. Tech. Rep. 98/14, DIKU, Copenhagen, 1998. Electronic version available as http://www.diku.dk/publikationer/tekniske.rapporter/1998/98-14.ps.gz.

[188] SPIVEY, M. J., GROSJEAN, M., AND KNOBLICH, G. Continuous attraction toward phonological competitors. *Proceedings of the National Academy of Sciences of the United States of America 102*, 29 (2005), 10393-10398.

[189] STANNETT, M. X-Machines and the Halting Problem: Building a Super-Turing Machine. *Formal Aspects of Computing 2* (1990), 331-341.

[190] STANNETT, M. Computation over arbitrary models of time. Tech. Rep. CS-01-08, Dept. of Computer Science, University of Sheffield, Sheffield, UK, 2001. Electronic version available from http://citeseer.ist.psu.edu/630977.html.

[191] STANNETT, M. Computation and Hypercomputation. *Minds and Machines* *13* (2003), 115-153.

[192] STEIN, L. A. Challenging the Computational Metaphor: Implications for How We Think. *Cybernetics and Systems: An International Journal 30* (1999), 473-507.

[193] STEINHART, E. Logically Possible Machines. *Minds and Machines 12* (2002), 259-280.

[194] STEINHART, E. Supermachines and Superminds. *Minds and Machines 13* (2003), 155-186.

[195] STEWART, I. The Dynamics of Impossible Devices. *Nonlinear Science Today 1*, 4 (1991), 8-9.

[196] SYROPOULOS, A. Fuzzifying P Systems. *The Computer Journal 49*, 5 (2006), 619-628.

[197] SYROPOULOS, A., AND DOUMANIS, E. On C Systems. Unpublished manuscript, 2005.

[198] TALLIS, R. *Why the Mind Is Not a Computer: A Pocket Lexicon of Neuromythology*. Imprint Academic, Exeter, UK, 2004.

[199] TENNANT, N. On Turing Machines Knowing Their Own Gödel-Sentences. *Philosophia Mathematica 9* (2001), 72-79.

[200] TEUSCHER, C., AND SIPPER, M. Hypercomputation: Hype or Computation. *Communications of the ACM 45*, 8 (2002), 23-24.

[201] THAGARD, P. Cognitive science. In *The Stanford Encyclopedia of Philosophy*, E. N. Zalta, ed. Summer 2007. Electronic document available at http://plato.stanford.edu/archives/sum2007/entries/cognitive-science/.

[202] THOMSON, J. F. Tasks and Super-Tasks. *Analysis 15* (1954), 1-13.

[203] TOKUDA, E., ASAHI, N., YAMADA, T., AND AMEMIYA, Y. Analog Computation Using Single-Electron Circuits. *Analog Integrated Circuits and Signal Processing 24*, 1 (2000), 41-49.

[204] TREMBLAY, J.-P., AND SORENSON, P. G. *The Theory and Practice of Compiler Writing*. McGraw-Hill, Singapore, 1985.

[205] TSUIKI, H. Real number computation through Gray code embedding. *Theoretical Computer Science 284* (2002), 467-485.

[206] TURING, A. M. On Computable Numbers, with an application to the Entscheidungsproblem. *Proceedings of the London Mathematical Society 42* (1936), 230-265. The paper is available on-line at http://www.abelard.org/turpap2/tp2-ie.asp and at http://www.thocp.net/biographies/papers/turing_oncomputablenumbers_1936.pdf.

[207] TURING, A. M. Computing Machinery and Intelligence. *Mind 59* (1950), 433-435. The paper is available on-line at http://cogprints.org/499/00/turing.html.

[208] VAN LEEUWEN, J., AND WIEDERMANN, J. On the Power of Interactive Computing. In *Theoretical Computer Science. Exploring New Frontiers of Theoretical Informatics: International Conference IFIP TCS 2000*, J. van Leeuwen, O. Watanabe, M. Hagiya, P. Mosses, and T. Ito, eds., vol. 1872 of *Lecture Notes in Computer Science*. Springer-Verlag, Berlin, 2000, pp. 619-623.

[209] VAN LEEUWEN, J., AND WIEDERMANN, J. The Turing Machine Paradigm in Contemporary Computing. In *Mathematics Unlimited-2001 and Beyond*, B. Enquist and W.Schmid, eds. Springer-Verlag, Berlin, 2001, pp. 1139-1155.

[210] VAN REGENMORTEL, M. V. H. Editorial: Biological complexity emerges from the ashes of genetic reductionism. *Journal of Molecular Recognition 17* (2004), 145-148.

[211] VELUPILLAI, K. V. The unreasonable *in*effectiveness of mathematics in economics. *Cambridge Journal of Economics 29* (2005), 849-872.

[212] VICKERS, S. *Topology via Logic.* Cambridge University Press, Cambridge, UK, 1989.

[213] VSEMIRNOV, M. Hilbert's Tenth Problem Web-page. Web page's URL: http://logic.pdmi.ras.ru/Hilbert10/, 2000.

[214] WAKEFIELD, J. C. The Chinese Room Argument Reconsidered: Essentialism, Indeterminacy, and Strong AI. *Minds and Machines 13* (2003), 285-319.

[215] WEGNER, P. Why interaction is more powerful than algorithms. *Communications of the ACM 40*, 5 (1997), 80-91.

[216] WEGNER, P. Interactive foundations of computing. *Theoretical Computer Science 192* (1998), 315-351.

[217] WEGNER, P., AND EBERBACH, E. New Models of Computation. *The Computer Journal 47*, 1 (2004), 4-9.

[218] WEGNER, P., AND GOLDIN, D. Computation Beyond Turing Machines. *Communications of the ACM 46*, 4 (2003), 100-102.

[219] WEIHRAUCH, K. *Computable Analysis: An Introduction.* Springer-Verlag, Berlin, 2000.

[220] WEINBERG, S. Is the Universe a Computer? *The New York Review of Books 49*, 16 (2002), 43-47.

[221] WEIZENBAUM, J. ELIZA-A Computer Program For the Study of Natural Language Communication Between Man and Machine. *Communications of the ACM 9*, 1 (1966), 36-45.

[222] WELCH, P. D. On the Possibility, or Otherwise, of Hypercomputation. *The British Journal for the Philosophy of Science 55*, 4 (2004), 739-746.

[223] WELLS, B. Pseudorecursive Varieties of Semigroups-I. *International Journal of Algebra and Computation 6*, 4 (1996), 457-510.

[224] WELLS, B. Is There a Nonrecursive Decidable Equational Theory. *Minds and Machines 12* (2002), 303-326.

[225] WELLS, B. Hypercomputation by definition. *Theoretical Computer Science 317* (2004), 191-207.

[226] WHEELER, J. A. Information, Physics, Quantum: The Search for Links. In *Complexity, Entropy and the Physics of Information*, W. H. Zurek, ed. Westview Press, Jackson, Tennessee, USA, 1990, pp. 3-28.

[227] WIEDERMANN, J. Characterizing the super-Turing computing power and efficiency of classical fuzzy Turing machines. *Theoretical Computer Science 317* (2004), 61-69.

[228] WOLFRAM, S. *A New Kind of Science.* Wolfram Media, Inc., Champaign, IL, USA, 2002.

[229] WOODS, D., AND NAUGHTON, T. J. An optical model of computation. *Theoretical Computer Science 334*, 1-3 (2005), 227-258.

[230] YANOFSKY, N. S. Towards a Definition of an Algorithm. Electronic document available from http://arxiv.org/math/0602053, 2006.

[231] YAO, A. C.-C. Classical Physics and the Church-Turing Thesis. *Journal of the ACM 50*, 1 (2003), 100-105.

[232] ZHENG, X., AND WEIHRAUCH, K. The Arithmetical Hierarchy of Real Numbers. *Mathematical Logic Quarterly 47*, 1 (2001), 51-65.

[233] ZIEGLER, M. Computability and Continuity on the Real Arithmetic Hierarchy and the Power of Type-2 Nondeterminism. In *New Computational Paradigms: First Conference on Computability in Europe, CiE 2005, Amsterdam, the Netherlands, June 8-12, 2005. Proceedings*, S. B. Cooper, B. Löwe, and L. Torenvliet, eds., no. 3526 in Lecture Notes in Computer Science. Springer-Verlag, Berlin, 2005, pp. 562-571.

[234] ZIEGLER, M. Computational Power of Infinite Quantum Parallelism. *International Journal of Theoretical Physics 44*, 11 (2005), 2059-2071.

[235] ZIEGLER, M. Real Hypercomputation and Continuity. *Theory of Computing Systems 41* (2007), 177-206.

[236] ZUSE, K. *Rechnender Raum.* Friedrich Vieweg & Sohn, Braunschweig, Germany, 1969. English translation available at ftp://ftp.idsia.ch/pub/juergen/zuserechnenderraum.pdf.

Name Index

Subject Index